Oracle8 DBA : Network Administration

The Cram Sheet

This Cram Sheet contains the distilled, key facts about Oracle8 in the area of network administration. Review this information right before you enter the test room, paying special attention to the subjects that you've found to be a bit more difficult to remember. You can transfer any of these facts from your head onto a blank piece of paper before beginning the exam.

NETWORK OVERVIEW

1. In a two-tier (client/server or simple) network architecture, the client is directly connected to the server.

2. An n-tier architecture has a middle tier (application server) between the client and the server.

3. The n-tier architecture provides translation services between network protocols, scalablility, and intelligent agent services.

4. Net8 supports communication between client applications and Oracle databases, regardless of the operating system.

BASIC NET8 ARCHITECTURE

5. The six layers of the Net8 protocol stack on the client are application, OCI, Two-Task Common, TNS, OPA, and Network Protocol.

6. The six layers of the Net8 protocol stack on the server are server, OPI, Two-Task Common, TNS, OPA, and Network Protocol.

7. The Two-Task Common layer is responsible for conversion of character set and data types when these are different between the client and server.

8. The TNS (Transparent Network Substrate) layer contains the Network Interface (NI), Network Routing (NR), Network Naming (NN), Network Administration (NA), and Network Services (NS Main and NS(2)). The TNS layer provides the interface to industry standard protocols.

SERVER CONFIGURATION

9. The listener.ora file is used to configure the listener process on the server. Multiple listeners can be configured on the same server, but each must have a different name and port number.

10. The listener resolves connection requests by either spawning a new process, or redirecting the request to an existing process.

11. The **PRESPAWN_MAX** parameter sets the maximum number of processes the listener will create.

12. The following commands are issued using the lsnrctl utility: **start**, **stop**, **reload**, **services**, **status**, **set password**, **set**, and **show**.

13. If a **lsnrctl** command is issued with no listener name specified, the default listener name is assumed.

14. When using a password, the lsnrctl utility requires that you start lsnrctl and then issue the **SET PASSWORD** command before issuing

commands such as **stop**, **reload**, **set save_config_on_stop**, **services** and **change_password**.

CLIENT CONFIGURATION

15. The host naming method uses the default TCP/IP protocol, port 1521, and a hostname as the connection string.

16. The sqlnet.ora and tnsnames.ora files on the client are used to configure the local naming method (TNSNAMES). The client supplies a connect string (alias) which is resolved to a connect descriptor. The connect descriptor provides the protocol, hostname (or address), and connect data (SID) for the connection.

17. The sqlnet.ora file is used to configure a client to use Oracle Names (ONAMES).

18. The default setting for the **NAMES.DIRECTORY_PATH** parameter in the sqlnet.ora file is **TNSNAMES**, **ONAMES**, **HOSTNAME**. This means it will attempt to use local naming first, Oracle Names second, and finally the host naming method for a connection.

19. External naming is supported for the following naming services: Cell Directory Services (CDS), Netware Directory Services (NDS) and Network Information Services (NIS).

ORACLE NAMES

20. Oracle Names provides a method to centralize the configuration and resolution of connection strings. It simplifies administration, increases efficiency, eliminates redundancy, and provides location transparency.

21. When you use Oracle Names, a connection request is directed to the Names Server to obtain the address information. The address information is returned to the client and the client then sends the request to the Database Server using that address information.

22. The names.ora file is used to configure Oracle Names.

23. The namesctl utility is used to start and stop the names server processes. The **reorder_ns** command creates a file that lists the names servers and their addresses in the order of fastest-to-slowest response times (based on the results of a **ping** command).

24. Client-side cache (started with the **namesctl start_client_cache** command) is used to allow workstations to store address information in the local cache. This improves performance because the client does not have to send a request for address information to the Oracle names server for every connection request. The TTL parameter determines the time to live for the connection information.

25. Cache replication occurs between regional servers to propagate changes. The root region replicates information to other root regions

26. A regional database is a repository for storing Oracle Names information.

MULTITHREADED SERVER (MTS) OPTION

27. The MTS option is used to reduce the number of processes against an instance by providing a method to share processes. This is especially useful in OLTP environments.

28. The user sends a request to the server using Net8, and the request is redirected by the listener process to a dispatcher process. The dispatcher places the request into the request queue in the SGA where it is picked up by a shared server process. The shared server processes the request and places the response in the SGA response queue for that dispatcher. The dispatcher picks up the response and returns it to the user.

29. The following database initialization parameters are used to configure MTS: **LOCAL_LISTENER**, **MTS_SERVICE**, **MTS_DISPATCHERS**, **MTS_MAX_DISPATCHERS**, **MTS_SERVERS**, and **MTS_MAX_SERVERS**. The following is an example of the database initialization parameter specification for MTS:

```
LOCAL_LISTENER = mts1
MTS_SERVICE = prod1
MTS_DISPATCHERS =
"(PROTOCOL=TCP)(DISPATCHERS=3)"
MTS_MAX_DISPATCHERS = 10
MTS_SERVERS = 3
MTS_MAX_SERVERS = 10
```

30. The number of shared_servers is increased (up to the **MTS_MAX_SERVERS** parameter value) and decreased (down to the **MTS_SERVERS** parameter value) automatically by

Oracle8 DBA: Network Administration

Barbara Ann Pascavage

Oracle8 DBA: Network Administration Exam Cram

The Coriolis Group, LLC
14455 N. Hayden Road
Suite 220
Scottsdale, Arizona 85260

480/483-0192
FAX 480/483-0193
http://www.coriolis.com

Library of Congress Cataloging-in-Publication Data
Pascavage, Barbara.
   Oracle8 DBA : network administration exam cram/by Barbara Pascavage
     p. cm.
   Includes index.
   ISBN 1-57610-578-4
   1. Electronic data processing personnel--Certification. 2. Microsoft software--Examinations--Study guides. 3. Computer networks--Management--Examinations--Study guides. I. Title.
QA76.3.P367 2000
005.75'85--dc21   99-052992
                                                 CIP

Printed in the United States of America
10 9 8 7 6 5 4 3 2 1

President, CEO
Keith Weiskamp

Publisher
Steve Sayre

Acquisitions Editor
Jeff Kellum

Marketing Specialist
Cynthia Caldwell

Project Editor
Stephanie Palenque

Technical Reviewer
Peter Teoh Teik Huat

Production Coordinator
Meg E. Turecek

Cover Design
Jesse Dunn

Layout Design
April Nielsen

CORIOLIS

14455 North Hayden Road ▪ Suite 220 ▪ Scottsdale, Arizona 85260

Coriolis: The Training And Certification Destination™

Thank you for purchasing one of our innovative certification study guides, just one of the many members of the Coriolis family of certification products.

Certification Insider Press™ has long believed that achieving your IT certification is more of a road trip than anything else. This is why most of our readers consider us their *Training And Certification Destination*. By providing a one-stop shop for the most innovative and unique training materials, our readers know we are the first place to look when it comes to achieving their certification. As one reader put it, "I plan on using your books for all of the exams I take."

To help you reach your goals, we've listened to others like you, and we've designed our entire product line around you and the way you like to study, learn, and master challenging subjects. Our approach is *The Smartest Way To Get Certified ™*.

In addition to our highly popular *Exam Cram* and *Exam Prep* guides, we have a number of new products. We recently launched *Exam Cram Audio Reviews*, audiotapes based on *Exam Cram* material. We've also developed *Practice Tests Exam Crams* and *Exam Cram Flash Cards*, which are designed to make your studying fun as well as productive.

Our commitment to being the *Training And Certification Destination* does not stop there. We just introduced *Exam Cram Insider*, a biweekly newsletter containing the latest in certification news, study tips, and announcements from Certification Insider Press. (To subscribe, send an email to **eci@coriolis.com** and type "subscribe insider" in the body of the email.) We also recently announced the launch of the Certified Crammer Society and the Coriolis Help Center—two new additions to the Certification Insider Press family.

We'd like to hear from you. Help us continue to provide the very best certification study materials possible. Write us or email us at **cipq@coriolis.com** and let us know how our books have helped you study, or tell us about new features that you'd like us to add. If you send us a story about how we've helped you, and we use it in one of our books, we'll send you an official Coriolis shirt for your efforts.

Good luck with your certification exam and your career. Thank you for allowing us to help you achieve your goals.

Keith Weiskamp
President and CEO

Look For These Other Books From The Coriolis Group:

Oracle DBA 7.3 to 8 Upgrade Exam Cram
Robert G. Freeman

Oracle DBA Exam Cram: Test 1 and Test 2
Michael R. Ault

Oracle DBA Exam Cram: Test 3 and Test 4
Michael R. Ault, Paul Collins, Barbara Ann Pascavage, Michelle Berard

Oracle8 Black Book
Michael R. Ault

Oracle8 DBA: Backup And Recovery Exam Cram
Debbie Wong

Oracle8 DBA: Database Administration Exam Cram
Paul Collins

Oracle8 DBA: Performance Tuning Exam Cram
Michael R. Ault and Josef Brinson

Oracle8 DBA: SQL And PL/SQL Exam Cram
Michael R. Ault

Oracle8 PL/SQL Black Book
Mark Gokman and Jonathan Ingram

I want to dedicate this book to my wonderful family.

Stanley Pascavage, the patriarch of our family. If I could have picked anyone to be my father, it would still be you. Thank you for believing in me and giving me your love and guidance.

Stan Pascavage, my brother. I know that if I ever need anything, you will be there to help me. Having a big brother like you means a lot.

Judy Butt, my sister. I consider you the heart of our family. You help to keep us together and always put family first.

I also want to dedicate this to the next generation, in order of their appearance in this world: David Yusko, Michael Pascavage, Christina Jenkins, Lisa Pascavage, Stanley (Joey) Pascavage, III.

I consider myself very fortunate to have all of you in my life.

❧

About The Author

Barbara Ann Pascavage (Chauncey Oracle 7, OCP 7.3, OCP 8.0) is a Senior Oracle Database Administrator at *The Washington Post*. She has been working with Oracle since 1987 and has been an Oracle DBA since 1991.Barbara is the co-author of *Oracle DBA Exam Cram: Test 3 and Test 4* with Michael R. Ault. She has presented at the International Oracle Users Group 1999 conference, as well as at local professional meetings.

Acknowledgments

The two people that I need to thank first are Michelle Berard and Michael R. Ault.

Michelle, thank you for getting me started with writing. Without you, I would never have gotten this opportunity. It is great to have someone so energetic, outgoing, intelligent, and fun to work with.

Mike, I think of you as a friend and mentor. You are so knowledgeable about Oracle and so willing to answer questions from everyone. Your work on the RevealNet pipeline is just one example of this. Thank you so much for all your help.

I need to thank my neighbors, Diana Wodder and Grace Marie Schmitt, for once again serving "Callie duty". My dog Callie is a very important part of my life. I really appreciate knowing that I have the two of you to help out when I can't be there.

My acknowledgments would not be complete if I failed to mention the great support I received from The Coriolis Group. Jeff Kellum, the acquisitions editor for this book, made sure I got started on the right track. Stephanie Palenque, associate project editor, kept me on target and pulled everything together. Tom Gillen, the copyeditor, corrected my grammar, showed me how to format things, and generally made this book much easier to read. Peter Teoh Teik Huat, the technical editor, checked my code and made sure that what I thought I had written was really what appeared on the page. I would also like to thank the other members of the Coriolis team who worked on this project: Cynthia Caldwell, marketing specialist; Meg Turecek, production coordinator; Jesse Dunn, cover designer; and April Nielsen, layout designer. You all did a fantastic job.

Contents At A Glance

Table Of Contents

Introduction

Welcome to *Oracle8 DBA: Network Administration Exam Cram*. This book will help you in preparing to take—and pass—the last of the five-part series of exams for the Oracle Certified Professional-Oracle8 Certified Database Administrator (OCP-DBA) certification. In this introduction, I'll talk about Oracle's certification programs and how the *Exam Cram* series can help you prepare for Oracle8's certification exams.

Exam Cram books help you understand and appreciate the subjects and materials you need to pass Oracle certification exams. These books are aimed strictly at test preparation and review, and do not teach you everything you need to know about a topic. Instead, I present and dissect the questions and problems that you're likely to encounter on a test.

Nevertheless, to completely prepare yourself for any Oracle test, I recommend that you begin by taking the Self-Assessment included in this book immediately following this Introduction. This tool will help you evaluate your knowledge base against the requirements for an OCP-DBA under both ideal and real circumstances.

Based on what you learn from that exercise, you might decide to begin your studies with either some classroom training or reading one of the many DBA guides that are available from Oracle or third-party vendors. I also strongly recommend that you install, configure, and work with the software or environment that you'll be tested on, because nothing beats hands-on experience and familiarity when it comes to understanding the questions you're likely to encounter on a certification test. Book learning is essential, but hands-on experience is the best teacher of all.

The Oracle Certified Professional (OCP) Program

The OCP program for DBA certification currently includes five separate tests, and Table 1 shows the required exams for the OCP certification:

➤ *Introduction to Oracle: SQL And PL/SQL (Exam 1Z0-001)*—Test 1 is the base test for the series. The knowledge that is tested in Test 1 will serve

Table 1   OCP-DBA Requirements*

All 5 of these tests are required		
Test 1	**Exam 1Z0-001**	Introduction to Oracle: SQL and PL/SQL
Test 2	**Exam 1Z0-013**	Oracle8: Database Administration
Test 3	**Exam 1Z0-015**	Oracle8: Backup and Recovery
Test 4	**Exam 1Z0-014**	Oracle8: Performance Tuning
Test 5	**Exam 1Z0-016**	Oracle8: Network Administration

* If you are currently an OCP certified in Oracle7.3, you need to take only the upgrade exam (Oracle8: New Features for Administrators, Exam 1Z0-010) to be certified in Oracle8.

as the foundation for all the other DBA tests. This test focuses on SQL and PL/SQL language constructs, syntax, and usage. It covers Data Definition Language (DDL) and Data Manipulation Language (DML). Also covered are basic data modeling, database design, and basic Oracle Procedure Builder usage.

➤ *Oracle8: Database Administration (Exam 1Z0-013)*—Test 2 deals with all levels of database administration in Oracle8 (primarily version 8.0.5 and above). Topics include architecture, startup and shutdown, database creation, managing database internal and external constructs (such as redo logs, rollback segments, and tablespaces), and all other Oracle structures. Database auditing, use of National Language Support (NLS) features, and use of SQL*Loader and other utilities are also covered.

➤ *Oracle8: Backup And Recovery (Exam 1Z0-015)*—Test 3 covers one of the most important parts of the Oracle DBA's job: database backup and recovery operations. This test focuses on backup and recovery motives, architecture as it relates to backup and recovery, back-up methods, failure scenarios, recovery methodologies, archive logging, supporting 24x7 shops, troubleshooting, and use of Oracle8's standby database features. The test also covers the use of Oracle's Recovery Manager (RMAN), which is new in Oracle8.

➤ *Oracle8: Performance Tuning (Exam 1Z0-014)*—Test 4 covers all aspects of tuning an Oracle8 database (which includes application as well as database tuning). The test relies on knowledge in diagnosis of tuning problems; optimal configurations for databases; shared pool tuning; buffer cache tuning; Oracle block usage; tuning rollback segments and redo mechanisms; monitoring and detection lock contention; tuning sorts; tuning in OLTP, DSS, and mixed environments; and load optimization.

➤ *Oracle8: Network Administration (Exam 1Z0-016)*—Test 5 covers all parts of the Net8 product: NET8 Assistant, Oracle Names Server, the listener process, name-resolution methods, MTS, Connection Manager, Intelligent Agent, Advanced Networking Option, configuration files, and troubleshooting.

To obtain an OCP certificate in database administration, you must pass all five exams. You do not have to take the tests in any particular order, although it is usually better to do so because the knowledge that is tested does build from each exam. The core exams require you to demonstrate competence with all phases of Oracle8 database lifetime activities. If you already have your Oracle 7.3 certification, you need to take only one exam—Oracle8: New Features for Administrators (Exam 1Z0-010)—to upgrade your status.

It's not uncommon for the entire process to take a year or so, and many individuals find that they must take a test more than once to pass. The primary goal of the *Exam Cram* series is to make it possible, given proper study and preparation, to pass all of the OCP-DBA tests on the first try.

Finally, certification is an ongoing activity. Once an Oracle version becomes obsolete, OCP-DBAs (and other OCPs) typically have six months to get recertified on current product versions. (If you do not get recertified within the specified time period, your certification becomes invalid.) Because technology keeps changing and new products continually supplant old ones, this should come as no surprise.

The best place to keep tabs on the OCP program and its various certifications is on the Oracle Web site. The current root URL for the OCP program is **http://education.oracle.com/certification**. This site changes frequently, so, if this URL doesn't work, try using the Search tool on Oracle's site (**www.oracle.com**) with either *OCP* or the quoted phrase *Oracle Certified Professional Program* as the search string. This will help you find the latest and most accurate information about the company's certification programs.

Taking A Certification Exam

Alas, testing is not free. You'll be charged $125 for each test you take, whether you pass or fail. In the United States and Canada, tests are administered by Sylvan Prometric. Sylvan Prometric can be reached at 1-800-891-3926, any time from 7:00 A.M. to 6:00 P.M., Central Time, Monday through Friday. If you can't get through at either of these numbers, try 1-612-896-7000 or 1-612-820-5707.

To schedule an exam, call at least one day in advance. To cancel or reschedule an exam, you must call at least one day before the scheduled test time (or you may be charged the $125 fee). When calling Sylvan Prometric, please have the following information ready:

➤ Your name, organization, and mailing address

➤ The name of the exam you want to take

➤ A method of payment (The most convenient approach is to supply a valid credit card number with sufficient available credit. Otherwise, payments by check, money order, or purchase order must be received before a test can be scheduled. If the latter methods are required, ask the Sylvan representative for more details.)

An appointment confirmation will be sent to you by mail (if you register more than five days before an exam) or by fax (if fewer than five days). A Candidate Agreement letter, which you must sign to take the examination, will also be provided.

On the day of the test, try to arrive at least 15 minutes before the scheduled time. You must supply two forms of identification, one of which must be a photo ID.

All exams are completely closed book. In fact, you will not be permitted to take anything with you into the testing area. I suggest that you review the most critical information about your test immediately prior to entering the room. (*Exam Cram* books provide a brief reference—the Cram Sheet, located inside the front of this book—that lists in distilled form the essential information from the book.) You will have some time to compose yourself, to mentally review this critical information, and even to take a sample orientation exam before you begin the real thing. I suggest you take the orientation test before your first exam. They're all more or less identical in layout, behavior, and controls, so you probably won't need to do this after the first test.

When you complete an Oracle8 certification exam, the testing software will tell you whether you've passed or failed. Results are broken into several topic areas. Whether you pass or fail, I suggest you ask for—and keep—the detailed report that the test administrator prints for you. You can use the report to help you prepare for another go-round, if necessary. Even if you pass, the report shows areas you may need to review to keep your edge. If you need to retake an exam, you'll have to call Sylvan Prometric, schedule a new test date, and pay another $125.

Tracking OCP Status

Oracle generates transcripts that indicate the exams you have passed and your corresponding test scores. After you pass the necessary set of five exams, you'll be certified as an Oracle8 DBA. Official certification can take anywhere from four to six weeks (although generally four weeks), so don't expect to get your credentials overnight. Once certified, you will receive a package with a Welcome Kit that contains a number of elements:

➤ An OCP-DBA certificate, suitable for framing

➤ A license agreement to use the OCP logo. Once the agreement is sent into Oracle and your packet of logo information is received, it allows you to use the logo for advertisements, promotions, documents, letterhead, business cards, and so on. An OCP logo sheet, which includes camera-ready artwork, comes with the license.

Many people believe that the benefits of OCP certification go well beyond the perks that Oracle provides to newly anointed members of this elite group. I am starting to see more job listings that request or require applicants to have an OCP-DBA certification, and many individuals who complete the program can qualify for increases in pay and/or responsibility. As an official recognition of hard work and broad knowledge, OCP certification is a badge of honor in many IT organizations.

How To Prepare For An Exam

At a minimum, preparing for OCP-DBA exams requires that you obtain and study the following materials:

➤ The Oracle8 Server version 8.0.5 Documentation Set on CD-ROM

➤ The exam prep materials, practice tests, and self-assessment exams on the Oracle certification page (**http://education.oracle.com/certification**). Find the materials, download them, and use them!

➤ This *Exam Cram* book. It's the first and last thing you should read before taking the exam.

In addition, you'll probably find any or all of the following materials useful in your quest for Oracle8 DBA expertise:

➤ *OCP Resource Kits*—Oracle has a CD-ROM with example questions and materials to help with the exam; generally, these are provided free by requesting them from your Oracle representative. The discs have also been offered free for the taking at most Oracle conventions, such as IOUGA-Alive! and Oracle Open World.

➤ *Classroom Training*—Oracle, TUSC, LearningTree, and many others offer classroom and computer-based, training material that you will find helpful in preparing for the exam. But a word of warning: These classes are fairly expensive (in the range of $300 per day). However, they do offer a condensed form of learning to help you "brush up" on your Oracle knowledge. The tests are closely tied to the classroom training provided by Oracle, so I would suggest at least taking the introductory classes to get the Oracle-specific (and classroom-specific) terminology under your belt.

➤ *Other Publications*—You'll find direct references to other publications and resources in this book, and there's no shortage of materials available about Oracle8 DBA topics. To help you sift through some of the publications out there, each chapter ends with a "Need To Know More?" section that provides pointers to exhaustive resources covering that chapter's subject matter.

➤ *The Oracle Administrator and PL/SQL Developer*—These online references are available from RevealNet, Inc., an Oracle and database online reference provider. These online references provide instant lookup on thousands of database and developmental topics and are an invaluable resource for studying and learning about Oracle. Demo copies can be downloaded from **www.revealnet.com**. Also available at the RevealNet Web site are the DBA and PL/SQL Pipelines, online discussion groups where you can obtain expert information from Oracle DBAs worldwide. The costs of these applications run about $400 each (current pricing is available on the Web site) and are worth every cent.

These required and recommended materials represent an unparalleled collection of sources and resources for Oracle8 DBA topics and software. In the section that follows, I explain how this book works and give you some good reasons why this book should also be on your required and recommended materials list.

About This Book

Each *Exam Cram* chapter follows a regular structure, along with graphical cues about especially important or useful material. Here's the structure of a typical chapter:

➤ *Opening Hotlists*—Each chapter begins with lists of the terms, tools, and techniques that you must learn and understand before you can be fully conversant with the chapter's subject matter. I follow the hotlists with one or two introductory paragraphs to set the stage for the rest of the chapter.

➤ *Topical Coverage*—After the opening hotlists, each chapter covers a series of topics related to the chapter's subject. Throughout this section, I highlight the material that is most likely to appear on a test using a special Exam Alert layout, like this:

This is what an Exam Alert looks like. Normally, an Exam Alert stresses concepts, terms, software, or activities that will most likely appear in one or more certification test questions. For that reason, any information found offset in this Exam Alert format is worthy of unusual attentiveness on your part. Indeed, most of the facts appearing in the Cram Sheet appear as Exam Alerts within the text.

Occasionally, in *Exam Crams*, you'll see tables called "Vital Statistics." The contents of Vital Statistics tables are worthy of extra study, because they contain informational tidbits that might show up in a test question.

Even if material isn't flagged as an Exam Alert or included in a Vital Statistics table, *all* the contents of this book are associated, at least tangentially, to something test-related. This book is tightly focused for quick test preparation, so you'll find that what appears in the meat of each chapter is critical knowledge.

I have also provided tips that will help build a better foundation of knowledge for database administration. Although the information may not be on the exam, it is highly relevant and will help you become a better test-taker.

This is how tips are formatted. Keep your eyes open for these, and you'll become a test guru in no time!

➤ *Practice Questions*—This section presents a series of mock test questions and explanations of both correct and incorrect answers. I also try to point out especially tricky questions by using a special icon, like this:

Ordinarily, this icon flags the presence of an especially devious question, if not an outright trick question. Trick questions are calculated to trap you if you don't read them carefully, and more than once at that. Although they're not ubiquitous, such questions make regular appearances in the Oracle8 exams. That's why I say exam questions are as much about reading comprehension as they are about knowing DBA material inside out and backward.

➤ *Details and Resources*—The "Need To Know More?" section at the end of each chapter provides direct pointers to Oracle and third-party resources that offer further details on the chapter's subject matter. In addition, these sections try to rate the quality and thoroughness of each topic's coverage. If you find a resource you like in this collection, use it (but don't feel compelled to use all these resources). On the other hand, I recommend only the resources that I use on a regular basis, so none of my recommendations will be a waste of your time or money.

The bulk of the book slavishly follows this chapter structure, but I would like to point out a few other elements. Chapter 12 includes a sample test that provides a good review of the material presented throughout the book to ensure you're ready for the exam. Chapter 13 provides an answer key to the sample test. Additionally, you'll find the glossary and an index that you can use to define and track down terms as they appear in the text.

Finally, look for the Cram Sheet, which appears inside the front of this *Exam Cram* book, because it is a valuable tool that represents a condensed and compiled collection of facts, figures, and tips that I think you should memorize before taking the test. Because you can dump this information out of your head onto a piece of paper before answering any exam questions, you can master this information by brute force, remembering it only long enough to write it down after you walk into the test room. You might even want to look at it in the car or in the lobby of the testing center just before you walk in to take the test.

How To Use This Book

If you're prepping for a first-time test, I've structured the topics in this book to build upon each other. Therefore, some topics in later chapters make more sense after you've read earlier chapters. That's why I suggest you read this book from front to back for your initial test preparation.

If you need to brush up on a topic or you have to prepare for a second try, use the index or table of contents to find the topics and questions that you need to study. Beyond the tests, I think you'll find this book useful as a tightly focused reference to some of the most important aspects of topics associated with being a DBA, as implemented under Oracle8.

Given all the book's elements and its specialized focus, I've tried to create a tool that you can use to prepare for—but especially to pass—the Oracle OCP-DBA set of examinations. Please share your feedback on the book with me, especially if you have ideas about how I can improve it for future test-takers. I'll consider everything you say carefully, and I try to respond to all suggestions. You can reach me via email at **bpascavage@aol.com**. Or you can send your questions or comments to **cipq@coriolis.com**.

For up-to-date information on certification, online discussion forums, sample tests, content updates, and more, visit the Certification Insider Press Web site at **www.certificationinsider.com**.

Thanks, and enjoy the book!

Self-Assessment

. . . .

I've included a Self-Assessment in this *Exam Cram* to help you evaluate your readiness to tackle Oracle8 OCP-DBA certification. It should also help you understand what you need to master the topic of this book—namely, Exam 1ZO-016 (Test 5), "Oracle8: Network Administration." But before you tackle this self-assessment, let's talk about the concerns you may face when pursuing an Oracle8 OCP-DBA, and who an ideal Oracle8 OCP-DBA candidate might be.

Oracle8 OCP-DBAs In The Real World

In the next section, I describe an ideal Oracle8 OCP-DBA candidate, knowing full well that only a few actual candidates meet this ideal. In fact, our description of that ideal candidate might seem downright scary. But take heart, because, although the requirements to obtain an Oracle8 OCP-DBA may seem pretty formidable, they are by no means impossible to meet. However, you should be keenly aware that it does take time, requires some expense, and consumes a substantial effort.

You can get all the real-world motivation you need from knowing that many others have gone before you. You can follow in their footsteps. If you're willing to tackle the process seriously and do what it takes to obtain the necessary experience and knowledge, you can take—and pass—the certification tests. In fact, the *Exam Crams* and the companion *Exam Preps* are designed to make it as easy as possible for you to prepare for these exams. But prepare you must!

The same, of course, is true for other Oracle certifications, including:

➤ Oracle7.3 OCP-DBA, which is like the Oracle8 OCP-DBA certification but requires only four core exams.

➤ Application Developer, Oracle Developer Rel 1 OCP, which is aimed at software developers and requires five exams.

➤ Application Developer, Oracle Developer Rel 2 OCP, which is aimed at software developers and requires five exams.

➤ Oracle Database Operators OCP, which is aimed at database operators and requires only one exam.

➤ Oracle Java Technology Certification OCP, which is aimed at Java developers and requires five exams.

The Ideal Oracle8 OCP-DBA Candidate

Just to give you some idea of what an ideal Oracle8 OCP-DBA candidate is like, here are some relevant statistics about the background and experience such an individual might have. Don't worry if you don't meet these qualifications (or, indeed, if you don't even come close), because this world is far from ideal, and where you fall short is simply where you'll have more work to do. The ideal candidate will have:

➤ Academic or professional training in relational databases, Structured Query Language (SQL), performance tuning, backup and recovery, and Net8 administration.

➤ Three-plus years of professional database administration experience, including experience installing and upgrading Oracle executables, creating and tuning databases, troubleshooting connection problems, creating users, and managing backup and recovery scenarios.

I believe that well under half of all certification candidates meet these requirements. In fact, most probably meet less than half of these requirements (that is, at least when they begin the certification process). But, because all those who have their certifications already survived this ordeal, you can survive it, too—especially if you heed what this Self-Assessment can tell you about what you already know and what you need to learn.

Put Yourself To The Test

The following series of questions and observations is designed to help you figure out how much work you'll face in pursuing Oracle certification and what kinds of resources you may consult on your quest. Be absolutely honest in your answers, or you'll end up wasting money on exams you're not ready to take. There are no right or wrong answers, only steps along the path to certification. Only you can decide where you really belong in the broad spectrum of aspiring candidates.

Two things should be clear from the outset, however:

➤ Even a modest background in computer science will be helpful.

➤ Hands-on experience with Oracle products and technologies is an essential ingredient to certification success.

Educational Background

1. Have you ever taken any computer-related classes? [Yes or No]

    If yes, proceed to question 2; if no, proceed to question 4.

2. Have you taken any classes on relational databases? [Yes or No]

    If yes, you will probably be able to handle Oracle's architecture and network administration discussions. If you're rusty, brush up on the basic concepts of databases and networks.

    If the answer is no, consider some basic reading in this area. I strongly recommend a good Oracle database administration book such as *Oracle8 Administration and Management* by Michael R. Ault (Wiley, 1998). Or, if this title doesn't appeal to you, check out reviews for other, similar titles at your favorite online bookstore.

3. Have you taken any networking concepts or technologies classes? [Yes or No]

    If yes, you will probably be able to handle Oracle's networking terminology, concepts, and technologies (but brace yourself for frequent departures from normal usage). If you're rusty, brush up on basic networking concepts and terminology.

    If your answer is no, you might want to check out the Oracle technet Web site (**http://technet.oracle.com**) and read some of the white papers on Net8. If you have access to the Oracle MetaLink Web site, download the Oracle Net8 Administration manual.

4. Have you done any reading on relational databases or networks? [Yes or No]

    If yes, review the requirements from questions 2 and 3. If you meet those, move to the next section, "Hands-On Experience."

    If you answered no, consult the recommended reading for both topics. This kind of strong background will be of great help in preparing you for the Oracle exams.

Hands-On Experience

Another important key to success on all of the Oracle tests is hands-on experience, especially with Net8 Assistant. If I leave you with only one realization after taking this Self-Assessment, it should be that there's no substitute for time spent installing, configuring, and using the various Oracle products upon which you'll be tested repeatedly and in depth.

5. Have you installed, configured, and worked with Net8? [Yes or No]

> If yes, make sure you understand basic concepts as covered in Exam 1Z0-013, "Oracle8: Database Administration" (Test 2) and advanced concepts as covered in Exam 1Z0-014, "Oracle8: Performance Tuning" (Test 4). You should also study the Net8configuration and administration for Exam 1Z0-016 (Test 5), "Oracle8: Network Administration."

 You can download the candidate certification guide, objectives, practice exams, and other information about Oracle exams from the company's Training and Certification page on the Web at **http://education.oracle.com/certification**.

> If you haven't worked with Oracle, you must obtain a copy of Oracle8 or Personal Oracle8. Then, learn about the database and Net8.

 For the Oracle exams, the Candidate Guide for the topics involved are a good study resource. You can download it free from the Oracle Web site (**http://education.oracle.com**). You can also download information on purchasing additional exam practice tests ($99 per exam).

If you have the funds or your employer will pay your way, consider taking a class at an Oracle training and education center.

Before you even think about taking any Oracle exam, make sure you've spent enough time with Net8 to understand how it may be installed and configured, how to maintain such an installation, and how to troubleshoot Net8 when things go wrong. This will help you in the exam—as well as in real life.

Testing Your Exam-Readiness

Whether you attend a formal class on a specific topic to get ready for an exam or use written materials to study on your own, some preparation for the Oracle certification exams is essential. At $125 a try, pass or fail, you want to do everything you can to pass on your first try. That's where studying comes in.

I have included in this book several practice exam questions for each chapter and a sample test, so if you don't score well on the chapter questions, you can study more and then tackle the sample test at the end of the book. If you don't earn a score of at least 80 percent after this test, you'll want to investigate the other resources I mention in this section.

For any given subject, consider taking a class if you've tackled self-study materials, taken the test, and failed anyway. If you can afford the privilege, the opportunity to interact with an instructor and fellow students can make all the difference in the world. For information about Oracle classes, visit the Training and Certification page at **http://education.oracle.com**.

If you can't afford to take a class, visit the Training and Certification page anyway, because it also includes free practice exams that you can download. Even if you can't afford to spend much at all, you should still invest in some low-cost practice exams from commercial vendors, because they can help you assess your readiness to pass a test better than any other tool. All of the following companies offer practice exams on their Web sites for less than $100 apiece (and some for significantly less than that):

➤ Selftest Software at **www.selftestsoftware.com**

➤ CramSession at **www.cramsession.com**

6. Have you taken a practice exam on your chosen test subject? [Yes or No]

    If yes—and you scored 80 percent or better—you're probably ready to tackle the real thing. If your score isn't above that crucial threshold, keep at it until you break that barrier.

    If you answered no, obtain all the free and low-budget practice tests you can find (or afford) and get to work. Keep at it until you can comfortably break the passing threshold.

There is no better way to assess your test readiness than to take a good-quality practice exam and pass with a score of 80 percent or better. When we're preparing ourselves, we shoot for 80-plus percent, just to leave room for the "weirdness factor" that sometimes shows up on Oracle exams.

Assessing Your Readiness For Oracle8: Network Administration Exam (Test 5)

In addition to the general exam-readiness information in the previous section, other resources are available to help you prepare for the Oracle8: Network Administration exam. For starters, visit the RevealNet pipeline (**www. revealnet.com**) or **technet.oracle.com**. These are great places to ask questions and get good answers, or simply to observe the questions that others ask (along with the answers, of course).

Oracle exam mavens also recommend checking the Oracle Knowledge Base from RevealNet. You can get information on purchasing the RevealNet software at **www.revealnet.com**.

For Oracle8: Network Administration preparation in particular, I'd also like to recommend that you check out one or more of these books as you prepare the exam:

➤ Ault, Michael. *Oracle8 Administration and Management.* Wiley, 1998.

➤ Loney, Kevin. *Oracle8 DBA Handbook.* Oracle Press, 1998.

➤ Kreines, David C., and Laskey, Brian. *Oracle Database Administration.* O'Reilly, 1999.

➤ Toledo, Hugo. *Oracle Networking.* Oracle Press, 1996.

Stop by your favorite bookstore or online bookseller to check out one or more of these books. The first two are—in our opinion—the best general, all-around references on Oracle8 available, and the third complements the contents of this *Exam Cram* very nicely. While the fourth book is somewhat dated, it provides excellent basic information on networking.

One last note: Hopefully, it makes sense to stress the importance of hands-on experience in the context of the Network Administration exam. As you review the material for that exam, you'll realize that hands-on experience with Oracle8 commands, tools, and utilities is invaluable.

Onward, Through The Fog!

Once you've assessed your readiness, undertaken the right background studies, obtained the hands-on experience that will help you understand the products and technologies at work, and reviewed the many sources of information to help you prepare for a test, you'll be ready to take a round of practice tests.

When your scores come back positive enough to get you through the exam, you're ready to go after the real thing. If you follow our assessment regime, you'll not only know what you need to study, but when you're ready to make a test date at Sylvan. Good luck!

Oracle OCP
Certification Exams

. . . .

Terms you'll need to understand:

√ Radio button

√ Checkbox

√ Exhibit

√ Multiple-choice question formats

√ Careful reading

√ Process of elimination

Techniques you'll need to master:

√ Assessing your exam-readiness

√ Preparing to take a certification exam

√ Practicing (to make perfect)

√ Making the best use of the testing software

√ Budgeting your time

√ Saving the hardest questions until last

√ Guessing (as a last resort)

As experiences go, taking tests is not something that most people eagerly anticipate, no matter how well they're prepared. However, in most cases, familiarity helps ameliorate test anxiety. (In plain English, this means you probably won't be as nervous when you take your fourth or fifth Oracle certification exam as you will be when you take your first.)

But, no matter whether it's your first test or your tenth, understanding the exam-taking particulars (how much time to spend on questions, the setting you'll be in, and so on) and the testing software will help you concentrate on the material rather than on the environment. Likewise, mastering a few basic test-taking skills should help you recognize—and perhaps even outfox—some of the tricks you're bound to find in some of the Oracle test questions.

In this chapter, I'll explain the testing environment and software, as well as some proven test-taking strategies you should be able to use to your advantage.

Assessing Exam-Readiness

Before you take any Oracle exam, I strongly recommend that you read through and take the Self-Assessment included with this book (it appears just before this chapter, in fact). This will help you compare your knowledge base to the requirements for obtaining an OCP, and it will also help you identify parts of your background or experience that may be in need of improvement, enhancement, or further learning. If you get the right set of basics under your belt, obtaining Oracle certification will be that much easier.

Once you've gone through the Self-Assessment, you can remedy those topical areas where your background or experience may not measure up to an ideal certification candidate. But you can also tackle subject matter for individual tests at the same time, so you can continue making progress while you're catching up in some areas.

Once you've worked through an *Exam Cram*, have read the supplementary materials, and have taken the practice test at the end of the book, you'll have a pretty clear idea of when you should be ready to take the real exam. Although I strongly recommend that you keep practicing until your scores top the 70 percent mark, 75 percent would be a good goal to give yourself some margin for error in a real exam situation (where stress will play more of a role than when you practice). Once you hit that point, you should be ready to go. But if you get through the practice exam in this book without attaining that score, you should keep taking practice tests and studying the materials until you get there. You'll find more information about other practice test vendors in the Self-Assessment, along with even more pointers on how to study and prepare. But now, on to the exam itself!

The Testing Situation

When you arrive at the Sylvan Prometric testing center where you've scheduled your test, you'll need to sign in with a test coordinator. You'll be asked to produce two forms of identification, one of which must be a photo ID. Once you've signed in and your time slot arrives, you'll be asked to leave any books, bags, or other items you brought with you, and you'll be escorted into a closed room. Typically, the room will be furnished with anywhere from one to six computers, and each workstation is separated from the others by dividers that are designed to keep you from seeing what's happening on someone else's computer.

You'll be furnished with a pen or pencil and a blank sheet of paper, or in some cases, an erasable plastic sheet and an erasable felt-tip pen. You're allowed to write down any information you want on this sheet, and you can write stuff on both sides of the page. I suggest that you memorize as much as possible of the material that appears on the Cram Sheet (inside the front of this book), and then write that information down on the blank sheet as soon as you sit down in front of the test machine. You can refer to the sheet any time you like during the test, but you'll have to surrender it when you leave the room.

Most test rooms feature a wall with a large window from which the test coordinator will monitor the room. The test coordinator will have loaded the Oracle certification test that you've signed up for, and you'll be permitted to start as soon as you're seated in front of the machine.

All Oracle certification exams permit you to take up to a certain maximum amount of time (usually 90 minutes). The computer maintains an on-screen counter/clock so that you can check the time remaining any time you like. Each exam consists of between 60 and 70 questions that are randomly selected from a pool of questions.

The passing score varies per exam and the questions selected. For the Oracle8: Network Administration Exam, the passing score is 69 percent.

All Oracle certification exams are computer-generated and use a multiple-choice format. Although this might sound easy, the questions are constructed not just to check your mastery of basic facts and figures about Oracle8 DBA topics, but also to evaluate one or more sets of circumstances or requirements. Often, you'll be asked to give more than one answer to a question; likewise, you may be asked to select the best or most effective solution from a range of choices, all of which technically are correct. The tests are quite an adventure, and they involve real thinking. This book will show you what to expect and how to deal with the problems, puzzles, and predicaments you're likely to find on the tests (in particular, Test 1Z0-016: "Oracle8: Network Administration").

Test Layout And Design

A typical test question is depicted in Question 1. It's a multiple-choice question that requires you to select a single correct answer. Following the question is a brief summary of each potential answer and why it was either right or wrong.

Question 1

You issue this lsnrctl command:

```
lsnrctl services
```

What task has been accomplished?

○ a. The listener process is stopped.

○ b. The uptime is listed for the listener process.

○ c. A list of the number of connections completed and refused by the listener process is displayed.

○ d. No task was accomplished because a listener name was not designated.

The correct answer is c. The services command produces a list of the number of connections that have been completed and refused for the default process (listener). The command to stop the listener process is lsnrctl stop. The uptime is displayed using the lsnrctl status command. If no listener name is specified then the default name LISTENER is assumed, and the command is executed for that process.

This sample question corresponds closely to those you'll see on Oracle certification tests. To select the correct answer during the test, you position the cursor over the radio button next to answer c and click the mouse to select that particular choice. The only difference between the certification test and this question is that the real questions are not immediately followed by the answers.

Next, I'll examine a question in which one or more answers are possible. This type of question provides checkboxes, rather than radio buttons, for marking all appropriate selections.

Question 2

> What are three ways to configure name resolution? [Choose the three best answers]
>
> ❏ a. Host naming
>
> ❏ b. ANO
>
> ❏ c. Connection concentration
>
> ❏ d. Local naming
>
> ❏ e. Centralized naming
>
> ❏ f. Connection pooling

The correct answer for this question is a, d, and e. The host-naming method uses defaults for name resolution. The local-naming method depends upon a tnsnames.ora file. Centralized naming is the configuration of a central place for configuration and administration of address information (Oracle Names). ANO is the Advanced Networking Option which provides additional security options through data encryption, cryptographic checksumming, and support for authentication services. Connection pooling and connection concentration are methods of sharing connections to support a large user population in an OLTP environment.

For this type of question, all the parts to the answer must be selected to answer the question correctly.

These two basic types of questions can appear in many forms and they constitute the foundation on which all the Oracle certification exam questions rest. More complex questions may include so-called "exhibits," which are usually tables or data-content layouts of one form or another. You'll be expected to use the information displayed in the exhibit to guide your answer to the question.

Other questions involving exhibits may use charts or diagrams to help document a workplace scenario that you'll be asked to troubleshoot or configure. Paying careful attention to such exhibits is the key to success. Be prepared to toggle between the picture and the question as you work. Often, both are complex enough that you might not be able to remember all of either one.

Using Oracle's Test Software Effectively

A well-known test-taking principle is to initially read over the entire test from start to finish, but to answer on this pass only those questions that you feel absolutely sure of. On subsequent passes, you can dive into more-complex questions, knowing how many such questions you have to deal with.

Fortunately, Oracle test software makes this approach easy to implement. At the bottom of each question, you'll find a checkbox that permits you to mark that question for a later visit. (Note that marking questions makes review easier, but you can return to any question by clicking the Forward and Back buttons repeatedly until you get to the question.) As you read each question, if you answer only those you're sure of and mark for review those that you're not, you can keep going through a decreasing list of open questions as you knock the trickier ones off in order.

There's at least one potential benefit to reading through the test before answering the trickier questions. Sometimes you find information in later questions that sheds light on earlier ones. Other times, information you read in later questions might jog your memory about Oracle8 facts, figures, or behavior that also will help with earlier questions. Either way, you'll come out ahead if you defer those questions about which you're not absolutely sure of.

Keep working on the questions until you are absolutely sure of all your answers or until you know you'll run out of time. If you still have unanswered questions, you'll want to zip through them and guess. Not answering a question at all only guarantees you'll get no credit for it, and a guess has at least a chance of being correct. (Oracle scores blank answers and incorrect answers as equally wrong.)

At the very end of your test period, you're better off guessing than leaving questions blank or unanswered.

Taking Testing Seriously

The most important advice I can give you about taking any Oracle test is this: Read each question carefully. Some questions are deliberately ambiguous; some use double negatives; others use terminology in incredibly precise ways. I've taken numerous practice tests and real tests, and, in nearly every test, I've missed at least one question because I didn't read it closely or carefully enough.

Here are some suggestions on how to deal with the tendency to jump to an answer too quickly:

➤ Make sure you read every word in the question. If you find yourself jumping ahead impatiently, return to the beginning of the question and start over.

➤ As you read, try to restate the question in your own terms. If you can do this, you should be able to pick the correct answer(s) much more easily.

➤ When returning to a question after your initial read-through, reread every word again. Otherwise, the mind falls quickly into a rut. Sometimes seeing a question afresh after turning your attention elsewhere lets you see something you missed before, but the strong tendency is to see only what you've seen before. Try to avoid this natural tendency at all costs.

➤ If you return to a question more than twice, try to articulate to yourself what you don't understand about the question, why the answers don't appear to make sense, or what appears to be missing. If you chew on the subject for a while, your subconscious might provide the details that are lacking, or you may notice a "trick" that will point to the right answer.

Above all, try to deal with each question by thinking through what you know about being an Oracle8—utilities, characteristics, behaviors, facts, and figures. By reviewing what you know (and what you've written down on your information sheet), you'll often recall or understand things sufficiently to determine the answer to the question.

Question-Handling Strategies

Based on the tests I've taken, a couple of interesting trends in the answers have become apparent. For those questions that take only a single answer, usually two or three of the answers will be obviously incorrect, and two of the answers will be plausible. But, of course, only one can be correct. Unless the answer leaps out at you (and if it does, reread the question to look for a trick, because sometimes those are the ones you're most likely to get wrong), begin the answering process by eliminating those answers that are obviously wrong.

Things to look for in the "obviously wrong" category include spurious command choices or table or view names, nonexistent software or command options, and terminology you've never seen before. If you've done your homework for a test, no valid information should be completely new to you. In that case, unfamiliar or bizarre terminology probably indicates a totally bogus answer. As long as you're sure what's right, it's easy to eliminate what's wrong.

Numerous questions assume that the default behavior of a particular Oracle utility (such as the listener control utility) is in effect. It's essential, therefore, to know and understand the default settings for the listener, Oracle Names, Connection Manager, MTS, Intelligent Agent, and ANO. If you know the defaults and understand what they mean, this knowledge will help you cut through many knots.

Likewise, when dealing with questions that require multiple answers, you must know and select all of the correct options to get credit. This, too, qualifies as an example of why careful reading is so important.

As you work your way through the test, another counter that Oracle thankfully provides will come in handy: the number of questions completed and questions outstanding. Budget your time by making sure that you've completed one-fourth of the questions one-quarter of the way through the test period (between 13 and 17 questions in the first 22 or 23 minutes). Check again three-quarters of the way through (between 39 and 51 questions in the first 66 to 69 minutes).

If you're not through after 85 minutes, use the last five minutes to guess your way through the remaining questions. Remember, guesses are potentially more valuable than blank answers, because blanks are always wrong and a guess might turn out to be right. If you haven't a clue with any of the remaining questions, pick answers at random, or choose all a's, b's, and so on. The important thing is to submit a test for scoring that has an answer for every question.

Mastering The Inner Game

In the final analysis, knowledge breeds confidence, and confidence breeds success. If you study the materials in this book carefully and review all of the questions at the end of each chapter, you should be aware of those areas for which additional studying is required.

Next, follow up by reading some or all of the materials recommended in the "Need To Know More?" section at the end of each chapter. The idea is to become familiar enough with the concepts and situations that you find in the sample questions to be able to reason your way through similar situations on a real test. If you know the material, you have every right to be confident that you can pass the test.

Once you've worked your way through the book, take the practice test in Chapter 12. The test will provide a reality check and will help you identify areas that you need to study further. Make sure you follow up and review materials related to the questions you miss before scheduling a real test. Only when you've covered all the ground and feel comfortable with the whole scope of the practice test should you take a real test.

If you take my practice test (Chapter 12) and don't score at least 80 percent correct, you'll want to practice further. At a minimum, download the practice tests and the self-assessment tests from the Oracle Education Web site's download page. If you're more ambitious or better funded, you might want to purchase a practice test from a third-party vendor. I've had good luck with tests from Self Test Software. See the next section in this chapter for contact information.

Armed with the information in this book and with the determination to increase your knowledge, you should be able to pass the certification exam. But, if you don't work at it, you'll spend the test fee more than once before you finally do pass. If you prepare seriously, the exam should go flawlessly. Good luck!

Additional Resources

By far, the best source of information about Oracle certification tests comes from Oracle itself. Because its products and technologies—and the tests that go with them—change frequently, the best place to go for exam-related information is online.

If you haven't already visited the Oracle certification pages, do so right now. As I'm writing this chapter, the certification page resides at **http://education. oracle.com/certification.** (See Figure 1.1.)

> *Note: The certification page might not be there by the time you read this, or it may have been replaced by something new and different, because things change regularly on the Oracle site. Should this happen, please read the section titled "Coping With Change On The Web," later in this chapter.*

The menu options in the left column of the page point to the most important sources of information in the certification pages. Here's what to check out:

➤ *FAQs*—Chances are that your question is a Frequently Asked Question. If so, yours will probably get answered here.

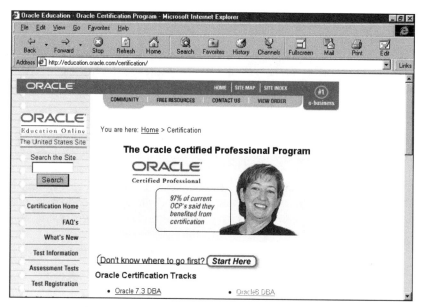

Figure 1.1   The Oracle certification page should be your starting point for further investigation of the most current exam and preparation information.

➤ *What's New*—Any new tests will be described here.

➤ *Test Information*—This is a detailed section that provides many jump points to detailed test descriptions for the several OCP certifications.

➤ *Assessment Tests*—This section provides an online questionnaire that you must complete before downloading the latest copy of the assessment test.

➤ *Test Registration*—This section provides information for phone registration and a link to the Prometric Web page for online registration. Also, this section provides a list of testing sites outside the USA.

➤ *Candidate Agreements*—Just what are you agreeing to be by becoming Oracle certified?

➤ *Oracle Partners*—This link provides information about test discounts and other offers for Oracle Partner companies.

Of course, these are just the high points of what's available in the Oracle certification pages. As you browse through them—and I strongly recommend that you do—you'll probably find other things I didn't mention here that are every bit as interesting and helpful.

Coping With Change On The Web

Sooner or later, all the specifics I've shared with you about the Oracle certification pages, and all the other Web-based resources I mention throughout the rest of this book, will go stale or be replaced by newer information. In some cases, the URLs you find here might lead you to their replacements; in other cases, the URLs will go nowhere, leaving you with the dreaded "404 File not found" error message.

When that happens, please don't give up. There's always a way to find what you want on the Web, if you're willing to invest some time and energy. To begin with, most large or complex Web sites—and Oracle's qualifies on both counts—offer a search engine. As long as you can get to Oracle's home page (and I'm sure that it will stay at **www.oracle.com** for a long while yet), you can use this tool to help you find what you need.

The more particular or focused you can make a search request, the more likely it is that the results will include information you can use. For instance, you can search the string "training and certification" to produce a lot of data about the subject in general, but, if you're looking for the Preparation Guide for the Oracle DBA tests, you'll be more likely to get there quickly if you use a Boolean search string such as this:

```
"DBA" AND "preparation guide"
```

Likewise, if you want to find the training and certification downloads, try a string such as this one:

```
"training and certification" AND "download page"
```

Finally, don't be afraid to use general search tools such as **www.search.com**, **www.altavista.com**, or **www.excite.com** to search for related information. Even though Oracle offers the best information about its certification exams online, plenty of third-party vendors offer information, training, and assistance in this area, and with the advantage that they do not have to follow a party line like Oracle does. So, if you can't find something where the book says it lives, start looking around. If worse comes to worse, you can always email me! I just might have a clue. My email address is bpascavage@aol.com.

Third-Party Test Providers

Example assessment tests are available from some third-party companies. I suggest obtaining and taking as many of these as you can so that you become completely familiar and confident with test taking. Among these third-party providers are:

➤ *RevealNet, Inc.*—The Oracle Administrator program has a complete review section for the DBA examination with example test questions. A fully functional, 15-day demo can be downloaded from the Web site (www.revealnet.com) free of charge. You can also call RevealNet at 1-800-738-3254 or 202-234-8557. RevealNet's address is RevealNet, Inc., PO Box 5560, Rockville, MD 20855.

➤ *Self Test Software*—Self Test also offers sample Oracle tests for all five of the OCP-DBA tests. Self Test is located at 4651 Woodstock Road, Suite 203-384, Roswell, GA, 30075. The company can be reached by phone at 770-641-9719 or 1-800-200-6446, and by fax at 770-641-1489. Visit Self Test's Web site at www.selftestsoftware.com; you can even order the software online.

➤ *DBDomain*—Formerly ORAWorld, this company provides study guides for the OCP exams. Contact them via its Web site (www.dbdomain.com), by phone (1-800-235-3030) or fax (1-805-929-8906), or by standard mail (PO Box 239, Arroyo Grande, CA, 93421-0239). DBDomain is associated with Animated Learning, Incorporated.

Network Overview

Terms you'll need to understand:

√ Two-tier architecture

√ N-tier architecture

√ Net8 Assistant

√ Oracle Names

√ Connection Manager

√ Advanced Networking Option

√ Security Server

√ Gateways

Techniques you'll need to master:

√ Understanding the issues involved in analyzing your network needs

√ Understanding the solutions available for configuration of Net8

This chapter provides you with an overview of how Oracle Net8 operates and covers the various methods that can be used to set up network connections. It also introduces Oracle Names, Connection Manager, Advanced Networking Option, Security Servers, and Oracle Gateways.

Oracle8 And The Network

Client applications need a method of connecting with the Oracle8 databases. The purpose of Net8 is to configure, establish, and maintain the connection between the user application and the Oracle database. Net8 provides:

➤ An open API,

➤ Network protocol independence,

➤ Platform independence,

➤ Security options, and

➤ Diagnostic and configuration tools.

At the implementation stage, it is important to plan the network and determine the Net8 options that you will implement. In order to determine how to configure your network properly, you will need to understand your application environment, the number of users, the network protocol, and so forth.

The process of connecting to an Oracle8 database begins with the client application requesting a connection to the Oracle database. At the server end, a listener process picks up the connection request and makes the connection to the database.

In the following sections, I'll discuss the network connection configurations and the features of each.

 It is important that you be able to identify when a simple (or two tier) configuration is desirable versus when an n-tier configuration should be used.

Two-Tier Network Connection

The simplest connection method is a two-tier architecture (Figure 2.1), also known as the *client/server architecture* or *simple network configuration*. The client connects directly to the Oracle database via the network.

In order to use this simple client/server configuration, the client and server must use the same network protocol. For example, if the server is using TCP/IP, then the client must also use TCP/IP.

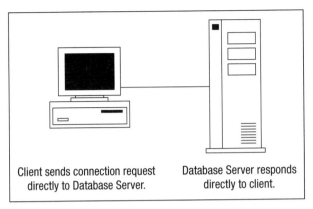

Figure 2.1   A two-tier (simple) configuration.

The simple, two-tier architecture works best in environments that have a small client population (usually less than a hundred clients). A common error is to use the two-tier connection method for an environment with hundreds or thousands of users. In such a situation, the server may not be able to handle this many connection requests. The clients either will not be able to make a connection or they will experience very slow performance as the server becomes overloaded. If the server becomes overloaded, it may be necessary to change to an n-tier configuration (discussed in the next section) to support the client population.

In a two-tier network configuration, the client workstation is often a fat client: It contains the application as well as the Net8 executables. This is a much more complex and decentralized configuration to maintain. Changes in the network or Oracle database servers may require changes to every client workstation.

N-Tier Network Connection

For environments that require many simultaneous connections, you should use the n-tier network connection method because it adds a middle tier or application server between the client and server. This middle tier is also known as the *agent*. See Figure 2.2.

The client issues a connection request. This request is transmitted over the network and is picked up by the agent. The middle tier contains the actual applications and can hold data that the client applications need. The middle tier sends the requests on to the database server.

For the most efficient accessibility of applications, the n-tier network connection configuration is recommended. An application can be placed on the agent, making it accessible to all the clients across your organization. This is a much

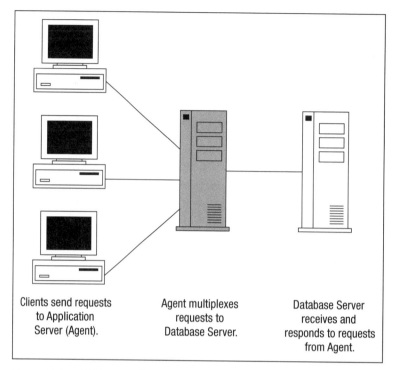

| Clients send requests to Application Server (Agent). | Agent multiplexes requests to Database Server. | Database Server receives and responds to requests from Agent. |

Figure 2.2 N-tier configuration.

easier method to maintain and distribute applications. With a two-tier configuration, every workstation needs to be individually configured for each new application, as well as each upgrade. With the use of an n-tier configuration, distribution, upgrades, and maintenance are performed at the middle-tier level. This centralization of maintenance is very desirable in a large, complex environment.

The use of a middle tier provides the following benefits:

➤ Translation services

➤ Scalability

➤ Intelligent agent services

Translation Services

Translation services provide a method to bridge the gap between clients and legacy systems and the Oracle database. Applications that are needed to integrate between legacy systems and the Oracle database can be set up on the middle tier or agent. Also, the middle tier can be configured to provide a bridge between different network protocols.

Scalability

Scalability should be considered from two aspects: user population and application.

From the aspect of the user population, using an n-tier approach allows for growth in the user population. Adding additional application servers as the population grows reduces the burden on the database server. The use of a middle tier supports the configuration of thin clients or workstations that are much less powerful. This feature reduces the overall cost of adding users, as well as the maintenance costs associated with fat-client configurations. A thin-client configuration requires less initial work in the configuration of additional users.

The middle tier can be used to perform load balancing, and the clients can be assigned to one of several application servers. By setting up multiple application servers and spreading the clients among them, an n-tier architecture can be configured to handle very large user environments. See Figure 2.3.

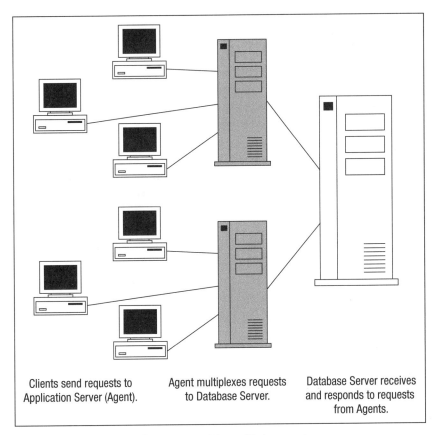

| Clients send requests to Application Server (Agent). | Agent multiplexes requests to Database Server. | Database Server receives and responds to requests from Agents. |

Figure 2.3   N-tier configuration with multiple agents.

The n-tier approach takes the burden of the applications off the database server and the client workstations. It provides scalability in managing the requests between the database server and the clients. Because the middle tier can hold data for the application, this approach can reduce the need to access the database.

Because the application server stores and retrieves data, the network time required is reduced and performance is improved. This is very useful in data warehouse operations in which the data is static and used mainly for analysis and business decisions. The data can be retrieved from the server and manipulated at the application server. This is also very important in an OLTP environment in which performance is crucial.

Intelligent Agent Services

The middle tier can be used to set up an intelligent agent that maps the client requests to multiple servers, collects and collates the results, and returns a single response to the client. In complex environments, this can greatly reduce the transmission of data over the network (and thus provide better performance).

Network Configuration

The increase in the growth of Web-based applications, workflow systems, and mobile clients has resulted in an increased need to access databases that involve a variety of network environments using multiple network protocols. Net8 provides a method to support connections throughout a very complex environment, and it supports multiple operating systems with multiple protocols. You can use Net8 to resolve connection issues with applications that use a variety of syntax. Net8 also provides a way to support large user environments that require very complex, heterogeneous applications and hardware platforms set up over a geographically widespread area.

Some key issues when configuring any network environment are:

➤ Scalability issues

➤ Security requirements

➤ Network protocols

➤ Platform

➤ Integration of applications

➤ Administration requirements (monitoring and troubleshooting)

An analysis of network requirements must address each of the above issues. Table 2.1 displays some of the questions that must be addressed for each of the areas listed above.

Table 2.1	Analyzing network requirements and connectivity issues.
Requirement	**Issues To Be Considered**
Scalability	How many users are there? How many transactions are expected? What are the size and frequency of the transactions? How often will you be adding additional client locations? Do you need the ability to increase the number of clients?
Security	How sensitive is the data? What is the level of security required? What tools will you need to enforce the security requirements?
Network	What network protocols must be supported? Is this a heterogeneous or homogeneous environment? What configuration options are available for your network?
Administration	How often will you be adding new locations? Where is the client population located? Are the users geographically dispersed over a large area or are they located in one central place? How many locations are there? How often do you expect to upgrade? What resources will be available for administration of the network configuration?
Monitoring	What networking resources are available? What resources will you need to troubleshoot network problems?
Platform	What hardware and operating systems will be used?
Integration of applications	Is there a need to support legacy applications?

Good initial planning and analysis are vital in configuring a network that meets the needs of the users. This initial planning of your current and projected needs affect the configuration of your network and the Net8 options you choose to implement.

Scalability

The initial analysis should look at the client population. Do you need a highly scalable environment to accommodate a growing client population? It is very easy to underestimate the number of clients that will use your application. If your initial application is used by only a few clients and then grows to a very large client base, it may be necessary to move from a simple two-tier architecture to an n-tier architecture with a middle-tier agent.

In planning your network, you must consider the number and size of your transactions. Does your user population execute many transactions? If the number of transactions is very large, you need to consider the impact on your network of the transmission of many simultaneous requests between the client and database server. The amount of data transmitted directly contributes to the load on the network. Will you need to support transmissions of large amounts of data in response to user requests? If you are configuring a data warehouse, an OLTP system, or a messaging system, you will need a scalable architecture to support the large amounts of data and the resultant heavy use of the Oracle database server.

When determining the workload that must be supported, you should consider the number of locations, the geographical location of each node, and the number of transactions going over the network. Will you be sending data over long distances? What will be the impact of poor network response time?

What is the configuration of the client? Are you going to have a fat client or a thin client? If you intend to have a thin client, you need to review the requirements of your application and determine if they can be met with a thin client or if an application server will be needed. Also, the cost of using thin clients versus fat clients must be considered. Will an n-tier architecture with one or multiple agent(s) cost more than the total cost of fat-client workstations? Consider the cost in light of the current application use as well as the future, projected use.

Security

How sensitive is the data? What is the level of security required? What tools will you be using to obtain the required security level? If you intend to send encrypted data over the network, you will need to look at the options available from Oracle and other vendors, and you need to consider the integration with the Oracle database. Will Net8 integrate with your current tools or those you intend to purchase?

Network

Net8 provides protocol independence by supporting a variety of network protocols. Net8 supports a variety of network protocols, including the following network protocols:

➤ TCP/IP

➤ Novell SPX/IPX

➤ IBM LU6.2

➤ DECnet

You need to look at your current network configuration and plan how you will integrate Oracle into it. Will you need translation services between multiple network protocols, or will you have one homogeneous network environment?

Administration

How often will you be adding new locations? Where is the client population located? Are your users geographically dispersed over a large area or are they located in one central place? How many locations are there? The configuration decisions you make for your network must consider such administration aspects, including the size and location of the client base.

Will you be able to have one consistent method for setting up Oracle database servers and the client environment? Will each location require a different network configuration? How do you plan to provide support for each location?

How often do you expect to upgrade? What resources will be available to administer the network configuration? Network administration is also impacted by the geographical configuration of your network. When you consider the resources that will be needed, you must include both staff and equipment. What staff is or will be available? What experience levels are available? If you need to upgrade on a regular basis, then you need to consider options such as setting up multiple agents instead of a simple (two-tier) configuration.

Monitoring

What networking resources are available? What resources will you need to troubleshoot network problems? Does each location have the staff and toolset that will be needed? If the network environment is geographically dispersed, this will impact what you will need to monitor as well as how your network will be configured.

Platform

What hardware and operating systems will be used? Oracle is noted for its ability to support a heterogeneous environment, as it supports a variety of hardware platforms with an open API. The client and applications do not have to perform any translations or conversions of data between Oracle databases on various hardware/operating systems. These conversions are performed invisible to the client.

While Oracle will transparently support a heterogeneous environment, you still need to think about the actual versions of the hardware and operating systems to be included in your Oracle network configuration. Are the Oracle products you intend to use supported on the platforms you are planning on using? You need to check Oracle product certification levels and include this in your plans.

Oracle Net8 will accept both SQL*Net 2 and Oracle Net8 calls. Oracle's SQL*Net 2 will support calls from Oracle Net8. However, if you are using SQL*Net 2 instead of Oracle Net8, some options will not be available to you. For instance, you need to consider the impact of not having the Advanced Networking Option and other new features of Net8 if you decide to have a mixed-version environment.

Integration Of Applications
Do you need to support legacy data? What integration is needed between the legacy systems and the Oracle database application? You need to plan a configuration that will include the integration of your legacy systems. You also need to decide if you will be phasing out the support for legacy systems or if you need to maintain this support over the long term.

Summary Of Planning Issues
It is important to ask all the above questions. Based on this information, you can plan a network configuration. This information is essential in making a determination of the Oracle8 networking options you will implement in your environment.

Oracle8 Networking Components And Tools

Net8 provides an enhanced GUI toolset to configure and troubleshoot the network configuration. The enhanced tools generate default configurations that are suitable to most environments. Net8 also provides enhanced security options.

The next sections provide an introduction to the following Oracle Network options:

➤ Net8 Assistant

➤ Oracle Names

➤ Connection Manager

➤ Oracle Security Server

➤ Oracle Open Gateway

➤ Net8 Trace Assistant

Net8 Assistant

Net8 provides a GUI tool to configure the files that are required in setting up your Oracle network services. This new GUI tool is named Net8 Assistant. The Net8 Assistant can be used to manage the Advanced Networking Option and the Oracle Security Server in addition to the standard Oracle Net8 configurations.

The Net8 Assistant includes an Oracle Service Name Wizard. This tool is used to configure files that the client workstation will need in order to establish a connection to an Oracle database.

Oracle Names

Oracle Names is a method to centrally store all the addresses for all the databases in the user environment. Oracle Names acts as the distributed name server. Address information for all the databases is contained in the name server(s), which allows the client to access all the databases configured on a network by using only one address in the sqlnet.ora file, also known as the *client profile*.

The sqlnet.ora file has the address information for the name server. When the client application requests a connection to a database, the default is to look at the sqlnet.ora file to determine how the connection request is to be handled. If a name server is specified, a request is passed to that name server in order to obtain the location information. This information is passed back to the client, and the client application then connects to the database server. Oracle Names makes use of a client-side cache of connection information to speed up the connection process. See Figure 2.4.

A name server provides the ability to centralize the administration and maintenance of your network configuration. Changes to the environment can be made at one central location (the name server) instead of at each application server and/or client workstation. This makes administration of the network much easier and faster.

You can configure one or multiple name servers. If multiple name servers are used, the address information for all the name servers can be placed in the client profile. The client connection process will attempt to use the first name server listed. If that server is unavailable, the client process will contact the next name server to obtain the required address information.

By using multiple name servers, you can configure your environment so that, if one server is not available, the users will still be able to obtain the required database's address information. This feature is especially useful during maintenance and upgrade processes, as the main name server can be taken down

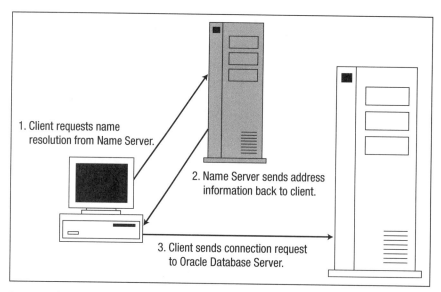

1. Client requests name resolution from Name Server.

2. Name Server sends address information back to client.

3. Client sends connection request to Oracle Database Server.

Figure 2.4 Using a single Oracle Name Server.

without disrupting the production environment. After that name server is upgraded or repaired, the second name server can be brought down for repair. The clients will not experience any disruptions connecting to the Oracle database server.

Multiple name servers are also beneficial in a very large user community. Load balancing can be configured by setting up multiple name servers and distributing the user population among them. See Figure 2.5.

Connection Manager

Connection Manager is a tool that is normally used with an n-tier configuration. It is installed on the middle tier or application server and provides support for a high-volume, multiuser environment. It also acts as a network control manager.

Connection Manager uses multiplexing to handle connection requests. A single connection to the database receives and handles the multiple connection requests. The first request for a connection to an Oracle server establishes the connection. This connection is then used by subsequent requests. See Figure 2.6, Multiplexing with Connection Manager.

Connection Manager supports cross-protocol connectivity in a manner that is transparent to the client. This cross-protocol connectivity allows clients using one

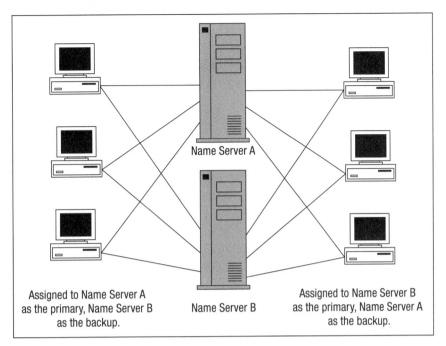

Figure 2.5   Configuration using multiple name servers.

network protocol to connect to a database server that uses a different network protocol. The Connection Manager provides the multiprotocol connectivity that was previously provided in the Oracle MultiProtocol Interchange.

In addition, the Connection Manager processes connection requests between the client and database server based on origin, destination, and SID. It can be used in a Web environment to provide firewall-like security using the Oracle8 application proxy functionality.

Advanced Networking Option

The Oracle8 Advanced Networking Option (ANO) works with both Net8 and SQL*Net 2.1.4 and later. It provides network security and integrates with non-Oracle security servers and biometric devices.

> *Note: The Advanced Networking Option is not packaged as part of Net8. It is sold as a separate option and is considered a separate product.*

Network Security Services

Network security safeguards data (and requests for data) that is transmitted over the network from being altered or read. The Advanced Networking Option provides security with data encryption and checksumming.

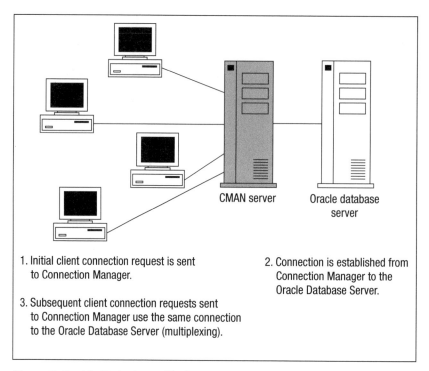

1. Initial client connection request is sent to Connection Manager.

2. Connection is established from Connection Manager to the Oracle Database Server.

3. Subsequent client connection requests sent to Connection Manager use the same connection to the Oracle Database Server (multiplexing).

Figure 2.6 Multiplexing with Connection Manager.

The Advanced Networking Option must be installed and configured on both the server and client in order to use encryption. The client must have the Advanced Networking Option installed in order to encrypt data that it sends over the network and to decode the transmissions it receives from the server. The Oracle database server must have the Advanced Networking Option installed in order to decode the messages from the client and to encrypt the data to be transmitted to the client. Both data and all sql commands transmitted over the network are then encrypted for secure transmission. See Figure 2.7.

Net8 can be integrated with third-party security packages to provide network security for user logins. The Advanced Networking Option integrates with both the Security Dynamics ACE Server and Kerberos. It also integrates with biometric devices such as Identix, which uses a fingerprint-scanning device for identification.

Oracle Distributed Computing Environment
Oracle Distributed Computing Environment (DCE) is a part of the Advanced Networking Option that can be used to enhance security. DCE allows applications to transparently access both Oracle7 and Oracle8 databases. It provides

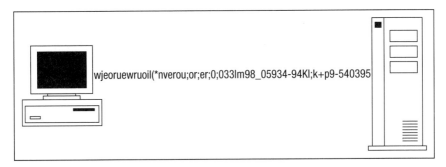

Figure 2.7 Encryption using Oracle Security Server.

support for a multivendor environment using Remote Procedure Calls (RPC). After a client has logged into the DCE, no username or password is required to access the database.

Oracle Security Server

The Oracle Security Server uses the X.509 certificate standard for security enforcement. The Security Server provides the authentication of users by validating identities of users attempting to access the Oracle database server. A single sign-on is handled by issuing a security "certificate" (an encrypted key) to authorize access. Security keys are centrally controlled and maintained. This centralized approach is extremely valuable in environments that span a wide geographic area with applications that may need to access multiple databases on a variety of servers.

The Oracle Security Server authentication can be configured using the Oracle Enterprise Manager. Using the Oracle Enterprise Manager, the administrator can define all user privileges within the Oracle Security Server. The administrator can create and maintain standard user logins and privileges across a very complex, multiserver, multidatabase environment. The Oracle Security Server ensures that the security is maintained and that users access the Oracle database within the privileges defined for them by the administrator. This also means that, if a user account needs to be terminated, it can be performed at one centralized point in a fast and efficient manner.

In order to use this advanced security option, you need to create a security server that stores the information on global security. Oracle recommends that the security server be set up in a separate database. Once configured, the Oracle Security Server can provide validation of users, Web servers, and other servers.

Oracle Open Gateway

The Oracle Open Gateway option provides a method to access data stored in non-Oracle databases as if the data were stored in an Oracle database. The two types of Oracle gateways are *transparent* and *procedural*.

The transparent gateway provides a seamless integration between Oracle and non-Oracle databases. Oracle has written transparent gateways to over 30 non-Oracle databases.

> *Note: Oracle Gateways are not packaged as part of Net8. Each gateway is sold as a separate option and is considered a separate product. Because of the complexity involved with developing Oracle Gateways, they are very expensive options.*

The procedural gateway allows the integration of non-Oracle products with an Oracle database using extensions to Oracle stored procedures. The procedural gateways can be used to integrate with message and monitoring products.

Net8 Trace Assistant

This Net8 Trace Assistant is used in conjunction with Net8 trace files for diagnostics. The Net8 Trace Assistant decodes and analyzes Oracle Net8 trace files. It also provides information on network problems and can assist you in identifying potential network bottlenecks.

Practice Questions

Question 1

In an environment that has several hundred clients connecting to an Oracle database, the best connection architecture is:

○ a. Simple

○ b. N-tier

○ c. TCP/IP

○ d. Oracle gateway

The correct answer is b: n-tier. The two types of architecture are two-tier (also called simple) and n-tier. The two-tier network is a direct connection between the server and client. The n-tier architecture uses an application server to reduce the burden on the database server. TCP/IP is a network protocol and not a connection architecture. An Oracle gateway is used for connections with non-Oracle databases with either a transparent or procedural interface.

Question 2

Which of the following are benefits of using an application server or agent? [Choose the three best answers]

❑ a. Translation services

❑ b. Scalability

❑ c. Intelligent agent services

❑ d. Data encryption

❑ e. Distributed name services

The correct answers are a, b, and c: translation services, scalability, and intelligent agent services. (Notice that the question is asking for multiple selections.) Data encryption is provided by the Advanced Networking Option. Oracle Names provides distributed name services. While Oracle Names should be placed on a separate server, that is not the answer that the exam expects because that is not a direct "benefit" of the agent or application server. Be careful not to read anything additional into the question. The n-tier architecture uses an agent located between the server and client to provide easy scalability, translation services, and intelligent agent services.

Question 3

> Which of the following network protocols are supported by Net8? [Choose the two best answers]
>
> ❑ a. TCP/IP
>
> ❑ b. Kerberos
>
> ❑ c. DECnet
>
> ❑ d. DCE

The correct answers are a and c: TCP/IP and DECnet. Kerberos and DCE are not network protocols. Kerberos is a security software product that can be integrated with Net8. DCE is the Distributed Computing Environment that comes with the Oracle Advanced Networking Option. When the question requires more than one item, both must be chosen in order for the answer to be considered correct. Look carefully at the question.

Question 4

> You have a geographically scattered environment with many clients signing on to databases on several different servers. What Oracle option will simplify your security administration by implementing a single sign-on for user authentication?
>
> ○ a. Connection Manager
>
> ○ b. Oracle Names Server
>
> ○ c. Advanced Networking Option
>
> ○ d. Oracle Security Server

The correct answer is d: Oracle Security Server. Connection Manager performs multiplexing of connections. The Oracle Names Server is used for name resolution for centralized resolution of addresses. The Advanced Networking Option is used to encrypt data over the network and to perform checksumming. The Oracle Security Server is used for single sign-on and centralized administration of security authentication. The Oracle Security Server performs authentication of the user and enforces the privileges defined by the administrator.

Question 5

You have a multivendor environment with both Oracle7 and Oracle8 databases. Your applications are using Remote Procedure Calls as the transport mechanism. Which Oracle product provides support for this type of connection?

○ a. Oracle Gateways

○ b. Oracle Distributed Computing Environment

○ c. Oracle Names

○ d. Connection Manager

The correct answer is b: Oracle Distributed Computing Environment. Remember that DCE uses RPC (Remote Procedure Calls) as the transport mechanism. Be careful not to let a word such as *connection* mislead you. The Connection Manager provides support for multiplexing.

Question 6

In order to use data encryption for Net8 connections, where do you have to install the Advanced Networking Option?

○ a. Only on the client

○ b. Only on the server

○ c. Both the client and server

○ d. Only on the Oracle Names Server

○ e. Only on the Security Server

The correct answer is c: both the client and server. Since the information must be encoded on transmission and decoded at the receiving end, the Advanced Networking Option must be installed at both sides.

Question 7

> Which architecture is used to support the Oracle Intelligent Agent?
>
> ○ a. N-tier
>
> ○ b. Two-tier
>
> ○ c. Simple
>
> ○ d. Client/server
>
> ○ e. Oracle Names

The correct answer is a: n-tier. The terms *two-tier*, *simple*, and *client/server* are all used to refer to the same architecture in which the client communicates directly to the server. Oracle Names is a method used for name resolution. Whenever possible, look at the answers and disregard the ones that are obviously incorrect. If you recognize several terms as synonymous, this eliminates them as the possible answer. Since only correct answers count, if you can narrow the scope to one or two, it is in your best interest to guess when you do not know.

Question 8

> What method does the Connection Manager use to handle connection requests?
>
> ○ a. Connection pooling
>
> ○ b. Multiplexing
>
> ○ c. Multithreading

The correct answer is b: multiplexing. The Connection Manager handles multiple connection requests with a single connection to the database (multiplexing).

Question 9

> Which Oracle8 tool provides a method to seamlessly connect between two different protocols?
>
> ○ a. Oracle Names
>
> ○ b. Connection Manager
>
> ○ c. DCE
>
> ○ d. MultiProtocol Interchange

The correct answer is b: Connection Manager. Connection Manager provides an interchange between two different network protocols. The Connection Manager replaces the Oracle7 MultiProtocol Interchange. Oracle Names is used to centrally resolve address information needed for a connection. The DCE (Distributed Computing Environment) is used to support multivendor environments using Remote Procedure Calls (RPC).

Question 10

Which Oracle8 tool provides a method to decode and analyze Oracle network trace files?

○ a. Advanced Network Option

○ b. Connection Manager

○ c. Net8 Trace Assistant

○ d. Net8 Assistant

○ e. Oracle Security Server

The correct answer is c: Net8 Trace Assistant. Be careful not to jump to conclusions based on the way the question is worded. The word *decode* in the above question does not deal with security. The Net8 Trace Assistant is a diagnostic tool that decodes Oracle Net8 trace files and provides an analysis of the network to identify possible bottlenecks. The Advanced Network Option and Oracle Security Server are used to provide enhanced security features. The Net8 Assistant is used to configure the Oracle8 network files.

Need To Know More?

 The first place to look for more information is the *Oracle Net8 Administrator's Guide* Release 8.0. Oracle Corporation. Chapter 1 "Introducing Net8" gives a good overview of Net8.

 Loney, Kevin. *Oracle8 DBA Handbook*. Oracle Press, 1998. ISBN 0-07-8822406-0. Chapter 13 provides an excellent overview of the Net8 configurations.

Basic Net8 Architecture

Terms you'll need to understand:

√ Service name

√ Listener

√ tnsnames.ora

√ sqlnet.ora

√ Oracle Call Interface (OCI)

√ Two Task Common

√ Transparent Network Substrate (TNS)

√ Oracle Program Interface (OPI)

√ Oracle Protocol Adapters (OPA)

√ Host naming

√ Local naming

Techniques you'll need to master:

√ Understanding of the files associated with networking

√ Knowledge of the location of the network parameter files

√ Understanding of the components of Net8

√ Understanding the actions performed by each layer of the protocol stack

√ Understanding of how Net8 connections are established

In this chapter, I lay the groundwork necessary to understand the architecture of Oracle Net8. I'll explain each layer in the protocol stack and introduce the various files used at the server and client levels. You will begin to gain an understanding of the requirements necessary to establish a connection using Oracle Net8. The following chapters will build on the basics you will learn in this chapter.

Oracle Net8 Communication

Net8 is comprised of multiple layers that handle various aspects of the connection between client applications and the Oracle database. Net8 provides three functions:

➤ Connection actions,

➤ Transmission of data, and

➤ Exception handling operations.

Connection Actions

When a client requests a connection to the Oracle database, the client application process provides the username, password, and service name.

The service name, also called a service alias or alias, is an easy to use and remember name for a connect descriptor. The connect descriptor provides the information needed to identify the network protocol and destination to be used in establishing a connection to an Oracle database. After Net8 resolves the service name to the connect descriptor, it begins the process of sending the connection request to the server. The username and password are provided to the database to authenticate the security for connection to the Oracle database.

The resolution of the service name into a connect descriptor is performed using one of the following methods:

➤ Local tnsnames.ora file (local naming)

➤ Oracle Names Server specified in the sqlnet.ora file

➤ Host naming

In order for the client to connect to an Oracle database, the database server must have a listener process active on the database server. The listener is configured to detect incoming requests for specific database instances.

The connection request is sent to the listener at the address specified by the service name; the request is then handled by the active listener process configured on the server. When a connection request is received, the listener determines where to direct the connection request.

Keep in mind that, in a client/server configuration, without the listener process active on the server side, no connection can be established between the client application and Oracle database.

If necessary, the listener spawns a process that connects the client application with the specified Oracle database. If a process that can handle the request already exists, the listener will redirect the connection to that process instead of spawning a new process. The address of the server process is returned to the client and the listener is no longer involved. This address (connection information) is maintained on the client for the database commands that are issued by the client application. The client process communicates directly with the server process. The client SQL or PL/SQL commands are executed on the server side and the results are returned to the client. The following list provides an easy review of the sequence of actions used to establish a connection between a client application and Oracle database server:

1. Listener process on server must be configured and active.

2. Client application provides username, password, and service name (e.g., sqlplus scott/tiger@prod1).

3. Service name is resolved into a connection descriptor using host naming, local naming, or Oracle Names.

4. Connection information is passed from the client to the server listener process.

5. The listener process determines where the request should be directed.

6. The listener redirects the request to an existing connection or spawns a new process to handle the request.

7. The process address information is passed back to the client.

8. The client process communicates directly to the server process. The listener is no longer involved.

Files Required For Connection Operations

The following files are used for the connection actions:

➤ *listener.ora*—Located on the database server. It contains all the information necessary to identify the Oracle database and establish an initial connection. It also contains information used for diagnosing connection problems involving the listener.

➤ *tnsnames.ora*—Located on the client. The tnsnames.ora file provides address and connection information for each service name.

➤ *sqlnet.ora*—Located on the client and/or server. The sqlnet.ora file contains profile information, and it may also include parameters used for diagnosing problems. If Oracle Names is used, the sqlnet.ora file contains information on the Oracle name server location.

The listener.ora file is always required on the Oracle database server for all variations of Net8 connections. However, the tnsnames.ora and sqlnet.ora files are used for different types of connections and are not always required. See Table 3.1 for a review of each of these files.

The tnsnames.ora file may be placed on both the server and the client. It is used on the server when a user is signed on to one server, but connecting to a database on another server using Net8. It is also used for connections between databases that use database links. A distributed database and Oracle advanced replication both make use of database links and require a tnsnames.ora file on the server.

The default location for the Net8 files on a Unix server is the $ORACLE_HOME/network/admin directory. On an NT workstation or server, the default location is in the $ORACLE_HOME\net80\admin directory. The environmental variable TNS_ADMIN can be used to override the default location of the Net8 parameter files.

Terminating A Net8 Connection

The connection to an Oracle database through Net8 can be terminated in three ways:

➤ By the user application

➤ By a time-out mechanism

➤ By an abnormal disconnection

Table 3.1	Connection configuration files.	
File	**Location**	**Purpose**
listener.ora	Server	Parameter file for the listener process with connection information for each SID
tnsnames.ora	Client	Service name and connect descriptor (address information)
sqlnet.ora	Client and server	Client profile information; connection and diagnostic parameters; name server location

When the client has completed transferring data or commands to the Oracle database, that application can close the connection normally.

Net8's Dead Connection Detection feature periodically sends out a packet to check that the client connection is valid and has not terminated abnormally. When a dead connection is discovered, all uncommitted transactions are rolled back and all locks held by the user are released. This feature reduces the waste of resources caused by having multiple dead connections, uncommitted data, and outstanding locks. Without Dead Connection Detection, abnormally terminated connections continue to lock the database objects and can cause performance problems.

The Oracle database background process (pmon) may recognize that a connection has been terminated. It will issue an error message (ORA-3113: "end-of-file on communication channel") and clean up the orphan processes.

Transmission Of Data

The transmission of data between the client application and database server is typically performed in a synchronous manner. With a synchronous transmission, each transmission sent must be completely received before the next transmission can be sent.

Oracle's Multithreaded Server (MTS) option handles multiple client requests in an asynchronous manner, which means that the multiple transmissions can be handled simultaneously instead of serially. With the development of the MTS option, SQL*Net version 2 added asynchronous capabilities. Net8 has continued that support for asynchronous transmissions for use with the MTS option. The Multithreaded Server option will be covered in a later chapter.

Exception Handling Operations

A break in the connection can be initiated by a user (for example, by the interrupt key, usually Ctrl+C) or the database (such as invalid data with SQL*Loader). The two types of requests for a break in the connection are inband and outband.

The inband break is a transmitted request for the connection to terminate. Inband breaks are messages transmitted as part of the normal communication between the client and the server.

The outband breaks 9also called "out-of-band" or "OOB" breaks) are connection-termination requests that are "urgent." The outband breaks send a signal outside of the normal transmissions and cause an immediate break in the connection. Outband breaks can break the connection faster because the break message is sent using urgent data messages.

Oracle Net8 Substrates

Net8 uses a six-level protocol stack to establish and maintain the connection between the client application and the Oracle database. The Net8 protocol stack is used to establish connections between the client and server. See Figure 3.1. This chapter covers the client and server protocol stacks and the protocol stack used between two servers (Network Program Interface).

 The protocol stack is defined differently in various references. Because the exam is directly based on the Oracle Net8 class, I have described the protocol stack layers as they are explained in the Oracle class. This will not be an exact match to the information in the Oracle Nert8 Administration manual.

Client Protocol Stack

This section covers each layer of the protocol stack on the client. Table 3.2 provides a review of the functions of the six layers in the client protocol stack.

Application

The Application layer is the front-end application presented to the user. It is application specific and can be either a character or graphic display. The Developer/2000 Oracle Forms and Reports are examples of the application layer. The Application layer identifies the commands or operations to be performed

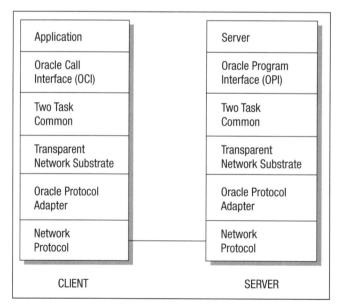

Figure 3.1   Communication protocol stack.

Table 3.2   Protocol layers on the client.

Stack Layer	Functions
Application	Front end at client side
Oracle Call Interface (OCI)	SQL command parsing, cursors, bind variables, execution, fetch data
Two Task Common	Datatype and character set conversions
Transparent Network Substrate (TNS)	Identify protocol and destination; send and receive functions; handle interrupts
Oracle Protocol Adapters (OPA)	Maps Oracle functions to network-specific protocols
Network Protocol	Machine-level connection; transmits packets across network

on the server and sends them to the next layer in the protocol stack (Oracle Call Interface).

Oracle Call Interface (OCI)

The Oracle Call Interface (OCI) layer contains the information necessary to perform an action at the database server. The OCI layer is responsible for passing database operations from the client application to the server. The Oracle Call Interface is also known as the User Program Interface (UPI).

The OCI layer handles the following functions:

➤ Parsing SQL and PL/SQL

➤ Controlling cursors (open and close)

➤ Binding variables

➤ Executing the SQL commands

➤ Fetching the data

Multiple OCI calls are bundled together for more efficient transmission to the server. The OCI layer passes control to Net8 for initiation of a connection to the database.

Two Task Common

In most environments, the application exits on a client (such as Windows 95) and the Oracle database is on a server (such as NT or Unix). If both the client application and Oracle database server support the same character set (such as

ASCII), then no translation is necessary. However, if the character sets do not match, the client and server cannot directly communicate.

The Two Task Common layer is used to perform datatype and character set conversions between the client and the server when the character sets do not match. If no conversions are necessary, this layer will be bypassed. (Oracle supports over a hundred different character sets.)

Transparent Network Substrate (TNS)

The Transparent Network Substrate (TNS) layer is the heart of Oracle networking. The TNS layer provides support for common industry-standard protocols. The TNS layer handles the send and receive functions. Also, if the connection is interrupted between the client and server, the TNS layer handles the connection interruption.

The following generic functions are included in the TNS layer:

➤ Server location

➤ Destination identification

➤ Interrupt codes

➤ Identification of network protocols used

The TNS layer has five components. See Table 3.3 for a review of the TNS layers. The five components of TNS are:

➤ The **Network Interface (NI)** is an interface to Net8. It is the layer responsible for executing break and reset requests for a connection.

➤ The **Network Naming (NN)** layer of TNS interprets a network alias address into an actual destination.

Table 3.3   Transparent Network Substrate (TNS) layers.

TNS Layer	Short Name	Purpose
Network Interface	NI	Interface to Net8; handles break and reset requests
Network Naming	NN	Converts alias address to destination
Network Routing	NR	Handles routing issues
Network Authentication	NA	Handles authentication between client and server
Network Session	NS	Establish handshake; manage buffers, multiplexing, pooling

➤ The **Network Routing (NR)** layer of TNS determines the route necessary between the client and the server.

➤ The **Network Authentication (NA)** layer of TNS handles authentication
between the client and server.

➤ The **Network Session (NS)** layer handles the handshake between the
client and server. This handshake is the actual network connection. The
NS layer manages any buffers that are established between the client and
server. In addition, if multiplexing and connection pooling are configured,
they are handled by the NS layer. (Mutiplexing and connection pooling are
covered in later chapters.) The Network Session (NS) actually has two layers:

   ➤ NS Main and

   ➤ NS(2)

The TNS layer passes information to the Oracle Protocol Adapter layer in the
protocol stack.

Oracle Protocol Adapter (OPA)

Oracle provides a variety of Oracle Protocol Adapters (OPAs); each works
with a specific network protocol (for example, TCP/IP). The OPA and the network protocol must be installed on both the client application and database server.
This layer maps the Oracle functions to the network-specific protocol calls.

The OPA layer consists of the following components:

➤ NT Main

➤ NT (2)

➤ NT OS

The OPA is the Network Transport (NT) layer, which maps generic function
calls between the OPA and the industry-standard protocol.

Network Protocol

The final layer of the protocol stack on the client is the network-specific protocol,
which handles the actual machine-level connection process. The sole function
of the network protocol is to pass data (packets) from the client to the server.

Server Protocol Stack

The protocol stack on the server side also has six layers, and these layers corre-
spond closely with those of the client. The following are the layers of the protocol
stack on the database server side:

➤ The **Server** layer receives and executes SQL commands and returns results to OPI.

➤ The **Oracle Program Interface (OPI)** layer is the counterpart to OCI, and it processes SQL code and returns data.

➤ The **Two Task Common** layer handles datatype and character set conversions.

➤ The **Transparent Network Substrate (TNS)** layer handles send and receive functions and interrupts.

➤ The **Oracle Protocol Adapters (OPA)** layer maps Oracle functions to network-specific protocols.

➤ The **Network Protocol** layer is the machine-level connection, and it transmits packets across the network.

Server

The Oracle Server layer receives the SQL command, performs the requested action, and begins the transmission of the result set back through the protocol stack and over to the client side. The Server layer interfaces with the OPI layer. It resolves the SQL statement and passes the information to the OPI layer.

Oracle Program Interface (OPI)

The Oracle Program Interface (OPI) is the counterpart to the client Oracle Call Interface (OCI) layer. It passes the request to the Oracle Server layer. It receives the results from the Server layer and formats the results for transmittal back through the protocol stack and to the client.

Other Layers Of Server Protocol

The Network Protocol on the server picks up the packet transmitted to the server from the client and begins the process of working up the protocol stack to the server. The functionality of the layers on the server side is equivalent to the layers on the client side. The Two Task Common, Transparent Network Substrate (TNS), Oracle Protocol Adapters (OPAs), and Network Protocol perform the same functions on the server as on the client.

 The real difference between the protocol stack of the client and that of the server is the work that is preformed on that machine. The server has the server layer, and the client has the application layer. The client sends the requests (Oracle Call Interface),

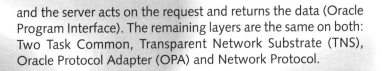

and the server acts on the request and returns the data (Oracle Program Interface). The remaining layers are the same on both: Two Task Common, Transparent Network Substrate (TNS), Oracle Protocol Adapter (OPA) and Network Protocol.

Network Program Interface

In distributed transactions between two servers, the process is the same except there is no OCI or OPI layer. Transmission of SQL commands and data is performed using a Network Program Interface (NPI). The NPI is server specific, and it performs the actions of the OCI/OPI layers.

Name-Resolution Methods

Name resolution is the determination of the address information for a service name or alias that is assigned to a database connect descriptor. The use of a service name allows the connection between the client application and Oracle database server by using a single descriptor. This descriptor is then interpreted into all the information necessary to initiate the connection request. Without the use of service names and name resolution, every application would have to contain information such as the hostname and database SID and network protocol information. By using name resolution, all this information is contained in a file that is then referenced by all the applications.

Before determining which naming method you'll use, you must analyze your environment with consideration of the benefits and limitations of each method. See Table 3.4 and Table 3.5.

The four methods of name resolution—host naming, local naming, Oracle Names, and external naming—are explained in the following sections.

Table 3.4   Choosing a name-resolution method.

Method	File Required	Process Used For Name Resolution
Host naming	sqlnet.ora	Name resolution using port 1521 and global names; requires TCP/IP
Local naming	tnsnames.ora	File on the client
Oracle names	sqlnet.ora	Oracle Names
External naming	sqlnet.ora	Oracle Native Naming Adapters

Table 3.5 Name-resolution methods.	
Name-Resolution Method	**Environmental Considerations**
Host naming	Simple configuration with default port and TCP/IP network hostname-resolution utility or file used for centralized maintenance. Minimal configuration required.
Local naming	Heterogeneous environment with multiple network protocols. Requires configuration of tnsnames.ora on each client.
Oracle names	Centralized administration in a heterogeneous network environment. Requires configuration of an Oracle Names Server.
External naming	Support third-party software that may be in use for both Oracle and non-Oracle software.

Host Naming

Host naming uses third-party name-resolution services, such as Domain Name Server (DNS) or an /etc/hosts file. Host naming can be used only with the TCP/IP network protocol. In order to use the host naming method, you must use the default port number 1521 for the listener and global names must be used for the database and hostname. Multiple databases can be supported on each server with multiple alias hostnames in the name-resolution service. With the host naming method, it is not necessary to have the tnsnames.ora file on the client. All the necessary parameters are in the client sqlnet.ora configuration file. See Table 3.6.

Table 3.6 Host naming requirements.
Defaults for host naming
Port
Network Protocol
SID
Host
1521
TCP/IP
Global name
Service name

The client application initiates a connection request using a hostname or hostname alias as the service name or connect string. Net8 creates a connection address by using the third-party product to resolve the hostname. The database name defaults to the hostname alias, the protocol is defaulted to TCP/IP, and the port defaults to 1521. Net8 makes a connection to the server and is picked up by the listener process. The listener process makes a connection to a database that matches the hostname or hostname alias.

The benefit of using the host naming method is that there is no configuration involved. When Net8 is installed on the server, a default listener.ora file is created to listen for TCP/IP connections on port 1521 with a database name that matches the hostname. Additional databases can be added as long as a hostname alias is created to match the database global name.

Be sure you understand the requirements of host naming. The requirements are also the weakness of using host naming.

The host naming method should be used only for very simple network and database environments. Host naming will not work in a complex, heterogeneous environment. Neither is host naming supported in an environment that requires the use of connection pooling or application failover configurations.

Local Naming

Local naming requires a tnsnames.ora file on the client to obtain the address information for the service name. A connection in a distributed database configuration also uses the tnsnames.ora file for resolution of the service name defined in the database link.

The client application initiates a connection request using the service name (or alias) as the connect string. Net8 checks the local client for a tnsnames.ora file to obtain the address information. Net8 then makes the connection request using the hostname, port, network protocol, and database specified in the tnsnames.ora file. A listener process on the server receives the request and makes the connection to the database.

Local naming requires that any change in the connection address information be made on all client workstations and/or all application servers.

Oracle Names

Oracle Names provides a method to centralize address information for all database connections. The sqlnet.ora file is used to direct Net8 to the Oracle name server or centralized naming file to determine the connection address information. (Configuration of Oracle Names requires creating an Oracle name server, which is covered in Chapter 6.)

The client application initiates a connection request using the service name (or alias) as the connect string. Net8 is redirected to an Oracle name server for resolution of the address information. Net8 then uses the address information supplied by the Oracle name server to send the request to the appropriate server. The listener process receives the request and directs it to the database according to the address information received.

The use of a names server is recommended for complex, volatile environments.

External Naming

The external naming method uses a supported, third-party naming service to resolve the name supplied in the connect descriptor. The native naming adapter must be obtained from the vendor that provides the naming service software. Oracle service names must be loaded into the native name service using that service's tools. Oracle's support for native naming adapters includes industry-standard naming services, such as Network Information Service (NIS) and NetWare Directory Service (NDS).

The client application initiates a connection request using the service name (or alias) as the connect string. A native naming adapter sends the request to the third-party naming service. The address of the native naming service is provided to Net8, which then sends out a connection request using that address information. The listener process receives the request and directs it to the appropriate database.

Configuration of the external naming method requires that the native naming adapter be installed on the client and that the client profile information specify the external naming adapter. The sqlnet.ora configuration file contains the parameters necessary for connections using native naming services.

When using a native naming adapter, there should not be a tnsnames.ora file on the client. If a tnsnames.ora file is available, Oracle will default to attempting to make a standard Net8 connection using that tnsnames.ora file for name resolution.

Practice Questions

Question 1

Which file is needed to resolve service names when a local naming method is used?

- ○ a. sqlnet.ora
- ○ b. tnsnames.ora
- ○ c. listener.ora
- ○ d. names.ora

The correct answer is b. The tnsnames.ora file contains service names that map to connect descriptors. The connect descriptor for each service name provides the address information required to establish a connection between the client and the Oracle database server. The address information includes the hostname, SID, and protocol.

Question 2

Net8 provides which functions? [Choose the three best answers]

- ❑ a. Connection actions
- ❑ b. Native name server loading utilities
- ❑ c. Exception handling operations
- ❑ d. TCP/IP
- ❑ e. Transmission of data
- ❑ f. MultiProtocol Interchange

The correct answers are a, c, and e. To answer this question, use the process of elimination. Oracle's native naming adapters provide the ability to use external name servers, but they do not provide any utilities for loading this information. To load information into a native name server, you must use the tools provided by the third-party software vendor. TCP/IP is a network protocol, so you can immediately eliminate that as a possible answer. The MultiProtocol Interchange is not part of Net8—which leaves the following, correct answers: connection actions, exception handling operations, and transmission of data.

Question 3

> In order to establish connections between the client application and the Oracle database server, which of the following must always be true?
>
> ○ a. A tnsnames.ora file must exist on the client.
>
> ○ b. The Oracle listener must be active on the server.
>
> ○ c. A sqlnet.ora file must exist on both the client and server.
>
> ○ d. A listener.ora file must exist on the client.

The correct answer is b. The Oracle listener must be active on the server. Depending upon the type of name-resolution method used, the tnsnames.ora file may not be necessary for the client workstation. While the sqlnet.ora file may be on both the server and the client, it is not mandatory for all connections. The tnsnames.ora file is not mandatory for establishing a connection between the client and server. The listener.ora file is used to configure the listener on the server, not on the client. (Be careful to read the question closely.) Without a listener process on the Oracle database server, you cannot establish the connection.

Question 4

> What is the default location of the tnsnames.ora file on an NT workstation for Oracle8?
>
> ○ a. $ORACLE_HOME/network/admin
>
> ○ b. orawin95/network/admin
>
> ○ c. orant\network\admin
>
> ○ d. ORACLE_HOME\NET80\ADMIN

The correct answer is d. ORACLE_HOME\NET80\ADMIN. While the default ORACLE_HOME on an NT server is *orant*, the subdirectory for Oracle8 is not *network*. On an NT server, the directory names use the version number. On a Unix server, the default location is $ORACLE_HOME/network/admin. The default location can be overridden by the TNS_ADMIN environmental variable. Remember that for Oracle8 the version is now part of the directory name (net80).

Question 5

What is the name of the Net8 feature that can be configured to check for processes that have abnormally terminated?

○ a. listener

○ b. Dead Connection Detection

○ c. Native naming adapter

○ d. pmon

○ e. TNS

The correct answer is b. Dead Connection Detection checks for a connection between the server and the client. If it finds that the connection has terminated abnormally, the connection will be closed. The Oracle database performs a rollback of any uncommitted transactions and releases all locks. The Oracle pmon background process cleans up any operating-system processes spawned by the listener for that connection.

Question 6

What layer of the protocol stack is responsible for closing cursors on the client side?

○ a. OCI

○ b. OPI

○ c. TNS

○ d. NI

○ e. Two Task Common

The correct answer is a. The Oracle Call Interface is responsible for parsing SQL code, controlling cursors, binding variables, executing the SQL command, and fetching data. The OCI is on the client side. The OPI (Oracle Program Interface) is the corresponding layer of the protocol stack on the server side.

Question 7

> What layers form the server-side protocol stack?
>
> ○ a. Application, OCI, Two Task Common, TNS, OPA, Network Protocol
>
> ○ b. Server, OPI, Two Task Common, TNS, OPA, Network Protocol
>
> ○ c. Server, NPI, TNS, OPA, Network Protocol
>
> ○ d. Server, OPI, Two Task Common, NI, TNS, Network Protocol

The correct answer is b. The server side includes many of the same layers as the client (two task common, TNS, OPA, and network protocol). It also contains the Oracle Program Interface and the server layers. The client side Oracle Call Interface (OCI) corresponds to the server Oracle Program Interface (OPI) layer.

Question 8

> What component of TNS is responsible for executing break and reset requests?
>
> ○ a. NI
>
> ○ b. NN
>
> ○ c. NR
>
> ○ d. NA
>
> ○ e. NS

The correct answer is a. The NN (Network Naming) layer converts alias addresses to destination information. The NR (Network Routing) layer handles routing issues. The NA (Network Authentication) layer establishes the authentication. The NS (Network Services) layer establishes the handshake between the server and client. The NI (Network interface layer handles the break and reset requests.

Question 9

Which of these components is not part of the OPA?

○ a. NT Main

○ b. NT (2)

○ c. NT OS

○ d. NR

The correct answer is d. The NR layer is part of the TNS protocol stack layer. Note that the question is written in the negative. The NT Main, NT (2), and NT OS make up the Oracle Protocol Adapter (OPA). You should also think about the answers you have given to other questions. Note the previous question on TNS included NR as a possible answer.

Question 10

For a distributed transaction, which protocol layer is used for server-to-server distributed database connections?

○ a. OCI

○ b. OPI

○ c. NPI

○ d. TNS

○ e. Net8

The correct answer is c. The NPI (Network Progeram Interface) layer performs the function of both the OCI (Oracle Call Interface) and OPI (Orcle Program Interface) layers. If you do not recognize the TNS layer, review the section on the protocol stack layers and Table 3.2.

Question 11

In order to use the host naming method, which of the following must be true? [Choose the two best answers]

❏ a. It must use the default port number 1526.

❏ b. It must use global names.

❏ c. The TCP/IP protocol must be on both the client and server.

❏ d. No listener.ora file is required.

❏ e. The environment must be heterogeneous.

The correct answer is b and c. The host naming method requires the use of global names for the database and TCP/IP installed on both the client and server. Host naming requires very little configuration and is useful in a simple network environment. It uses the default settings. The default port number for Oracle is 1521. Port 1526 is the port number used by SQL*Net 2 for a second listener connection, which was automatically generated by the SQL*Net 2.3 Easy Configuration tool. The listener.ora file is required. The default listener.ora file created at installation can be used. The host naming method should not be used in a complex, heterogeneous environment.

Question 12

The tnsnames.ora file is required when connecting with which of the following methods?

○ a. Native naming adapters

○ b. Oracle Names

○ c. Host naming

○ d. Local naming

The correct answer is d. The local naming method requires a tnsnames.ora file on each client for name resolution. The other methods listed above use the sqlnet.ora file on the client. When using native naming adapters, no tnsnames.ora file should be on the client. For Oracle Names, the sqlnet.ora provides the information necessary to locate the Oracle Names server, which will provide the name resolution service.

Need To Know More?

 The first place to look for more information is the *Oracle Net8 Administrator's Guide* Release 8.0. Oracle Corporation. Chapter 2 "Understanding Net8."

 Toledo, Jr., Hugo. *Oracle Networking*. Oracle Press, 1996. ISBN 0-07-882165-7. Chapter 3 "SQLNet," Chapter 4 "TNS Applications." This book does not include information on Net8. However, the information provided on SQLNet 2 and the protocol stack is still relevant to Net8.

 "Net8/SQL*Net—How It Works." RevealNet Oracle Administration Knowledge Base. Network Management.

Net8 Server Configuration

Terms you'll need to understand:

√ Bequeathed process

√ Prespawned dedicated server processes

√ Dispatchers

√ listener.ora

√ Queue size

√ Logging

√ Tracing

√ lsnrctl

√ Reload

Techniques you'll need to master:

√ Understanding the listener files and their parameters

√ Understanding the listener control utility commands

√ Setting up multiple listeners and when to use them

√ Configuring the server listener process with
  Net8 Assistant

As you learned in the previous chapter, you cannot make a Net8 connection unless you have an active listener process on the server to accept the request. In this chapter, you'll learn how to configure the listener process on the server. The Oracle 8: Network Administration exam includes questions on the new GUI interface, Net8 Assistant. Thus, it is important that you know not only how the listener process works—including the contents of the files used by the listener process—but also how to use the Net8 Assistant.

Listener Process And Configuration

The Oracle listener is the process, running on a server, that is used to make a connection from a client or application. If the client is using local naming, the tnsnames.ora file includes the host and port designations as well as the protocol and SID. The listener waits for connection requests for specific databases using specified protocols. If a listener is not active, the client connection request cannot be serviced. The lsnrctl utility is used to start, stop, and monitor the listener process.

The default port for a listener process is 1521. This port number represents a virtual device, not an actual physical one. No two devices should be assigned to any one port: If port 1521 is assigned to another application, you must use another port number for the listener process. As we discussed in the previous chapter, you must use port 1521 if you are going to use host naming on the client.

Listener Connection Processes

When the listener process receives a connection request, it must determine which of the following two actions to take:

➤ Spawn a new process (bequeath)

➤ Redirect the connection to an existing process

The connection decision made by the listener process is transparent to the client. If an existing process can be used for the client connection, the listener will redirect the connection request to that process. If it is necessary to spawn (create) a new process, the listener will then bequeath (pass) the connection to the newly spawned process. (When a new process is spawned, it is a dedicated process for that client or application.)

If you want to find out which decision the listener has made for a connection request, you have to turn on tracing and analyze the results. You can then determine whether the listener is spawning new processes or redirecting the connection requests to an existing process.

Bequeath Session Method

A *bequeathed* session occurs when the listener creates a new dedicated process for a connection request. In order to use this method, the listener must be running on the same server (or node) as the database: The listener cannot bequeath a connection to another server.

The following steps describe how the listener process responds to a connection request by spawning a new process (bequeath session):

1. The client or application sends a connection request to the listener based on the network address in the connect descriptor for that service name.

2. The listener receives the connection request and determines if it can be serviced or not. If it cannot be serviced, the connection request is refused. The listener continues listening for new connection requests.

3. If the listener determines that a dedicated session will be used for the connection request, it spawns a new process for that session.

4. The listener bequeaths (passes) the connection for that session to the newly created operating-system process.

5. The connection between the client and Oracle database uses the new dedicated server process directly. The listener is no longer involved in the connection between the client or application and the Oracle database.

6. The listener continues waiting for incoming connection requests.

Prespawned Dedicated Processes

Whenever the listener process must spawn a new process, the server is burdened with additional overhead, which naturally has some performance impact. To reduce this overhead and speed up the connection process, it is possible to "precreate" processes. These are called *prespawned dedicated processes*.

When the listener is started, it will prespawn dedicated server processes based on the **PRESPAWN_MAX** and **PRESPAWN_LIST** parameters in the listener.ora file. The default for **PRESPAWN_MAX** is 0, meaning that no processes are prespawned. The disadvantage of using prespawned processes is that they consume system resources. The listener will replace the prespawned processes as they are used and will always keep the specified number of processes available for incoming connection requests. (Additional information on the parameters for prespawned dedicated processes is covered later in this chapter.)

While this increases the speed of making the connections, it is more work for the listener. The listener must not only determine if it should redirect or spawn a new process, but it must also track the prespawned processes.

The listener maintains a log with information on the processes that have been prespawned. The listener will redirect a new connection request to a pre-spawned dedicated server process instead of spawning a new process. The following steps describe how the listener process responds to a connection request by redirection to an existing process:

1. The listener process spawns dedicated server processes, up to the maximum number specified in the **PRESPAWN_MAX** parameter in the listener.ora file. The listener maintains a log of the prespawned processes and client/server connections.

2. The client or application sends a connection request to the listener based on the network address in the connect descriptor for that service name.

3. The listener receives the connection request and determines if it can be serviced or not. If it cannot be serviced, the connection request is refused. The listener continues listening for new connection requests.

4. If the listener decides it can service the request by redirection, it sends a REDIRECT message to the client. This message contains the address of one of the available prespawned processes.

5. The client disconnects from the listener process and connects to the address for the specified prespawned process.

6. The listener spawns another server process and continues waiting for incoming connection requests.

Redirection To Dispatcher Processes

There is another method to redirect connection requests to processes that currently exist. By configuring your database to use the multithreaded server option (covered in the Chapter 7), you can create processes called *dispatchers*. Dispatchers are shared among several connections, thus reducing the overhead of dedicated processes for every connection. The following describes how the listener responds to a connection request by redirection to a dispatcher:

1. When the database is started, dispatchers are created according to the **MTS_DISPATCHERS** parameter in the init.ora file for the database.

2. The address for each dispatcher is registered with the listener process.

3. The client or application sends a connection request to the listener based on the network address in the connect descriptor for that service name.

4. The listener receives the connection request and determines if it can be serviced or not. If it cannot be serviced, the connection request is refused. The listener continues listening for new connection requests.

5. If the listener decides it can service the request by redirection to a dispatcher, it sends a REDIRECT message to the client with the address of the least-used dispatcher process.

6. The client disconnects from the listener process and connects to the address for the specified dispatcher process.

7. The dispatcher sends a message to the listener process with a new load value. This load value is what the listener uses to determine which dispatcher is the least used for the next connection request. The listener continues waiting for incoming connection requests.

Note: The listener process should be started before the database startup in order for the dispatchers to register with the listener process.

Multiple Listeners

With the early versions of SQL*Net 2, database administrators were encouraged to have one listener on each server and to use that listener for all databases on that server. With SQL*Net 2.3, the default configurations on the client included two listener addresses—one using port 1521 and a second using port 1526. Oracle began to encourage the database administrator to consider multiple listeners on a server to load balance the database connection requests. (Load balancing spreads the connection requests among two or more listeners in order to reduce the number of incoming requests that must be handled by any single listener.)

If you are using multiple listeners on a server, each listener must have a unique name and a unique port. The default name for the listener process is LISTENER. When you are working with the lsnrctl utility, it will always assume that you are working with a process named LISTENER. If you have multiple listeners (or simply decide to use another name for your listener process), you will have to use the listener name when using the lsnrctl utility.

For each listener to be configured on a server, it must have a unique name and port. No two devices should ever be assigned to the same port. Remember that the port used by the listener is not actual physical hardware; it is a virtual port. Also remember that the port number assigned to the listener must match the port number the client uses in its connection request. The next chapter will cover the client-side configuration.

If you have multiple listeners for the same database—and both are included in the listener addresses for that service name—each connection request will be randomly assigned to the listeners. This supports load balancing of the requests between the listener processes.

Multiple listeners can be defined in one listener.ora file, as long as you define each one completely and separately within the file. Each listener must have a separate address as well as separate general parameters. Each parameter keyword in the listener.ora file must include the listener name.

For example, if you were setting up two listeners with the names Listener1 and Listener2, you would have a Listener1 address list and a Listener2 address list. You would have a SID_LIST_LISTENER1 and a SID_LIST_LISTENER2. If you wanted to configure a connection timeout for each, you would have a CONNECT_TIMEOUT_LISTENER1 and a CONNECT_TIMEOUT_LISTENER2. If you decided to accept the defaults for Listener1 and set general parameters only for Listener2, then you would have only the parameter with the Listener2 name (for example, STARTUP_WAIT_TIME_LISTENER2).

See Appendix A for a comprehensive sample copy of the listener.ora file. Review this carefully when you are preparing for the exam.

listener.ora File

The parameter file used to configure the listener process is called the listener.ora file. This file contains the information that the listener process needs when it is started. If there is no listener.ora file when the listener is started, it will create a listener.ora file using the default parameters. By default, the listener.ora file is located in the $ORACLE_HOME/network/admin directory for Unix servers. On an NT server, the default directory is $ORACLE_HOME\net80\admin. (ORACLE_HOME on an NT defaults to orant.) You can use the TNS_ADMIN environmental variable to override the default location for the listener.ora file. The listener.ora file must reside on the server on which the listener will be running.

 Experienced Oracle DBAs know that in a Unix environment, it is possible to configure a listener.ora file on one server with an address pointing to another server. However, for the purposes of this exam, you must answer that the listener.ora file must reside on the same server as the listener process.

The listener.ora file contains the following information:

➤ Address

➤ Databases

➤ General parameters

Address

A listener can be configured to listen for multiple network protocols. As you learned in the previous chapter, the IPC and TCP network protocols are the two protocols that are installed by default. Addresses for IPC and TCP are included in the default listener.ora file. See Listing 4.1 for an example of an **ADDRESS_LIST** in a listener.ora file.

The address begins with the specification of the listener name (**LISTENER** in Listing 4.1). This is followed by the **ADDRESS_LIST** parameter. (If only one address is specified, then the phrase **ADDRESS_LIST** can be omitted.) The next line—either directly after **LISTENER** or following **ADDRESS_LIST**— is an address and the values for that address. The first value in the address is the protocol. Depending upon the protocol, the address will have different values defined.

The IPC address in the address list is for InterProcess Communication connections. This address picks up connection requests from clients and applications that are on the same server (node) as the listener process. A connection using IPC requires a key value. (The key is equivalent to the service name of the database.) If the SID and the service name are the same, you can have just one address in the address list for IPC connections.

The TCP address requires that the host and port be included in the address. The host can be specified using either a hostname or an IP address. When the listener receives a client connection request, the port must match the port specified by the client or application attempting to connect to a SID on that server. If the port does not match, the listener will refuse the connection.

If you need to handle a large volume of connection requests, your listener process may become overloaded with a backlog of requests to be handled. You can configure a specific queue size to increase the amount of requests that can be queued and waiting for the listener to service them. Specifying a queue size allows the listener to handle a large number of concurrent connection requests. The **QUEUESIZE** parameter is supported only for TCP and DECnet. The default queue size for TCP is 17, and the maximum size that is supported is operating-system specific.

In order to configure a queue size, you must include the **QUEUESIZE** parameter in the address specification. Listing 4.1 shows an example of a TCP address configuration using the **QUEUESIZE** parameter.

Listing 4.1   Example of an **ADDRESS_LIST** in a listener.ora file.

```
LISTENER  =
     (ADDRESS_LIST =
        (ADDRESS = (PROTOCOL = IPC)(KEY = ORCL))
```

```
            (ADDRESS = (PROTOCOL = IPC)(KEY = PNKEY))
            (ADDRESS = (PROTOCOL = TCP)(HOST = prod1)(PORT = 1521))
            (ADDRESS = (PROTOCOL = TCP)(HOST=server1)
                       (PORT = 1523)(QUEUESIZE=10))
    )
```

Databases

A listener can be configured to listen for multiple databases. For each database to be serviced by the listener, a database identifier (SID) must be specified in the **SID_LIST**. (See Listing 4.2 for an example of a **SID_LIST** in the listener.ora file.) The designation of the databases begins with the parameter **SID_LIST_<listener_name>**. The next line is the **SID_LIST** keyword. If there is only one database SID, then the **SID_LIST** line may be omitted. For each database, there is a **SID_DESC**, which contains the descriptive information necessary for a connection. The **SID_DESC** contains three values:

➤ GLOBAL_DBNAME

➤ ORACLE_HOME

➤ SID_NAME

The GLOBAL_DBNAME is the name and domain of the database as specified in the init.ora parameter file. (A global database name is the unique name for a database in a hierarchical database structure.) This value is used by the listener to resolve the database when hostnaming is used.

Oracle supports multiple versions of the Oracle executables on a server, and the ORACLE_HOME is needed to identify the executables being used for the specified SID.

The SID_NAME is the Oracle identifier for the database and not the database name.

As previously mentioned, the **PRESPAWN_MAX** is used by the listener to determine the maximum number of prespawned dedicated server processes that can be created. The default is 0. The **PRESPAWN_MAX** should be equal to or greater than the sum of all the **POOL_SIZE** parameter values in the **PRESPAWN_LIST**. To use pre-spawned server processes, the following values should be configured in the **SID_DESC** entry:

➤ PRESPAWN_MAX

➤ PROTOCOL

➤ POOL_SIZE

➤ TIMEOUT

When one of the prespawned dedicated servers is used, another is created to replace it. The **PROTOCOL** is the network protocol for which dedicated server processes will be spawned. (This protocol must be listed in the **ADDRESS_LIST** parameter of the listener.ora file.) The **POOL_SIZE** parameter is the number of unused prespawned dedicated server processes that must be maintained for each **PROTOCOL**. The **POOL_SIZE** setting cannot be larger than the setting for **PRESPAWN_MAX**. The **TIMEOUT** parameter is the number of minutes an inactive prespawned dedicated server process will wait for the next connection. This timeout applies only to prespawned dedicated server processes that have already disconnected from a previously assigned connection; it does not apply to newly created processes. If this is set to 0, the processes will continue indefinitely, thereby wasting valuable resources. See Listing 4.3 for an example of how to specify prespawned dedicated server processes in your **SID_DESC**.

If you decide to configure prespawned dedicated processes, you must, at a minimum, specify the timeout value and the number of pre-spawned dedicated servers that the listener will create when it is started.

Listing 4.2   Example of a **SID_LIST** in the listener.ora file.

```
SID_LIST_LISTENER =
  (SID_LIST =
    (SID_DESC =
      (GLOBAL_DBNAME = PROD1.WORLD)
      (SID_NAME = PROD1)
      (ORACLE_HOME=/sqlhome/Prod/8.0.5)
    )
  )
```

Listing 4.3   Example of a **SID_DESC** with prespawned
                dedicated processes.

```
(SID_DESC =
      (GLOBAL_DBNAME = PROD1.WORLD)
      (SID_NAME = PROD1)
      (ORACLE_HOME=/sqlhome/Prod/8.0.5)
      (PRESPAWN_MAX=50)
      (PRESPAWN_LIST=
                    (PRESPAWN_DESC =
                            (PROTOCOL=TCP)(POOL_SIZE=5)(TIMEOUT=2)
                    )
      )
)
```

General Parameters

Prespawning (or precreating) dedicated server connections with the general parameter **PRESPAWN_MAX** is one way to control various aspects of the listener's behavior. You can also include other parameters in the listener.ora file to control various aspects of how the listener will function. Unlike the address list and the SID list, it is not necessary to include any general parameters, as they will default to a specific setting. All you have to do is include those parameters where you do not want to accept the default setting. See Listing 4.4 for an example of settings for typically used parameters in the listener.ora file.

Listing 4.4 Example of settings for general parameters in the listener.ora file.

```
CONNECT_TIMEOUT_LISTENER=10
LOG_DIRECTORY_LISTENER=/orax1/oracle/8.0.5/network/log
LOG_FILE_LISTENER=listener.log
PASSWORDS_LISTENER=password
TRACE_DIRECTORY_LISTENER=/orax1/oracle/8.0.5/network/trace
TRACE_FILE_LISTENER=listener.trc
TRACE_LEVEL_LISTENER = ADMIN
```

The **CONNECT_TIMEOUT_**<listener_name> parameter is used to set the number of seconds that a listener will wait for a valid query after a session has been started. This parameter is used to detect when a session has terminated abnormally during the connection process. The default is 10. If this is set to 0, there will be no timeout, and it will continue to wait forever.

The **LOGGING_**<listener_name> parameter determines if logging will be performed. (The default is to have logging ON.) This parameter is provided for situations in which the database administrator wants to turn logging OFF.

The **LOG_DIRECTORY_**<listener_name> parameter is used in conjunction with the **LOG_FILE_**<listener_name> parameter. Together, these control the directory to be used for the listener log and the file name for the log. The **LOG_FILE_**<listener_name> parameter will accept a full path and name specification. If you include the path in the **LOG_FILE_**<listener_name>, you do not have to include the **LOG_DIRECTORY_**<listener_name> parameter.

In certain operations (such as stopping the listener process), you may want additional security beyond the operating system sign-on. In this situation, you can use the **PASSWORDS_**<listener_name> parameter to set the password(s) for the listener process.

Some changes can be made dynamically to the listener process. The **SAVE_CONFIG_ON_STOP_**<listener_name> parameter indicates if these changes should be made permanent. If this is set to TRUE, then any changes made dynamically are saved in the configuration file. This parameter can also be set to ON to save the changes or OFF to disregard any changes. The default behavior is to revert to the original listener.ora settings when the listener is stopped or a reload command is issued.

The **SERVICE_LIST_<listener_name>** parameter is used to support non-database servers. This parameter is very similar to **SID_LIST_<listener_name>**, except this is not a mandatory parameter. The default setting is null. Detailed information on how to configure this depends upon the product to be supported.

 You need to be familiar with the **SERVICE_LIST** parameter. However, the Oracle8 Network Administration exam does not cover the configuration of this parameter.

The **STARTUP_WAIT_TIME_<listener_name>** parameter sets the number of seconds that the listener sleeps before it responds to the initial request for a status by the lsnrctl utility. This parameter is for situations in which the protocol supported is very slow to start. In this situation, the listener process may be running, but it is not yet available to resolve connections. The default value is 0.

The **TRACE_DIRECTORY_<listener_name>** and the **TRACE_FILE_<listener_name>** parameters are used together with the **TRACE_LEVEL_<listener_name>** parameter to obtain trace information. Remember that tracing has an impact on performance and that, depending upon the level of tracing, this impact can be significant. The **TRACE_LEVEL_<listener_name>** parameter can be set to one of the following values:

➤ OFF

➤ USER

➤ ADMIN

➤ SUPPORT

The **TRACE_LEVEL_<listener_name>** defaults to OFF, meaning that no trace files will be written. The USER level provides user trace information. The ADMIN level provides administrative-level tracing. The SUPPORT level generates the maximum amount of information and is the level that is requested by WorldWide Customer Support for problem resolution. This level provides very detailed information on the packets transferred and actions taken by the listener process.

The **TRACE_DIRECTORY_<listener_name>** parameter indicates the directory to which the trace files should be written, if you do not want to use the default. The default is ORACLE_HOME/network/trace for a Unix server and ORACLE_HOME\net80\trace for an NT server. **TRACE_FILE_<listener_name>** indicates the name of the file, and the full path can be included in the **TRACE_FILE_<listener_name>** parameter. If the full path for the file is included in the **TRACE_FILE_<listener_name>** parameter, then the **TRACE_DIRECTORY_<listener_name>** parameter is not necessary.

The **USE_PLUG_AND_PLAY_<listener_name>** parameter indicates to the listener process that a well-known names server is in use. This parameter defaults to OFF and should only be set to ON if you are certain that you have a well-known names server and want to use it. If this parameter is set to ON, the listener registers with the well-known names server and continues looking for a well-known names server until it finds one.

See Table 4.1 for an alphabetical list of the general parameters for the listener.ora file.

Server Configuration With Net8 Assistant

Net8 Assistant is the new GUI tool used to configure, monitor, and control Net8. The Oracle8 Network Administration exam includes questions on Net8 Assistant, so it is important that you are familiar with what it looks like and how it works. And this section provides just that.

If you have the opportunity to use Net8 Assistant in preparation for the test, this is certainly the best way to prepare. If you do not have this option, then carefully look at each of the figures provided in this chapter and study the steps for configuration.

When creating the listener.ora file, any syntax errors will result in a problem. If you omit a punctuation mark or misspell a keyword, the listener.ora file will be invalid and the listener will not start. Net8 Assistant creates the listener.ora file based on your input in each screen. Review the following steps that are used to create a listener using Net8 Assistant.

1. Start Net8 Assistant.

2. Click on Listeners.

3. Select Create from the Edit menu item at the top of the screen.

Table 4.1 List of general parameters in the listener.ora file.		
Parameter	**Default**	**Use**
connect_timeout_<listener_name>	10	Seconds listener waits for valid query after the session starts
log_directory_<listener_name>	current directory	Directory where the log file is to be written
log_file_<listener_name>	<listener_name>.log	The name of the log file for the listener
logging_<listener_name>	ON	Turns logging on and off
passwords_<listener_name>	null	Sets password(s) to secure certain activities
save_config_on_stop_<listener_name>	OFF	Save set command changes when listener is stopped
service_list_<listener_name>	null	Nondatabase service
startup_wait_time_<listener_name>	0	Sleep time before response to initial status request
trace_directory_<listener_name>	$ORACLE_HOME/ network/trace	Directory for trace files
trace_file_<listener_name>	<listener_name>.trc	Name of the trace file
trace_level_<listener_name>	OFF	Tracing level
use_plug_and_play_<listener_name>	OFF	Registers with well-known names server if set to ON

4. Type in the name of the listener.

5. Select Listening Locations from the pull-down menu.

6. Click on Add Address.

7. Supply the information required for the specified network protocol (for example, TCP requires the host and port).

8. Select Save Network Configuration from the File menu item at the top of the screen.

9. Select Database Services.

10. Fill in the global database name, Oracle_Home, and SID.

11. Choose the appropriate option for designating prespawned servers. If you are creating prespawned servers, configure the timeout and number for the servers.

12. Select Save Network Configuration from the File menu.

13. Set the general parameters from the pull-down menu, including logging, tracing, and authentication.

Starting Net8 Assistant

Because the Net8 Assistant is implemented using Java, it can be used on any client or server that supports the Java Virtual Machine and on which Net8 has been installed. If it is installed on a workstation, you can start te Net8 Assistant by clicking on the icon. If you are using it on a Unix server, you can run the netasst.sh shell script, which is located in the $ORACLE_HOME/admin/ bin directory.

Once you have started Net8 Assistant, you will notice four menu items in the toolbar at the top of the screen. The following list presents the options that are available under each menu item:

➤ File

   ➤ Open Network Configuration

   ➤ Save Network Configuration

   ➤ Save As

   ➤ Revert To Saved Configuration

   ➤ Exit

➤ Edit

   ➤ Create

   ➤ Delete

➤ Tools

   ➤ Test Service Name Connectivity

   ➤ Discover Oracle Names Servers

   ➤ Reload All Names Servers

➤ Help

   ➤ Help

   ➤ About Net8 Assistant

The following items have icons under the Network heading:

➤ Profile

➤ Service Name

➤ Listeners

➤ Oracle Names Servers

In the rest of this chapter, we will cover configuration using the Listeners icon. In later chapters, we will cover the Profile, Service Name, and Oracle Names Servers icons. See Figure 4.1 for the initial Net8 Assistant screen.

Basic Listener Configuration

To configure a listener, first click on the Listeners icon. Then click on the Edit menu item. The two options under the Edit item are Create and Delete. Select Create to begin configuration of the listener process. In the initial listener screen, you will be prompted for the listener name. See Figure 4.2. When you click on the OK button, the next listener configuration screen will be automatically displayed.

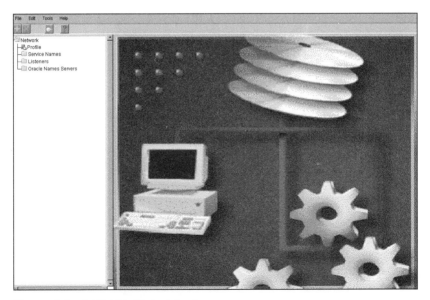

Figure 4.1   Initial Net8 Assistant screen.

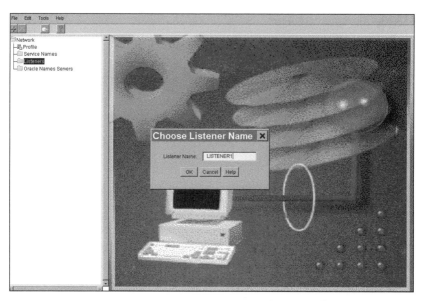

Figure 4.2 Initial listener creation screen.

The next step is to designate the listening locations. Pick the Listening Locations options from the pull-down list. Then click on the Add Address button. See Figure 4.3.

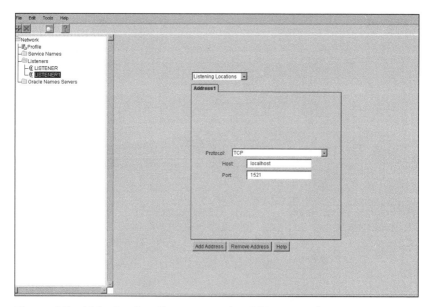

Figure 4.3 Listening locations screen for TCP protocol.

The next step is to select a protocol from the pull-down menu. This screen will change depending upon the protocol selected from the pull-down list. For example, if you choose the TCP protocol, you are requested to fill in the host name and port number. The information on this screen is used to create the ADDRESS_LIST section of the listener.ora file. See Table 4.2 for examples of protocols and the information required for each.

The final step in the initial configuration of the listener is to save this information. Select Save Network Configuration from the File menu.

Database Configuration

After you have made the initial listener configuration, it is time to add the databases. This is the SID_LIST section of the listener.ora file. Highlight the listener that you are configuring, and select Database Services from the pull-down menu. Click the Add Database button. Fill in the global database name, Oracle home directory, and the SID. If you do not intent to configure prespawned servers, select "Do Not Use Prespawned Dedicated Servers". If you decide to use prespawned servers, select "Use Prespawned Dedicated Servers". See Figure 4.4.

If you are using prespawned dedicated server processes, you will be presented with a screen to configure the parameters for the prespawned processes. See Figure 4.5. For each protocol, you need to set the number of prespawned servers and the timeout value. You will also need to set the maximum number of prespawned servers. Click on the OK button when you have finished.

After you have configured the prespawned servers, you need to save your configuration. Select Save Network Configuration from the File menu. If you are going to use the defaults for the general parameters, you are finished with the configuration process.

Configuring General Parameters

With the listener icon highlighted, choose General Parameters from the pull-down menu. The first tab reveals the General screen (Figure 4.6.), where you

Table 4.2	Examples of protocols supported and required fields.
Protocol	**Information Required**
TCP	Host and port
IPC	Key
SPX	Service
NMP	Machine name and pipe name

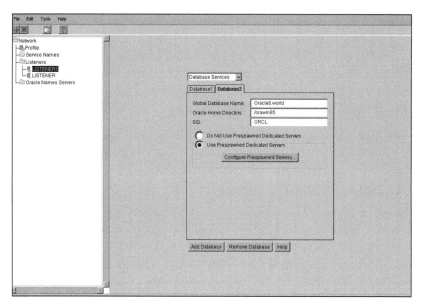

Figure 4.4 Add Database Services screen.

can enter the number of seconds for the startup wait time (**STARTUP_WAIT_ TIME_<listener_name>**) and the Connect Timeout (**CONNECT_ TIMEOUT_<listener_name>**). You can turn on the options for Save Configuration on Shutdown (**SAVE_CONFIG_ON_STOP_<listener_name>**), and you can choose the option of registering services with Oracle Names.

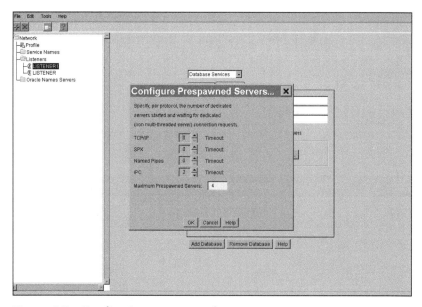

Figure 4.5 Configuring prespawned servers.

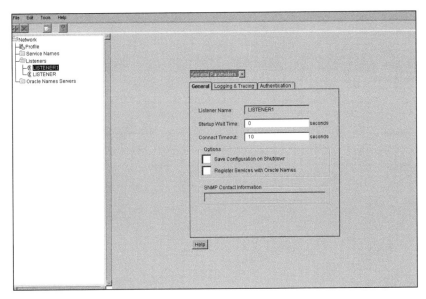

Figure 4.6   General listener parameters.

Next on the General Parameters screen is Logging & Tracing (Figure 4.7), through which you can enable or disable logging (**LOGGING_<listener_name>=OFF**). You can specify the log file name, the trace file name, and the trace level. This screen generates the entries for **LOG_FILE_<listener_name>**, **TRACE_FILE_<listener_name>**, and **TRACE_LEVEL_<listener_name>**.

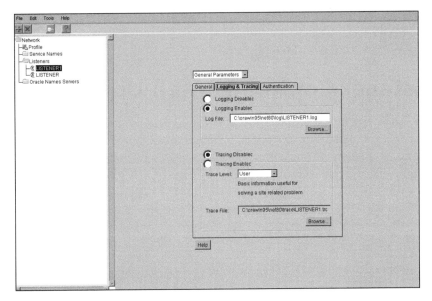

Figure 4.7   Logging & Tracing screen.

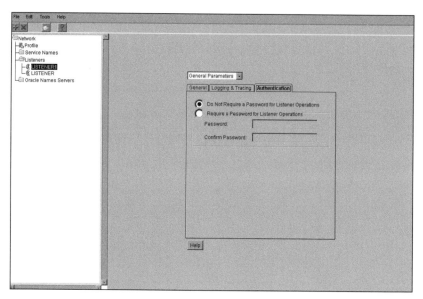

Figure 4.8   Authentication parameter screen.

The final General Parameters screen is Authentication (Figure 4.8), where you will set the password.

When you have finished configuring the general parameters, it is time to save the configuration. Select Save Network Configuration from the File option in the menu toolbar.

If you decide later that you want to change the parameter settings, you can go back to this screen and change the values. Remember to save your changes by selecting Save Network Configuration.

Listener Control (lsnrctl) Utility

The Listener Control Utility (lsnrctl) is the Oracle program to control the listener in command-line mode. (See Table 4.3 for a summary list of the lsnrctl commands.) Many of the commands can be issued at the operating-system prompt with the following statement:

```
$ lsnrctl command <listener_name>
```

On an NT platform, the command includes the version:

```
C:\ lsnrctl80 command <listener_name>
```

Table 4.3 Listener Control Utility commands.

Command	Action
CHANGE_PASSWORD	Dynamically change the password
DBSNMP_START	Start the SNMP subagent
DBSNMP_STATUS	Verify if the SNMP subagent is running
DBSNMP_STOP	Stop the SNMP subagent
EXIT	Return to the operating system
HELP	List the commands available in lsnrctl
QUIT	Return to the operating system
RELOAD	Shut down everything except the listener addresses and reread the listener.ora file
SAVE_CONFIG	Create a backup of the listener.ora file and update the file with current parameters
SERVICES	List information about the listener process connections
SET	List the values that can be dynamically changed
SET CONNECT_TIMEOUT	Dynamically change the amount of time a listener will wait for a valid connection when the session is started
SET CURRENT_LISTENER	Display or change the listener you are working with from within the lsnrctl utility
SET LOG_DIRECTORY	Dynamically change the directory for the log file
SET LOG_FILE	Dynamically change the file name for the log file
SET LOG_STATUS	Dynamically turn logging on or off
SET PASSWORD	Authentication of the user
SET SAVE_CONFIG_ON_STOP	Save the new configuration when exiting the lsnrctl utility
SET STARTUP_WAITTIME	Set the time the listener should sleep before responding to an initial status command
SET TRC_DIRECTORY	Dynamically change the location for the trace files
SET TRC_FILE	Dynamically change the name for the trace file
SET TRC_LEVEL	Dynamically change the level for tracing

(continued)

Table 4.2 lsnrctl commands (continued).	
Command	**Action**
SET USE_PLUG_AND_PLAY	Instructs the listener process to register with a well-known names server
SHOW	Display the current setting for the stated command
SPAWN	Start a program
START	Startup the listener
STATUS	Display basic information on the listener process
STOP	Shut down the listener process
TRACE	Begin tracing
VERSION	Display the current version of the listener and protocol adapter

If no listener name is provided at the command line, then the lsnrctl utility assumes that the listener is using the default name (LISTENER). Alternatively, you can start the lsnrctl utility and then issue the commands, for example:

```
$ lsnrctl
lsnrctl> command
```

For an NT server, use the following command.

```
C:\ lsnrctl80
lsnrctl80> command
```

You can obtain a list of the available commands with the **HELP** command (lsnrctl help <listener_name>). To close the lsnrctl utility and return to the operating-system prompt, you can use either **EXIT** or **QUIT**.

START And STOP Commands

START and STOP are the two functions that are used most often. The START command brings up the listener, and the STOP command shuts down the listener. If password protection is being used, then you must set the password before you can issue the STOP command. When using passwords for the listener, you cannot issue a STOP command at the operating-system level because the password can only be set within the lsnrctl utility.

When you are bringing down the listener process, you should issue a warning to all the network users that the listener will be stopped. While the listener is shut down, users will not be able to initiate new connections.

*Note: On some operating systems, any connections to the listener process that are in place when the **STOP** command is issued will continue to run. This causes a problem because the listener cannot be restarted until all the running processes have been stopped.*

STATUS Command

Another commonly used command is the **STATUS** command. See Listing 4.5 for an example of the response from the **STATUS** command. The **STATUS** command provides the following information:

➤ Version

➤ Address

➤ Start date

➤ Uptime

➤ Setting for logging

➤ Settings for tracing

➤ Database SIDs serviced by this listener

➤ Security

➤ Whether or not SNMP-based connections are accepted

Listing 4.5   Sample response from a lsnrctl **status** command.

```
LSNRCTL for IBM/AIX RISC System/6000Copyright (c) Oracle
Corporation 1997. All rights reserved.Connecting to
(ADDRESS=(PROTOCOL=TCP)(HOST=server1)(PORT=1521))
STATUS of the LISTENER
Alias    listener
Version TNSLSNR for IBM/AIX RISC System/6000: Version 8.0.5.0.0
Production
Start Date      03-MAR-99 12:36:23
Uptime  7 days 8 hr. 19 min. 37 sec.
Trace Level     OFF
Security        OFF
SNMP    OFF
Listener Parameter File /home/oracle/8.0.5/network/admin/listener.ora
Listener Log File       /home/oracle/8.0.5/network/log/listener.log
Services Summary
ORCL   has 1 service handler(s)
PROD   has 1 service handler(s)
The command completed successfully
```

SERVICES Command

The **SERVICES** command provides a detailed list of the services provided by the listener. It provides information on the number and types of services established, as well as the number of refused services. The services include dedicated servers, dispatchers, and prespawned (shadow) processes. See Listing 4.6 for an example of the results of the **SERVICES** command.

Listing 4.6   Results of a lsnrctl **services** command.

```
LSNRCTL for IBM/AIX RISC System/6000: Version 8.0.5.0.0
Production on 29-JAN-99 20:56:20Copyright (c) Oracle Corporation
1994. All rights reserved.

Connecting to (ADDRESS=(PROTOCOL=TCP)(HOST=server1)(PORT=1521))
Services Summary...
ORCL            has 1 service handler(s)
DEDICATED SERVER established:4616 refused:3
PROD            has 1 service handler(s)
DEDICATED SERVER established:200 refused:0

The command completed successfully
```

SHOW And SET Commands

The **SHOW** and **SET** commands are used to display and change the values of certain listener configuration parameters.

The **SHOW** command is used to display information on the current settings. The following list is of the settings that can be displayed using the **SHOW** command.

➤ current_listener

➤ connect_timeout

➤ log_file

➤ log_directory

➤ log_status

➤ save_config_on_stop

➤ snmp_visible

➤ startup_waittime

➤ trc_file

➤ trc_directory

➤ trc_level

➤ use_plug_and_play

The **SET** command is used to dynamically change settings for the listener process. The one exception is the **SET PASSWORD** command, which is used for authentication purposes only. The following commands can be used in conjunction with the **SET** command to dynamically make changes in the listener.

➤ CONNECT_TIMEOUT

➤ CURRENT_LISTENER

➤ LOG_DIRECTORY

➤ LOG_FILE

➤ LOG_STATUS

➤ SAVE_CONFIG_ON_STOP

➤ STARTUP_WAITTIME

➤ TRC_DIRECTORY

➤ TRC_FILE

➤ TRC_LEVEL

➤ USE_PLUG_AND_PLAY

Once you change parameters using the **SET** command, they remain in effect until the next time you stop the listener—unless you have **SAVE_CONFIG_ON_STOP** set to ON or TRUE. You can also issue the **SAVE_CONFIG** command to create a backup of the current listener.ora file and update the file with the new parameters.

Security In The Listener Control Utility

Security in the lsnrctl utility is achieved by requiring a password to execute commands such as stopping the database, displaying certain information, and changing certain settings. Not all actions within the lsnrctl utility require a password, even if the option to use password security is included. The default is not to have any passwords for the lsnrctl utility.

The **PASSWORD** command cannot be issued on the command line. Instead, you must start the lsnrctl utility and then issue the following command:

```
set password <password>
```

If passwords are configured, then the password must be set before issuing the following commands:

➤ CHANGE_PASSWORD

➤ RELOAD

➤ SAVE_CONFIG

➤ SERVICES

➤ SET SAVE_CONFIG_ON_STOP

➤ SET TRC_LEVEL

➤ SET USE_PLUG_AND_PLAY

➤ STOP

➤ TRACE

When you are using password protection for your listener, you have the option of using an encrypted or unencrypted password depending upon how you create the listener.ora file. You can designate one or more unencrypted passwords in the listener.ora file when you manually create the file. If you are using Net8 Assistant, you can create only a single encrypted password.

> *Note: The listener.ora file is a text file. If unencrypted passwords are used, this file should be protected by setting strict operating-system privileges on the file.*

In order to change the password dynamically, you must use the **CHANGE_PASSWORD** command. When you do, you will be prompted for the current password and then asked to confirm the new password. **CHANGE_PASSWORD** allows you to create a new password or change the encrypted password; it will not remove unencrypted passwords in the listener.ora file.

RELOAD Command

Another important command is the **RELOAD** command. In order to change the listener.ora file, you must first shut down (**STOP**) the listener. Using the **RELOAD** command allows you to manually change the listener.ora file and then have the changes take effect without actually stopping the listener. The **RELOAD** command shuts down everything except the listener addresses and rereads the listener.ora file.

SNMP Commands

If you are using an Oracle SNMP subagent, you can control it using the lsnrctl utility. You can start the Oracle SNMP subagent with the **DBSNMP_START** command, and you can shut it down with the **DBSNMP_STOP** command. In addition, you can determine if the Oracle SNMP subagent is running with the **DBSNMP_STATUS** command.

Practice Questions

Question 1

How can you determine if the listener has spawned a new process or redirected the request to an existing process to satisfy a connection request?

Trick! question

○ a. Check the log file.

○ b. Ask the client.

○ c. Check at the operating-system level.

○ d. Turn on tracing and analyze the trace file.

The correct answer is d. If you are experienced with SQL*Net 2 and know your operating system on the server, you may be able to determine whether or not new processes are being spawned by checking for processes at the operating-system level. However, this is not the best answer because it is not how Oracle provides the information to you. In order to correctly determine if a connect request is being serviced by spawning a new process or by redirecting to an existing process, it is necessary to turn on tracing and analyze the trace file.

Question 2

Which of the following is necessary for setting up multiple listeners on a server? [Choose the two best answers]

❑ a. Each listener must have a unique name and port.

❑ b. At least one of the listeners must be named LISTENER and use port 1521.

❑ c. Each listener must have its own configuration file on the server.

❑ d. Each listener must be separately defined in the listener.ora file.

❑ e. Each listener must be separately defined in the tnsnames.ora file

The correct answers are a and d. Each listener on a server must have a unique name and port number. All the listeners on a server can be defined within one listener.ora file. However, each must be separately defined within this file. You can use separate listener.ora files by setting the TNS_ADMIN to a different directory for each listener, but this is not required.

Question 3

> You are having problems and want to temporarily change the trace level for the listener process. You are using password protection for your listener process. Which of the following set of commands should you use?
>
> ○ a. **LSNRCTL SET TRC_LEVEL SUPPORT**
>
> ○ b. **LSNCRTL; SET PASSWORD; SET TRC_LEVEL SUPPORT**
>
> ○ c. **LSNRCTL; SET PASSWORD; SET TRACE_LEVEL ADMIN; SAVE_CONFIG**
>
> ○ d. **LSNRCTL STOP; LSNRCTL START**
>
> ○ e. You cannot dynamically change the level of tracing.

The correct answer is b. Since you have a password, you must first log into lsnrctl and set the password. The need for a password eliminates answers a and d. Answer c can be eliminated by two things: The command is "SET TRC_ LEVEL" and not "TRACE_LEVEL", and the SAVE_CONFIG makes the change permanent. Since the trace level can be dynamically changed, answer e is also incorrect.

Question 4

> The listener process receives a connection request and determines that it can be processed. Which of the following is true?
>
> ○ a. The listener will always redirect the request to a pre-spawned dedicated process.
>
> ○ b. The listener will always redirect the request to a dispatcher.
>
> ○ c. The listener will always spawn a new process and bequeath the connection to the dedicated process.
>
> ○ d. The listener will handle the request either by redirection or spawning a new process.
>
> ○ e. The listener will handle the request either by redirection to a dispatcher or by spawning a new process.

The correct answer is d. Be careful that you do not read anything additional into questions or answers like these. You must pick the best answer based only on the information that is provided in the question and in the answers. Answers a, b, and c can all be eliminated basically due to the presence of the word *always*. Answer a can be eliminated because, although the listener will redirect the request to a prespawned dedicated process, it does so *only if* it is using pre-spawned dedicated processes. The question does not specifically state that this is the situation. Similarly, b is eliminated because the listener will redirect the request to a dispatcher *if* the database is using the multithreaded option—a situation that, again, the question does not specify. Answer c is also eliminated with the same logic: The listener will spawn a new process and bequeath the connection to the dedicated process, *unless* it can redirect the connection request. Answer e assumes that the listener can use redirection only if there are dispatchers, which is not true because the listener can use redirection if it has prespawned dedicated server processes configured.

Question 5

> The listener process is receiving more requests than it can handle and is overloaded. What two items listed below can be used to allow the listener to handle the workload? [Choose the two best answers]
>
> ❑ a. Increase the queue size for the listener.
>
> ❑ b. Create multiple listeners for the same database.
>
> ❑ c. Add databases to the listener.
>
> ❑ d. Change the listener configuration to use prespawned processes.
>
> ❑ e. Change the level of tracing to SUPPORT.

The correct answers are a and b. Increasing the queue size will allow the listener to handle a larger number of requests, and creating multiple listeners for the same database allows for load balancing. Both of these will help the listener handle the workload. Adding databases to the listener (Answer c) actually increases the workload. Although changing the listener to use pre-spawned processes (Answer d) allows for faster connections, the listener will need to create and maintain information about these processes. Changing the level of tracing to SUPPORT (Answer e) also increases the workload because the listener must now write extensive tracing information to a file.

Question 6

You are having problems with the listener process. You need to obtain very detailed information for Oracle WorldWide Support to assist you in resolving the problem. What trace level should you use?

○ a. ADMIN

○ b. USER

○ c. OFF

○ d. SUPPORT

The correct answer is d. The USER and ADMIN levels provide information; however, they do not give as much detailed information as the SUPPORT level. The trace level should normally be set to OFF.

Question 7

What lsnrctl command can be used to allow manual changes to the configuration for the listener process without actually stopping the listener?

○ a. **SERVICES**

○ b. **STATUS**

○ c. **RELOAD**

○ d. You cannot change the configuration of the listener process without stopping the listener first.

The correct answer is c. The **RELOAD** command performs a shutdown of everything except the listener addresses and rereads the listener.ora file. While manual changes of the listener.ora file require the listener to be shut down, the **RELOAD** command performs this function without requiring an actual **STOP** command. The **SERVICES** and **STATUS** commands are used to obtain information on the listener process such as the current settings, whether or not the listener is running, how many connections have been established, and so forth.

Question 8

Which of the following is a Java-based tool that can be used to configure and monitor the listener process?

○ a. lsnrctl

○ b. Oracle Names

○ c. Advanced Networking Option

○ d. Net8 Assistant

○ e. Net8 Administrator

The correct answer is d, Net8 Assistant. The lsnrctl utility is not Java based. Oracle Names and the Advanced Networking Option are not used to configure and monitor the listener process. There is no tool called the Net8 Administrator.

Question 9

When using Net8 Assistant, what is the first step in creating the listener?

○ a. Select Listener from the menu toolbar.

○ b. Click on the Listener icon and then choose Create from the Edit menu item on the toolbar.

○ c. Click on the Profile icon and choose Create from the Tools menu.

○ d. Click on the Listener icon and choose Database Services from the pull-down menu.

○ e. Select Create from the Edit menu toolbar and then click on the Listener icon.

The correct answer is b. Click on the Listener icon and then choose Create from the Edit menu item on the toolbar. Screen shots and the steps for creating a listener with the Net8 Assistant are included in this chapter.

Question 10

> When using Net8 Assistant, what information do you fill in when adding a database?
>
> ○ a. Oracle home and SID
>
> ○ b. Global database name, Oracle home, and SID
>
> ○ c. SID, location, and Oracle home
>
> ○ d. Oracle home, port, and SID
>
> ○ e. Oracle home, port, global database name, and SID

The correct answer is b. Review the Figure 4.4 for adding a database service using the Net8 Assistant.

Question 11

> Where do you go in Net8 Assistant to set up a password for your listener?
>
> ○ a. Listener icon, Database Services pull-down menu, Authentication tab
>
> ○ b. Listener icon, General Parameters pull-down menu, Authentication tab
>
> ○ c. Listener icon, General Parameters pull-down menu, Authorization tab
>
> ○ d. Listener icon, Authentication pull-down menu, Password tab
>
> ○ e. Authentication icon, General Parameters pull-down menu, Password tab

The correct answer is b. Highlight the Listener icon, choose General Parameters from the pull-down menu, and select the Authentication tab. See Figure 4.8.

Question 12

You have finished filling in the information in Net8 Assistant for your listener configuration. What should you do before you exit Net8 Assistant?

○ a. Choose Save from the File menu.

○ b. Choose Execute from the Tools menu on the toolbar to create the listener.ora file.

○ c. Click on the SAVE button.

○ d. Choose Save Network Configuration from the File menu on the toolbar.

The correct answer is d. Review the steps for creating a listner with the Net8 Assistant.

Need To Know More?

 The first place to look for more information is the *Oracle Net8 Administrator's Guide* Release 8.0, Chapter 4 "Configuring Network Services" and Appendix A.1 "Listener Control Utility (LSNRCTL)."

 Kreines, David C. and Laskey, Brian. *Oracle Database Administration: The Essential Reference.* O'Reilly, 1999. Chapter 5 contains a sample listener.ora file and a brief description of the Net8 Assistant.

 "SQL*Net Configuration." RevealNet Oracle Administration Knowledge Base. Network Management. It also provides excellent sample listener.ora parameter file samples.

Net8 Client Configuration

Terms you'll need to understand:

√ HOSTNAME

√ sqlnet.ora

√ tnsnames.ora

√ Profiles

√ Oracle Service Name Wizard

Techniques you'll need to master:

√ How to configure the client to use host naming

√ How to configure the client to use local naming

√ How to configure the client using Net8 Assistant

In the previous chapter, you learned how to configure the listener on the server. Once you have an active listener to accept connection requests, you need to configure the client to correctly transmit the requests.

This chapter focuses on two methods for configuring the client: host naming and local naming. See Figures 5.1 and 5.2.

This chapter also briefly describes the external naming method and introduces you to Oracle Names (ONAMES). Oracle Names is covered in more detail in a later chapter.

Host Naming Configuration

You can configure the host naming (HOSTNAME) method with very little effort. However, it has very specific requirements. The connect string used by the client must match the **GLOBAL_DBNAME** parameter in the listener.ora file, and the hostname, not a service name, is used as the connect descriptor. There is no need to configure and maintain a tnsnames.ora file on the client. See Figure 5.1.

The host naming method requires the TCP/IP protocol, and you cannot use it with any other network protocol. Net8 with the TCP/IP protocol adapter and the TCP/IP network protocol must be installed on both the client and server. Since the host name uses an IP address translation method, you must have the IP address translation mechanism in place before configuring the client for host naming. One of the following must be used for the IP address translation:

➤ Domain Name Services (DNS)

➤ Network Information Services (NIS)

➤ Local hosts file

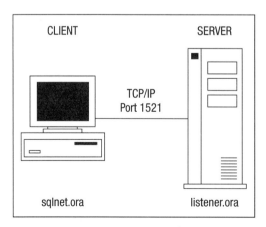

Figure 5.1   Host naming configuration.

In this section, I'll cover the two files necessary for host naming: sqlnet.ora and listener.ora.

I'll also cover the advantages and disadvantages of using the host naming method.

The sqlnet.ora File

The host naming method requires a sqlnet.ora file on the client, with the following parameters configured:

```
names.authentication_services
names.directory_path
```

The authentication services parameter must be set to the IP translation method (DNS or NIS), or a local hosts file must be available to resolve the service name.

To use the host naming method, you must place HOSTNAME as the first entry in the **NAMES.DIRECTORY_PATH** parameter in sqlnet.ora.

You can combine host naming with local naming and/or Oracle Names by including them in the **NAMES.DIRECTORY_PATH** setting. Net8 will try to resolve the connect string with the methods specified in this parameter in the order in which they are listed. The following is an example of the sqlnet.ora specification for host naming:

```
names.directory_path=(HOSTNAME)
names.authentication_service=(DNS)
```

In this example, **HOSTNAME** is the only method specified, and the DNS is specified as the translation mechanism.

The listener.ora File

The listener.ora default configuration uses port 1521 and defaults the **GLOBAL_DBNAME** to the hostname. Listing 5.1 is an example of the entry in a listener.ora file using the host names method.

Listing 5.1   SID entry in listener.ora file for host naming.

```
SID_LIST_LISTENER =
      (SID_LIST =
            (SID_DESC =
                  (GLOBAL_DBNAME = prod1svr)
                  (ORACLE_HOME=/orax1/oracle/8.0.5)
                  (SID_NAME=PROD)
            )
      )
```

When making a connection, the **GLOBAL_DBNAME** is specified as the connection string. The connection request for the PROD database, as it is specified in Listing 5.1, would be:

```
sqlplus username/password@prod1svr
```

The connect string, **prod1svr**, must also be a hostname for the server.

Advantages And Disadvantages Of The Host Naming Configuration

An obvious advantage to host naming is the easy configuration. By using Net8 Assistant and relying on the IP translation mechanism, configuration of the client is minimal. On the server side, the default listener.ora file that is created when the listener is started will be able to accept connection requests using the host naming method. Host naming is useful for very simple network environments with a small number of client connections.

The most obvious disadvantage to using the HOSTNAME method is that you are restricted to the use of one network protocol: TCP/IP. While local naming supports multiple protocols, the HOSTNAME method requires TCP/IP.

As I mentioned in the previous chapter, every listener process on the server must have its own unique port number assigned to it. Since you must use the default port (1521), you cannot have multiple listeners on the server with the HOSTNAME method.

Another disadvantage is that you will not be able to use the features provided by Connection Manager, because it is incompatible with host naming.

Local Naming Configuration

The local naming (TNSNAMES) method requires configuring a tnsnames.ora file on the client. The client uses the tnsnames.ora file to map the service name into a connect descriptor. Using Net8 Assistant, this local naming file is very easy to configure. See Figure 5.2.

The tnsnames.ora file is very sensitive to errors in syntax and punctuation. Keep this in mind if you decide to configure the tnsnames.ora file manually.

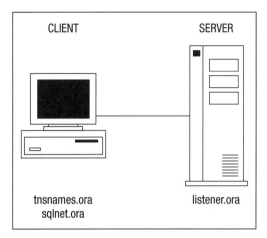

Figure 5.2   Local naming configuration.

On the server, the listener.ora file that was configured in the previous chapter can be used to accept connection requests that are generated by the local naming method. In this section, I'll cover the client files that are configured local naming: tnsnames.ora and sqlnet.ora.

The default location for both the tnsnames.ora and sqlnet.ora files is in the $ORACLE_HOME/network/admin directory for Unix clients and the ORACLE_HOME\net80\admin directory for NT clients. A Unix server can override this default by setting the TNS_ADMIN environmental variable.

I'll also cover the advantages and disadvantages of using the local naming method.

The tnsnames.ora File

The most important client file for local naming is tnsnames.ora, which must reside on every client in order to use local naming. This file contains two main sections:

➤ SERVICE NAME

➤ CONNECT DESCRIPTOR

See Appendix B for a complete example of the tnsnames.ora file.

SERVICE NAME

The SERVICE NAME is a name that maps to a CONNECT DESCRIPTOR. The client uses this name as the connect string in a connection request. A

SERVICE NAME may be anything that is easy for the client to use and remember. Unlike the host naming method, with the local naming method you are not restricted to using the **GLOBAL_DBNAME**. If you want to support multiple service names for connections to the same database, you must define each one separately.

The service name entry can include the domain name. If no domain is specified, the default domain is assumed. The default domain may be either the domain in which the client resides or the domain from which the client often requests services. If your configuration has multiple domains, you will need to include your domain name in the service name. When using some advanced database features, the domain must be specified—even if you are using the default domain. For example, advanced replication requires the use of global names, which includes the domain.

CONNECT DESCRIPTOR

The CONNECT DESCRIPTOR has two sections:

➤ ADDRESS_LIST or ADDRESS

➤ CONNECT_DATA

If there is only one ADDRESS, then the keyword ADDRESS_LIST is not required. For each ADDRESS, it is necessary to provide the network protocol information required for a connection. The keyword PROTOCOL indicates the network protocol in use. The remaining address information is based on the type of network protocol. Although you can configure multiple protocols for each service name, each protocol must be specified with a different ADDRESS entry.

When using the TCP/IP network protocol, the host and port must be specified. The host can be specified with either an IP address or a hostname. If you specify a hostname, then you must have some method available for the network to determine the IP address that is assigned to that hostname. For example, a local hosts file or a DNS can be used to point to the IP address for a hostname. Again, the port specified must match the port used by the listener process on the server. If the port does not match in the tnsnames.ora and listener.ora files, the connection request cannot be completed.

The CONNECT_DATA section contains the SID for the database connection.

You can configure your tnsnames.ora file to use multiple listeners on the server. Listing 5.2 shows multiple addresses with different port numbers. The service name will resolve to either address listed under the ADDRESS_LIST, allowing the listener processes on the server to perform load balancing. It is important to remember that, in order to use multiple listeners for a SID, you must have an address entry for each listener in your tnsnames.ora file for each applicable service name.

Listing 5.2   Service name entry in tnsnames.ora file for local naming with multiple listener entries.

```
PROD.world =
     (DESCRIPTION =
          (ADDRESS_LIST =
               (ADDRESS =
                         (PROTOCOL = TCP)
                         (HOST = prod1svr)
                         (PORT = 1521)
                )
               (ADDRESS =
                         (PROTOCOL = TCP)
                         (HOST = prod1svr)
                         (PORT = 1526)
          )
          (CONNECT_DATA =
               (SID=PROD)
     )
```

The sqlnet.ora File

The local naming method is the default first method for Net8 connections. Therefore, the sqlnet.ora file is not always required when using local naming. A sqlnet.ora file is created when you create a configuration for local naming with Net8 Assistant.

The sqlnet.ora file is required when performing diagnostics and when the default parameters are not sufficient. Many parameters can be set in the sqlnet.ora file to control how Net8 will behave when using local naming. This includes aspects of the connection on both the sending (client workstation) side and the receiving (server) side. Therefore, the sqlnet.ora file may be necessary on either the client-side workstation or the server side, depending upon what actions are being controlled. There are also parameters that can be set in the sqlnet.ora parameter file that are used to configure Net8 connections for advanced security functionality and Oracle Names. This section will not cover the sqlnet.ora parameters relevant to security and Oracle Names, as these are covered in later chapters. One sqlnet.ora file that contains parameters for the client and server sides can be created and placed on both the client and server. See Table 5.1 for an alphabetical list of the sqlnet.ora parameters covered here.

Table 5.1 sqlnet.ora parameters relevant to local naming.		
Parameter	**Default**	**Use**
AUTOMATIC_IPC	OFF	Controls use of IPC addresses
BEQUEATH_DETACH	NO	Controls use of signal handling
DISABLE_OOB	OFF	Disables out-of-band breaks
LOG_DIRECTORY_CLIENT	current directory	Directory where logs will be written
LOG_FILE_CLIENT	sqlnet.log	File name for the logs
NAMES.DEFAULT_DOMAIN	null	Specifies domain name to be used with service name
NAMES.DIRECTORY_PATH	TNSNAMES, ONAMES, HOSTNAME	The method and order for resolution of service names
SQLNET.EXPIRE_TIME	none	Time interval used to check if the session is alive
TNSPING.TRACE_DIRECTORY	$ORACLE_HOME/ network/trace	Directory for tnsping results
TNSPING.TRACE_LEVEL	OFF	Sets the trace level for the tnsping
TRACE_DIRECTORY_CLIENT	$ORACLE_HOME/ network/trace	Directory where trace files will be written
TRACE_FILE_CLIENT	sqlnet.trc	File name for the trace
TRACE_LEVEL_CLIENT	OFF	Level of tracing to be performed
TRACE_UNIQUE_CLIENT	OFF	Create a unique name for each trace file
USE_DEDICATED_SERVER	OFF	Forces dedicated connections

 Because this exam focuses on the sqlnet.ora placed on the client workstation, that is the focus of this chapter. It can contain parameters for both ends of the Net8 connection.

The **AUTOMATIC_IPC** parameter can be set to ON or OFF (the default). When set to ON, all connection requests are forced to attempt a connection using the interprocess communication (IPC) address first.

The **BEQUEATH_DETACH** parameter turns signal handling on or off when using Net8 in a Unix environment. This parameter can be set to YES or NO. The default is No, which leaves signal handling on.

In the chapter on Net8 Architecture, I mentioned out-of-band breaks, which some network protocols do not support. The **DISABLE_OOB** parameter can be set to On to disable out-of-band breaks. The default setting is OFF, meaning that out-of-band breaks are enabled by default.

The **LOG_DIRECTORY_CLIENT** and **LOG_FILE_CLIENT** parameters are used to control where the Net8 log files are written and also the name that is used for the log file. The **LOG_DIRECTORY_CLIENT** defaults to the current directory for the user, and the **LOG_FILE_CLIENT** will default to sqlnet.log.

The **NAMES.DEFAULT_DOMAIN** parameter is used to define the domain that is to be used with the service name. This parameter defaults to NULL, but it can be set to any valid domain name for your environment. If there is no specification for a default domain, the domain is assumed to be WORLD.

The **NAMES.DIRECTORY_PATH** determines which method is to be used for resolution of service names and the order in which the specified methods are applied. By specifying the methods in the **NAMES.DIRECTORY_PATH** parameter, you control the way Net8 interprets the connect string supplied by the user. Net8 will attempt to resolve the connect string with the first method specified. If this method fails, it moves through the list until all the specified methods have been attempted. If the connect string is not resolved successfully, an error is returned to the client. The values that can be used for the connection methods are:

➤ TNSNAMES

➤ ONAMES

➤ HOSTNAME

➤ DCE

➤ NIS

➤ Novell

The default is TNSNAMES, ONAMES, HOSTNAME. By default, if the provided connect string cannot be resolved as a service name in the tnsnames.ora file, then Net8 will try the Oracle names method. If that fails, Net8 will assume the connect string is a hostname and will attempt to resolve it using the host naming method. If you are using local naming, you can use the default specification because Net8 will attempt a to use the TNSNAMES method first. However, if you are using only TNSNAMES, there is no need for Net8 to attempt an ONAMES or HOSTNAME connection. In this case, you can set **NAMES.DIRECTORY_PATH**=(TNSNAMES).

The **SQLNET.EXPIRE_TIME** is used to check whether a session is still alive. If a connection terminates normally, this value is not applicable. However if a connection dies unexpectedly (abnormally terminates), this value will provide a method to clean up connection processes. The default value is NONE, which does not check the status of the sessions. The **SQLNET.EXPIRE_TIME** is configured in minutes and can be set between the minimum of 0 minutes to the maximum supported for your platform. Oracle recommends that this be set to 10 minutes. You should note that this parameter is configured on the receiving (server) side for the sqlnet connection.

If you decide to test your service name, you can use a **TNSPING** command. The **TNSPING.TRACE_DIRECTORY** is used to determine where the tnsping trace information will be written. This works in conjunction with the **TNSPING.TRACE_LEVEL**, which sets the level of tracing to be performed. The default location for the trace file is $ORACLE_HOME/network/trace, and the default level is OFF. The values available for the trace level are OFF, USER, ADMIN, and SUPPORT. See Table 5.2.

The **TRACE_FILE_CLIENT** and **TRACE_DIRECTORY_CLIENT** work with the **TRACE_LEVEL_CLIENT** to control how much trace information is to be written, where the Net8 trace files are written, and the name that is used for the trace file. The **TRACE_DIRECTORY_CLIENT** defaults to the $ORACLE_HOME/network/trace directory for Unix or $ORACLE_HOME\net80\trace for NT. The **TRACE_FILE_CLIENT** will default to sqlnet.trc, and the **TRACE_LEVEL_CLIENT** will default to OFF. The settings for the **TRACE_LEVEL_CLIENT** are the same as those used for the **TNSPING** .TRACE_LEVEL. See Table 5.2.

If you are troubleshooting your client connection and do not want to have the trace file overwritten each time, you can use the **TRACE_UNIQUE_CLIENT**

Table 5.2	Trace level options.
Setting	**Results**
OFF	No tracing information is generated
USER	User-level trace information
ADMIN	Administration-level trace information
SUPPORT	Detailed tracing information is provided for use by Oracle WorldWide Customer Support in problem resolution

parameter. This parameter defaults to OFF. By setting it to ON, the PID of the process is appended to the end of the trace file name.

Tracing on the server can be configured in the listener.ora file, but tracing on the client cannot be configured in the tnsnames.ora file. You must set the tracing and logging parameters in the sqlnet.ora file.

 Direct your logs to the $ORACLE_HOME/network/log directory and your trace files to the $ORACLE_HOME/network/trace directory. This will provide a more consistent placement and make troubleshooting easier.

The **USE_DEDICATED_SERVER** parameter is used to ensure that the connection request is resolved with a dedicated server process connection to the Oracle database. The default is OFF. To ensure that you have a dedicated server process, set this to ON.

Advantages And Disadvantages Of Local Naming

With the local naming method, you can configure Net8 using any supported network protocol: You are not limited to only TCP/IP. You can use SPX or DecNet or whatever you decide will work best in your environment.

Another advantage to local naming is that you can configure your client to make use of multiple listeners on the server.

The biggest disadvantage, however, of the local naming method is that it requires configuration on every client to maintain the tnsnames.ora file and sqlnet.ora files. Whenever there is a change in your configuration, this change must be made on every client workstation.

Cient Configuration With Net8 Assistant

Net8 Assistant is the GUI tool that Oracle provides with Net8 to configure the Net8 files. For client-side configuration, you can use Net8 Assistant to configure both the tnsnames.ora and sqlnet.ora files for host naming, local naming, external naming, and Oracle Names. The Profile configuration creates or modifies the sqlnet.ora file. The Service Names configuration creates or modifies the tnsnames.ora file.

You can start Net8 Assistant in the NT environment by choosing Start and then Programs. Under Programs, choose Oracle for NT. Under Oracle for NT, choose Oracle Net8 Assistant. You can also start Net8 Assistant by running the n8a.exe executable file.

On a Unix platform, you can run the executable file, net8asst.sh, to start Net8 Assistant.

The three major parts to the configuration of the client using Net8 Assistant are:

➤ Profile

➤ Service Name

➤ Oracle Service Name Wizard

Profile

The first step in configuring the client is to configure the profile. The profile screen is used to set up the naming methods and the order in which the methods will be used. By default, you will have the TNSNAMES and HOSTNAME methods listed under Selected Methods.

If you are using host naming, place the HOSTNAME method first under Selected Methods. If you are using local naming, be sure that TNSNAMES is the first method on the list for Selected Methods.

You may choose multiple methods and arrange them in any order. Use the arrow keys to move methods between Selected Methods and Available Methods. Use Promote and Demote to rearrange the order of the Selected Methods. This information is used to create the sqlnet.ora file with a **NAMES.DIRECTORY_ PATH** set to the values you have chosen in the order they are listed. See Figure 5.3.

You can continue to configure your profile now or use Net8 Assistant at a later time to configure or change your Profile. Highlight the Profile icon on the opening screen of Net8 Assistant. Select General from the pull-down menu. See Figure 5.4. Four tabs provide configuration of different parameters for your profile.

The Tracing tab is used to configure the parameters associated with tracing. The Trace Level field provides a pull-down list of the four trace levels: Off, User, Admin, and Support. Fill in the appropriate file name and directory. If you click on the Unique File Trace Name box, a checkmark appears in the box. This will set the **TRACE_UNIQUE_CLIENT** parameter to ON for unique trace file names.

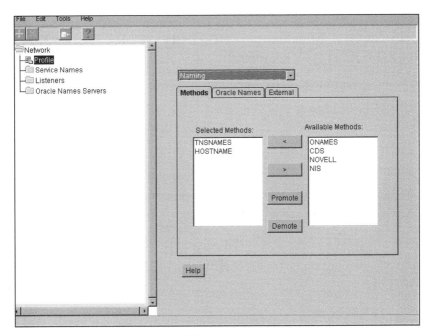

Figure 5.3   Net8 Assistant Profile configuration screen.

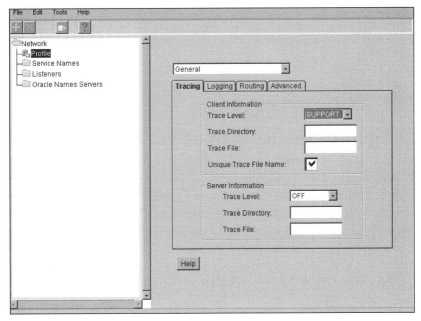

Figure 5.4   Net8 Assistant Profile General parameters screen.

The Logging tab is where you'll specify the directory and file name for your log files. This configures the **LOG_DIRECTORY_CLIENT** and **LOG_FILE_CLIENT** parameters.

The Routing tab configures the following:

➤ Use Dedicated Server configures the **USER_DEDICATED_SERVER** parameter

➤ Use IPC Addresses For Client configures the **AUTOMATIC_IPC** parameter

➤ Use Source Route Addresses configures connections using Connection Manager

The Advanced tab screen is where you can set the following options:

➤ TNS Time Out configures the **SQLNET.EXPIRE_TIME** parameter

➤ Client Registration ID is used for security configurations

➤ Turn Off UNIX Signal Handling configures the **BEQUEATH_DETACH** parameter

➤ Disable Out-Of-Band-Break configures the **DISABLE_OOB** parameter

For more information on each of these parameters, review the previous section in this chapter that discusses the sqlnet.ora file parameters. See Table 5.1.

If you are using the HOSTNAME method, you are finished configuration for the client. Choose Save Network Configuration from the File option on the toolbar to generate a sqlnet.ora file.

Configuring Service Names For Local Naming

If you are using local naming, after you have configured the method of connection in your profile, it is time to configure your service names. Highlight the Service Names icon and choose Create from the Edit menu item on the toolbar. Remember the service name is the name that is used to map to a connect descriptor. Net8 Assistant starts the Oracle Service Name Wizard to step you through the creation of service names. See Figure 5.5.

Oracle Service Name Wizard

The Oracle Service Name Wizard is a Java-based GUI application and is used for the following actions:

➤ Create new service names

➤ Modify service name information

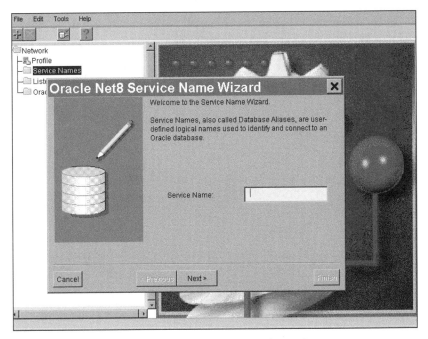

Figure 5.5   Oracle Net8 Service Name Wizard initial screen.

➤ Delete service names

➤ Test service names

The first screen of the Oracle Service Name Wizard prompts you for the service name. Type in the service name you have chosen for your database. Remember, you can use any name for your service name. This is just a convenient, easy name for your clients to use in the connection request. It is the connect descriptor that is attached to this service name that is used to make the connection. Click on the Next button to proceed.

The first step in configuring the service name is to choose the network protocol from the list provided. You must have the network protocol installed and operational before you can configure a service name to use that protocol. Click on the Next button to continue in your configuration. See Figure 5.6.

The screen you see next will vary depending upon the network protocol selected. If you are using TCP/IP, the next step is to specify the host name and port number for the service name. This screen will default to port 1521 for the TCP/IP port number. See Figure 5.7.

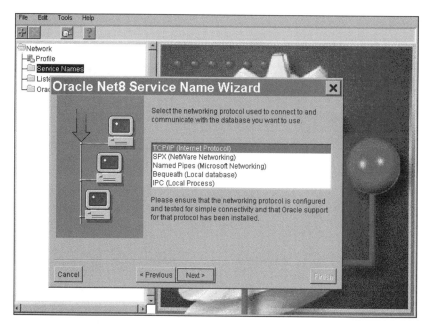

Figure 5.6 Oracle Net8 Service Name Wizard proctocol selection screen.

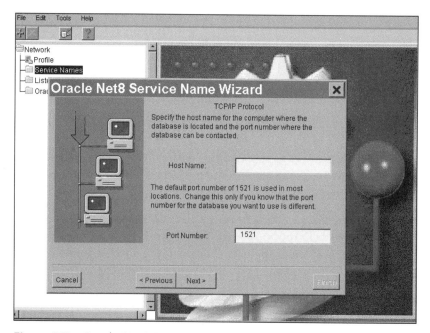

Figure 5.7 Oracle Net8 Service Name Wizard TCP/IP Protocol configuration.

If you choose IPC as the network protocol, you will be prompted for the IPC Key Value. If you Choose SPX/IPX, you will be prompted for an SPX service name. If you are using named pipes, you will be prompted for the server name and pipe name. If you are configuring the NT server to be both client and server, you may be using the bequeath method of connection. When using this method, you will be given an acknowledgement screen, but you will not be prompted for additional information.

With the exception of TCP/IP—which is the most widely used network protocol—the Net8 Exam will not cover all the possible entries you may have.

Once you have configured the protocol-specific information, click on the Next button to proceed to the next step: specifying the SID. See Figure 5.8. The default SID is ORCL. Be sure to specify the SID (Oracle system identifier) and not the database name or service name. Click on the Next button to continue.

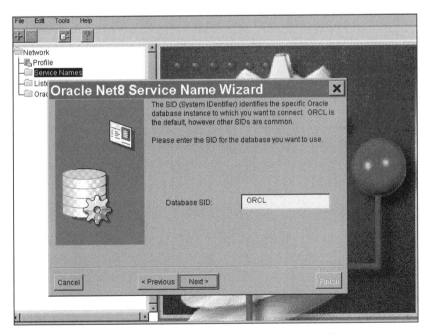

Figure 5.8   Oracle Net8 Service Name Wizard SID specification screen.

For easy configuration and maintenance, consider keeping your service name, database name, and SID consistent.

The final phase of the configuration for a service name is to perform the service test (Figure 5.9). Testing the service name is optional. You can choose to click on Finish without performing a service name test. When you click on the Test Service button, another screen will prompt you for a username and password. See Figure 5.10. Provide a username and password and then click on the Test button on this screen. After you receive the results of your test, click on the Done button.

After clicking on the Done button, the next screen will allow you to add additional addresses for your service name. See Figure 5.11. You can add addresses for your service name and delete any addresses that you do not want. If you are using multiple listeners, you should add the second address here. When you have completed configuring your service name, select Save Network Configuration from the File menu item on the toolbar. At this point, the tnsnames.ora and sqlnet.ora files are created.

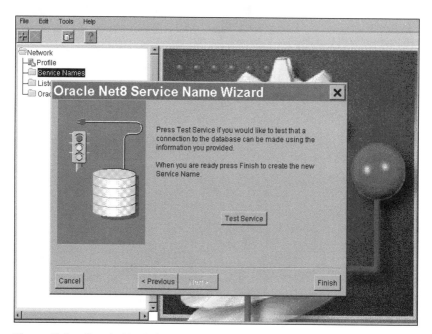

Figure 5.9 Oracle Net8 Service Name Wizard Test Service screen.

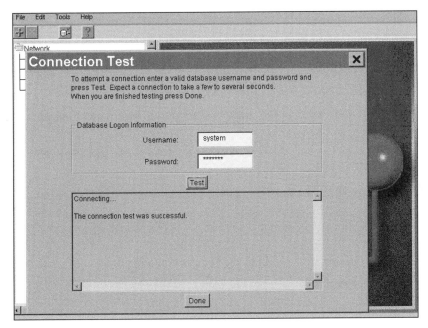

Figure 5.10   Oracle Net8 Assistant Connection Test screen.

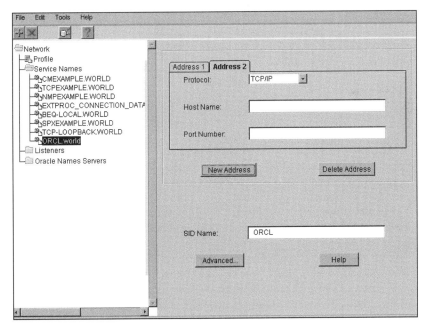

Figure 5.11   Oracle Net8 Assistant Service Name Address screen.

You need to go through this procedure for each service name to be included. Remember to select Save Network Configuration from the File menu item on the toolbar after you're finished configuring your additional service names. When you save the configuration, the tnsnames.ora file is updated to reflect the changes.

Below is a summary of the Net8 steps in cofiguration of local naming files.

1. Start Net8 Assistant.

2. Click on Profiles.

3. Configure Methods.

4. Set the general parameters for logging, tracing, routing, and advanced features.

5. For host naming, go to number 13. For local naming, begin configuration of database addresses by clicking on the Service Names icon.

6. Select Create from the Edit menu item on toolbar.

7. Type in a service name.

8. Choose the protocol.

9. If you choose TCP, you will be prompted to provide the host and port number for TCP protocols. The information required will differ for other network protocols.

10. Specify a SID.

11. Test the connection.

12. Add additional service names and service name addresses.

13. Select Save Network Configuration from the File menu item on the toolbar.

14. When the configuration is saved, the sqlnet.ora and/or tnsnames.ora files are created depending upon the method and configuration parameters.

While you can make service name modifications using Net8 Assistant, which calls the Oracle Service Name Wizard, it is more direct to go straight to the Oracle8 Service Name Wizard. On an NT server, go to Start. From there, choose Programs. From the Programs list, choose Oracle For NT. From here, choose Oracle Net8 Easy Config, which brings up the Service Name Wizard (Figure 5.12). If you prefer, you can start the Oracle Service Name Wizard from the file manager by clicking on the n8sw.exe executable file. For a Unix server, you can type in "net8wiz.sh" at the command-line prompt.

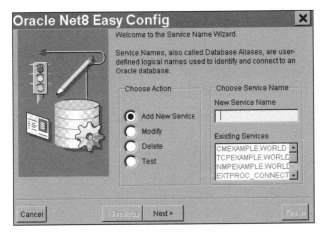

Figure 5.12   Oracle Service Name Wizard initial screen.

You can use the Oracle Service Name Wizard to perform the following tasks:

➤ Add new service names

➤ Modify existing service names

➤ Delete a service name

➤ Test connectivity for a service name

External Naming

Before you can begin configuring your client for external naming using Net8, you must have one of the following naming services available:

➤ Cell Directory Services (CDS, provided with the Advanced Networking Option)

➤ NetWare Directory Services (NDS, used for NetWare 4.1 or above)

➤ Network Information Service (NIS, available on many Unix servers)

You can use Net8 Assistant to configure the client for external naming. Highlight the Profile icon. Select Create from the Edit menu item on the toolbar. Select Naming from the pull-down menu and go to the Methods tab. Select the external naming service from the Available Methods list. Make this the only method under Selected Methods. Now go to the External tab to provide the necessary information on your external naming method. See Figure 5.13. Finally, select the Save Network Configuration menu item under File on the toolbar. Net8 Assistant will generate the sqlnet.ora file for using the external naming method.

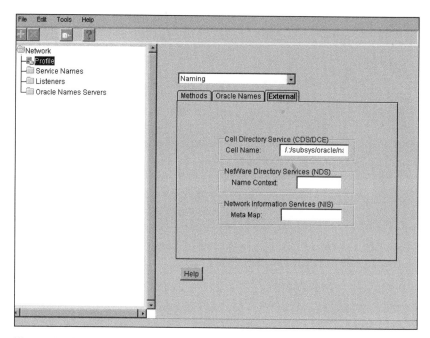

Figure 5.13 Net8 Assistant screen for configuration of external naming.

Oracle Names

Oracle Names is the service name resolution method that uses an Oracle Names Server for the central configuration and resolution of service names. This method requires only the sqlnet.ora file on the client.

Net8 Assistant can be used to configure Oracle Names. Highlight the Profile icon and select Create from the Edit menu item toolbar. Select Naming from the pull-down menu. On the Methods screen, you will see ONAMES on the Available Methods list. (*ONAMES* stands for Oracle Names.) Move ONAMES to the Selected Methods screen to add it to the sqlnet.ora entry for **NAMES.DIRECTORY_PATH** when you save your network configuration.

In a Chapter 6, we will go into detail on how to configure Oracle Names.

Practice Questions

Question 1

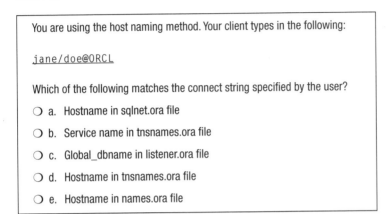

You are using the host naming method. Your client types in the following:

jane/doe@ORCL

Which of the following matches the connect string specified by the user?

- ○ a. Hostname in sqlnet.ora file
- ○ b. Service name in tnsnames.ora file
- ○ c. Global_dbname in listener.ora file
- ○ d. Hostname in tnsnames.ora file
- ○ e. Hostname in names.ora file

The correct answer is c. The host naming method does not use a tnsnames.ora file or a names.ora file. That eliminates all but answers a and c. There is no hostname in the sqlnet.ora file.

Question 2

You are using a Domain Name Server (DNS) with the TCP/IP protocol. What connection method makes use of the DNS and requires very little configuration on the client?

- ○ a. TNSNAMES
- ○ b. ONAMES
- ○ c. HOSTNAME
- ○ d. External naming

The correct answer is c. The key to this answer is the phrase "very little configuration." The HOSTNAME method relies heavily on using the defaults and requires TCP/IP with the default port 1521. The sqlnet.ora parameter **NAMES.AUTHENTICATION_SERVICES** can be set to use DNS.

Question 3

> Which of the following is the correct default for the **names.directory_path** in the sqlnet.ora file?
>
> ○ a. **NAMES.DIRECTORY_PATH**=(TNSNAMES,ONAMES,HOSTNAME)
>
> ○ b. **NAMES.DIRECTORY_PATH**=(HOSTNAME,TNSNAMES,ONAMES)
>
> ○ c. **NAMES.DIRECTORY_PATH**=(ONAMES,HOSTNAME,TNSNAMES)
>
> ○ d. **NAMES.DIRECTORY_PATH**=(HOSTNAME,ONAMES,TNSNAMES)
>
> ○ e. **NAMES.DIRECTORY_PATH**=(TNSNAMES,HOSTNAME,ONAMES)

The correct answer is a. Often, the hardest questions are the ones with very similar answers that depend upon information that has to be memorized. Net8 will attempt to resolve a connection string (service name) by looking for a local tnsnames.ora file (TNSNAMES). If it cannot find the service name in the tnsnames.ora file, it will look for the specification of an Oracle Name Server. Finally, it will attempt a connection with the defaults using the host naming method.

Question 4

> Which of the following make up an entry in the tnsnames.ora file? [Choose the two best answers]
>
> ❑ a. Service name
>
> ❑ b. address_list
>
> ❑ c. connect_data
>
> ❑ d. Connect descriptor
>
> ❑ e. Protocol
>
> ❑ f. Host
>
> ❑ g. Port

The correct answers are a and d. The purpose of the tnsnames.ora file is to map between service names and connect descriptors. Remember that you have to choose the best answer. While all the above answers are parts of the tnsnames.ora file, the service name and connect descriptor are the two parts to a full entry in the tnsnames.ora file. The service name is the alias or connect string. The host and port are part of an address if TCP is specified as the protocol. The address list contains the protocol connection information, but it is only a partial address and requires the connect data to be complete. The connect data is the SID specification. All of these are part of the description, which is called the connect descriptor.

Question 5

You are using local naming and need to obtain the most diagnostic information possible. Which is the correct file and parameter setting?

- O a. tnsnames.ora, **TRACE_LEVEL_CLIENT**=support
- O b. tnsnames.ora; **TRACE_LEVEL_CLIENT**=admin
- O c. sqlnet.ora; **LOG_FILE_CLIENT**=support
- O d. sqlnet.ora; **CLIENT_TRACE_LEVEL**=support
- O e. sqlnet.ora; **TRACE_LEVEL_CLIENT**=support

The correct answer is e. Tracing on the client is always handled by settings in the sqlnet.ora file, which eliminates both a and b as the answer. The log file will not obtain the tracing information you need. There is no parameter named **CLIENT_TRACE_LEVEL**. Remember the designation of client or server is at the end and not the beginning of the parameter name. THE **TRACE_LEVEL_CLIENT** parameter in the sqlnet.ora file should be set to "support" to obtain the most detailed information; the user and admin levels provide much less information.

Question 6

You are using Net8Assistant to configure local naming. What is the first step?

- O a. Define the service name.
- O b. Define the profile.
- O c. Specify the host and port for the protocol.
- O d. Install the TCP protocol on the client.

The correct answer is b. You need to define the profile to select TNSNAMES as your connection method. If you answered this quesion incorrectly, review the summary list provided for configuration of local naming with Net8.

Question 7

You are using Net8 Assistant to configure local naming. What is the first step to configure your service name?

○ a. Fill in the service name.

○ b. Select the protocol.

○ c. Enter the database SID.

○ d. Test the service.

○ e. Save network configuration.

The correct answer is a. Fill in the service name. If you answered this quesion incorrectly, review the summary list provided for configuration of local naming with Net8.

Question 8

You are using Net8 Assistant to configure local naming. What do you do after you have entered the database SID?

○ a. Fill in the service name.

○ b. Select the protocol.

○ c. Enter the host and port.

○ d. Test the service name.

○ e. Select the connection method.

The correct answer is d. Test the service name. While this test is not required, it is the next screen after the SID specification; therefore, it is the best answer. If you answered this quesion incorrectly, review the summary list provided for configuration of local naming with Net8.

Question 9

You are using Net8 Assistant to configure local naming. You have configured multiple listeners on the server using the TCP protocol for connections to your database. You want to take advantage of multiple listeners on the server. What should you do?

○ a. Add a service name for each listener address.

○ b. Highlight the specific service name icon and click on New Address.

○ c. Highlight the Profile icon and click on New Address.

○ d. Highlight the Service Name icon and choose Create from the Edit menu toolbar.

○ e. Use the Oracle Names Wizard to modify the port number for your service name.

The correct answer is b. Highlight the specific service name icon and click on New Address. To take advantage of multiple listeners, you need an address entry for each listener process. Net8 allows you to specify additional addresses for your service name to take advantage of multiple listeners.

Question 10

Which of the following tools is called by Net8 Assistant to configure service names?

○ a. Oracle Enterprise Manager

○ b. SQL*Net Easy Config

○ c. Oracle Service Name Wizard

○ d. Oracle Names Wizard

The correct answer is c. When you click on the Service Name icon and choose Create from the File menu, the Oracle Service Name Wizard is called. Be careful when you read the answers. Do not accidentally choose the Oracle Names Wizard instead of the Oracle Service Name Wizard. While the names are close, only one is correct. The Service Names Wizard screen is titled Oracle Net8 Easy Config and resembles the old SQLNet Easy Config tool. This can be confusing if you have used SQLNet 2.3. Take a close look at Figure 5.12.

Question 11

What two files are generated by Net8 Assistant when you configure a client for local naming? [Choose the two best answers]

❏ a. sqlnet.ora

❏ b. listener.ora

❏ c. names.ora

❏ d. tnsnames.ora

The correct answers are a and d. These are the two files used for local naming. The listener.ora file is needed on the server, and the names.ora file is used with Oracle Names, not for local naming.

Question 12

You are using Net8 Assistant to configure local naming. You have completed configuring the profile and service name and are ready to test your service name. What information do you need to provide for the connection test?

○ a. Username, password, service name

○ b. Username, password

○ c. Username, password, protocol

○ d. Protocol, host and port

○ e. The connection test does not require additional information.

The correct answer is b. The Connection Test screen requests a username and password. Be careful of questions that seem easy. Read them carefully. In this case, the question is not asking you for the information you would typically need to connect to a database (username, password, and service name). The Connection Test screen is testing a specific service name. Therefore, you do not need to enter the service name.

Need To Know More?

 The first place to look for more information is the *Oracle Net8 Administrator's Guide* Release 8.0. Chapter 5 "Configuring Network Clients," Appendix B.2 "Profile Parameters (SQLNET.ORA)," B.3 "Local Naming Parameters (TNSNAMES.ORA)."

 Loney, Kevin. *Oracle8 DBA Handbook*. Oracle Press, 1998. Chapter 13 "SQL*Net V2 and Net8" briefly covers service names and the tnsnames.ora parameters.

 RevealNet Oracle Administration Knowledge Base. Network Management.

6

Oracle Names Usage And Configuration

. . . .

Terms you'll need to understand:

√ Centralized naming

√ Root region

√ Cache replication

√ Regional database

√ names.ora

√ Client-side cache

√ namesctl

Techniques you'll need to master:

√ Configuring a names server

√ Configuring a client to use ONAMES

√ Understanding the Names Control utility commands

Previous chapters covered the local and host naming methods on both the client and server. Although the host naming method is very easy to configure, it has many limitations in how and when it can be used. While the local naming method provides much more flexibility than the host naming method does, it is also more difficult to configure and maintain.

Oracle Names is a method that provides the flexibility of local naming and the ability to centralize the maintenance of your configuration. A Names server can be configured on any node that has Net8 installed. You can configure and administer the Names server using the Names Control utility or Net8 Assistant.

An understanding of Oracle Names is important to do well in the Net8 Network Administration exam. In this chapter, I'll describe the Centralized Naming method using Oracle Names. Then I'll go into the configuration of both the Oracle Names Server and the client. Finally, I'll cover how to control and monitor the Oracle Names Server.

Centralized Naming

The Oracle Names (ONAMES) method provides a way to maintain a central storage for information and central point for configuration of network service names. With centralized naming, you won't have to maintain a tnsnames.ora file on every client and manually replicate changes to every client.

 Experienced Oracle DBAs know that you can avoid many of the problems associated with a tnsnames.ora file on each client by placing this file on a shared network drive and pointing the clients to that drive. However, for the purposes of this exam you should associate centralized naming with ONAMES.

Net8 on the client sends a message to the Oracle Names Server to obtain the required address information. The Names server looks up the information in the server cache and returns the address to the client. This address information is then used to send connection requests to the Oracle Database server. See Figure 6.1.

In a large, distributed, nonstatic environment, maintaining local naming is very difficult and host naming is too inflexible. The four major benefits to using centralized naming are that it:

➤ Simplifies administration

➤ Increases efficiency

➤ Eliminates redundancy

➤ Location is transparent for the clients

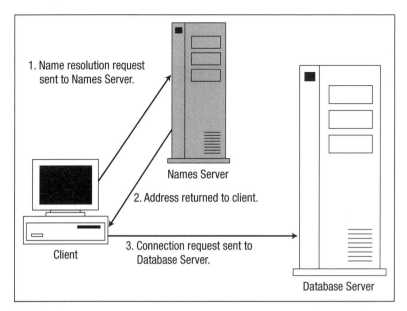

Figure 6.1   Address identification using an Oracle Names Server.

Centralizing the maintenance of the server addresses reduces the administrative burden. To add a new database, you only have to add the address at the Oracle Names Server level, which is obviously much more efficient than making a change on every node. Also, the redundancy of tnsnames.ora files on every node is eliminated. Changes to locations or IP addresses are also handled at the Oracle Names Server level. An added benefit is that these changes to the network configuration are transparent to the clients. One or multiple Names servers can be used to provide address information for many clients, including connection manager servers and database servers. See Figure 6.2.

Configuration Of Oracle Names Server

Oracle Names Servers are configured in a hierarchical fashion. The first level is referred to as the *root region*. Under the root region is one or more regional Names servers, each of which has one or more Names servers under it. Your network can have multiple hierarchies, each starting with a root region. Information is replicated between all the Names servers in a region and also between root regions using the Names server that is designated as the root.

Cache replication is the default method to keep the Names servers synchronized. Instead of having to maintain the information separately in all the Names servers, cache replication is used to replicate information. Listeners configured

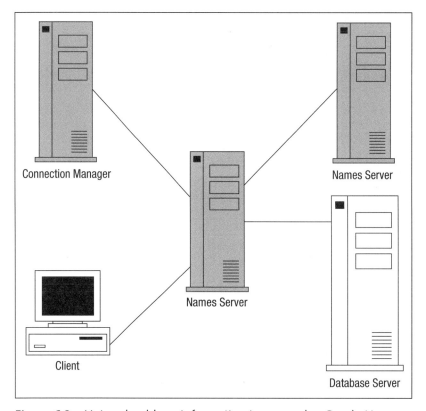

Figure 6.2 Network address information in a complex Oracle Names Server environment.

to find a Names server will forward information to all the available, registered Names servers. When a regional database is not configured, all the Names servers are included in one region and replication takes place between all the Names servers. Using a regional database is covered later in this chapter.

The following information is stored in a Names server:

➤ Names and addresses for other Names servers

➤ Service names

➤ Database links

➤ Aliases

➤ Oracle connection managers

Each Names server stores the names and addresses for all the other Names servers in its region.

The service names that are in the tnsnames.ora file for the local naming method are stored instead at the Names server. In addition to service names for Oracle databases, a Names server can store gateways to non-Oracle databases.

 You need to know that the Oracle Names Server can support gateways to non-Oracle databases. however, for the purposes of this exam, you do not need to know anything about how to configure or use this feature.

After the database address has been registered with the Names server, that name can then be used as a global database link.

Aliases, or alternative names, are also stored in the Names server. These aliases can be for databases or database links.

In addition, the Names server stores the names and addresses for all connection managers on the network. (Connection managers will be covered in Chapter 8.)

Although the Names server can be manually configured, the Net8 Network Administration exam will focus on how to configure it using Net8 Assistant. Therefore, that is the configuration method I'll cover in this chapter for the Names server. This section will cover:

➤ Basic Names server configuration

➤ Regional Names server configuration

➤ Service names

Basic Names Server Configuration

Before you configure your Oracle Names Server, you need to determine if this server will be the root region, a regional server, or a local server.

Start Net8 Assistant, and highlight the Oracle Names Servers icon. Then choose the Create option from the Edit menu item on the toolbar.

If you have previously created a Names server, you will get a message that one already exists. If you have never configured an Oracle Names Server, the following message will be displayed:

```
The NetAsst does not know of any Name Server in this region. Please
use the "Tools" menu, option "Discover Oracle Names Servers" to
detect existing name servers in this region. If no name servers
exist in this region, you may create one.
```

(You will periodically receive messages during the Net8 Assistant configuration for Oracle Names. These messages should be carefully read and acknowledged by choosing the OK or Next button, as appropriate.)

Net8 Assistant calls the Names Wizard to walk you through the configuration of your Names server.

> *Note: The Names Wizard is not the same as the Oracle Service Name Wizard. The Oracle Service Name Wizard is used in the creation of the tnsnames.ora file and configuration of the service names. The Names Wizard is for creating names.ora files and the Oracle Names Server.*

The first thing you need to do is specify the name for your Names server. This must be a unique name within the domain and should include the domain name if you are not using the default domain.

After supplying a name, you will be prompted for address information. Each Names server must have a unique address, and the values required for this address differ depending upon the network protocol that will be used. You will be prompted for the values required for the protocol you choose. If you choose TCP from the pull-down menu, you will need to supply a host and port.

The next area addressed by the Names Wizard relates to whether or not your configuration will be for a regional database. The default is the "Use A Region Database" option. For configuration without using a regional Names server, you must click on "Don't Use A Region Database".

The next question is whether this Names server is the first in the region. If there are other Names servers, then all the other Names servers in the region need to know about the new Names server. If this is the first Names server you are configuring, then it is also the first Names server in the region.

If this is not the first Names server in the region, choose the "Names Server Is Not First In Its Region" option. You will then need to find the other Names servers. If there are well-known Names servers in the region, you should choose "Discover Names Servers" from the Tools menu item, and Net8 will look for other Names servers. (This search may take some time.) You also have the option to specify an existing Names server in the region.

If you have another Names server in the region, you will need to select the appropriate network protocol for that Names server from the pull-down menu. Once again, depending upon the protocol chosen, the screen will change to prompt you for the appropriate values. After you provide this information, the Names Wizard will attempt to contact that Names server to verify its existence.

Next, the Names Wizard will ask if this server is in the root region. Naturally, the first name service created in a region will always be in the root region. For a very simple environment, you can have a configuration with only one Names server. If this is the case, that Names server will be in the root region.

After you answer the questions relating to the region, a screen announces that the configuration process is complete. Click on the Finish button to save the configuration information and to generate a names.ora file with the default settings. See Appendix D for a sample names.ora file.

Note that the names.ora file is created at this point. You do not need to use the Save Network configuration option in the File menu list on the toolbar.

You should browse through the names.ora file to ensure that it is correctly configured. By default, this file is located in the $ORACLE_HOME/network/admin directory for Unix servers. For NT servers, the default location is the $ORACLE_HOME\net80\admin directory.

Seview the steps below for basic configuration of a Names server using Net8 Assistant:

1. Highlight the Oracle Names Server icon.

2. Select Create from the Edit menu on the toolbar.

3. Enter a name for your Names server.

4. Select the network protocol from the pull-down list and supply the network-protocol-specific information.

5. Choose the Don't Use A Region Database option.

6. Indicate if the Names server is the first in the region.

7. Indicate if the Names server is in the root region.

8. Click on the Finish button to save the Names server configuration.

9. Start your Names server.

You can also use Net8 Assistant to delete Names servers. However, before you can delete a Names server, you must shut down the Names server process. Start Net8 Assistant and click on the icon of the Names server that you want to delete. Choose the Delete option from the Edit menu item on the toolbar. You will need to manually remove the names.ora file and any ckp*.* files that have been created on the server. The ckp*.* files are the checkpoint files discussed later in this chapter. After the files have been removed, remember to save your new configuration by choosing Save Network Configuration from the File menu item on the toolbar.

After you have completed configuring the Oracle Names Server, you can use either the Names Control utility or Net8 Assistant to start and stop it. (The Names Control utility will be covered later in this chapter.) To use Net8 Assistant, highlight the listener process, select Manage Data from the pull-down menu, and then select the Control tab. This tab allows you to start, shut down, and restart the Names server. In addition, you can use this screen to gather statistics and set a wait time for the Names server startup process. (These options will be covered in more detail later in this chapter.) Once you have selected your options, click on the Apply button.

Regional Names Server

Cache replication works best when there are fewer Names servers to be kept in synch. By defining a regional Names server, however, this replication process is much more efficient.

Each region must have at least one Names server, but you can configure multiple Names servers in a region for improved performance. Each region can also consist of one or more domains. When you have multiple Names servers in a region, you need to replicate information between the Names servers by one of two methods: continuous replication or a regional database. Information is collected about foreign regions and is saved in the Names server cache files. This collection of data is called checkpointing.

In a small or static environment, continuous replication between Names servers does not have a significant performance impact. For larger and more volatile environments, a regional database is recommended. Instead of requiring all the Names servers to continually communicate with all the other Names servers, they will all communicate with the regional database, which is the repository for the Names server information. (Information about all the Names servers is communicated to the regional database.) Each Names server will periodically check with the regional database to update its information on the other Names servers. Multiple regional databases can be created for high availability and better performance.

Before you can configure a regional database, you must execute an initialization script in the database that you have chosen to store your information. This script is named "namesini.sql". This script must be executed under the Oracle ID that will own the objects creeated for the regional database. It is located in the

$ORACLE_HOME/network/names directory for a Unix server and in the $ORACLE_HOME\net80\names directory for an NT server.

After you have initialized the database, start Net8 Assistant. Highlight the Names Server icon and choose Configure Server from the pull-down menu. Go to the Database tab and click on Region Database. At this point, you will need to provide Net8 Assistant with information on the Oracle database and user that will own the objects created.

Select the network protocol from the pull-down menu. Depending upon the network protocol chosen, you will be prompted for the appropriate network connection information. For TCP, you will need to supply a host and port. Regardless of the protocol chosen, you will need to provide the SID, session type, user, and password.

Service Names

After you have configured your Names server or regional Names server, you need to add service names. If you already have a valid tnsnames.ora file, you can load this into your regional database. Choose the load option and specify the full path and file name for the tnsnames.ora file. When you are finished, click on the Execute button to save the configuration.

Clicking on Execute in a Net8 Assistant screen always saves the configuration. You do not need to use the Save Network Configuration option in the File menu list on the toolbar.

You can also add each service name to the Names server. With the name service highlighted, choose the Manage Data option from the pull-down menu, and select the Service Names tab. This screen can be used to query, add, remove, and load service names. See Figure 6.3.

You will need to provide the name and address information for each service name. For the address information, choose the appropriate network protocol from the pull-down menu. You will be prompted for the appropriate values based on the protocol you select. You will also need to provide the SID name. This is the same information that would be supplied for configuration of a service name when using the local naming method.

In addition, you will need to select the session type, which must be either dedicated or dispatched.

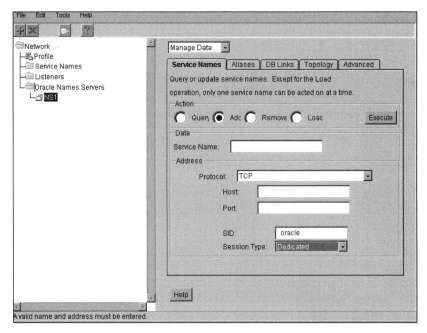

Figure 6.3   Net8 Assistant Service Names configuration for a Names server.

When you have provided the required information, click the Execute button. (There is no need to save this configuration or restart the Names server process. When you click on Execute, these processes are performed implicitly.)

For each service name, you need to repeat this process.

Configuration Of The Client For Oracle Names

In order to use an Oracle Names Server, you must configure the sqlnet.ora file on the client, and you can do this manually or with Net8 Assistant. First, I'll provide information on manual configuration, then I'll explain how to use Net8 Assistant to configure the client for an Oracle Names Server configuration. I'll also cover the client-side cache.

Manual Configuration

To manually configure the Oracle Names Server you must create a names.ora file that has all the necessary information without any syntax errors. (Only the main names.ora parameters will be covered here; additional parameters are covered under the Net8 Assistant Configuration section.)

The first parameter in the names.ora file should be the **NAMES.ADDRESSES,** which specifies the address for the Names server process to listen on. The default location is

```
(address=(protocol=tcp)(host=oranamesrvr0)(port=1575))
```

The **NAMES.ADMIN_REGION** is the data source for the Names server. This is the parameter that is used to identify the regional database. The default is NULL. If the default is used, then continuous replication is used between all the Names servers.

The **NAMES.AUTO_REFRESH_EXPIRE** parameter controls the time be-tween refreshes. When a refresh takes place, the Names server will query other regional database servers to refresh the address information. The default is 600 seconds, but it can be set as low as 60 seconds or as high as 1,209,600 seconds (equivalent to 2 weeks).

The **NAMES.AUTO_REFRESH_RETRY** specifies the number of attempts to be made to contact a Names server for new information. The default is 180 times, but it can be set as low as 60 retries or as high as 3,600.

The **NAMES.CACHE_CHECKPOINT_FILE** is the file name for check-point information. The default value is ckpcch.ora. When you delete a Names server, you must remember to delete this file manually, even if you are using Net8 Assistant for configuration purposes.

The **NAMES.CACHE_CHECKPOINT_INTERVAL** parameter indicates the interval, in seconds, for checkpoints of stored data. This is disabled by default. If enabled, the minimum value is 10 seconds and the maximum value is 259,200 (3 days). This parameter works with the **NAMES.CONFIG_CHECKPOINT_FILE** that indicates the file name used for checkpoint in-formation. The default is $ORACLE_HOME/network/names/ckpcfg.ora for a Unix server and $ORACLE_HOME\net80\names\ckpcfg.ora for an NT server.

The **NAMES.LOG_DIRECTORY** and **NAMES.LOG_FILE** are used to indicate the directory and file name for the logs. The default directory is oper-ating-system specific, and the file name will default to names. These parameters work with the **NAMES.LOG_STATS_INTERVAL** and **NAMES.LOG_UNIQUE** parameters. The **NAMES.LOG_STATS_INTERVAL** parameter specifies the number of seconds between statistical entries in the log file. The default is 0, which means it is turned off. The minimum value when this is turned on is 10 seconds. The default for **NAMES.LOG_UNIQUE** parameter is FALSE. If you do not want the log files overwritten, set this to TRUE. If you want to save your log files for informational purposes or in order to perform troubleshooting actions, then you must set the **NAMES.LOG_UNIQUE** to TRUE.

Tracing is controlled using the **NAMES.TRACE_DIRECTORY, NAMES .TRACE_FILE, NAMES.TRACE_LEVEL,** and **NAMES.TRACE_ UNIQUE** parameters, which determine the directory and file name to be used, the level for tracing, and whether or not the trace file name should be unique. If you keep your trace files unique, they will not be overwritten. This is useful for correcting problems that have been encountered.

Net8 Assistant Configuration

Highlighting the Profile icon is the first step within Net8 Assistant when configuring the client to use the Names server. Choose Naming from the pull-down menu. You can configure ONAMES as the first, last, or only method. This screen configures the value for the **NAMES.DIRECTORY_PATH** parameter in the sqlnet.ora file.

If you want to ensure the use of the Names server at all times, you should place ONAMES as the only method. However, you can choose to mix ONAMES with the tnsnames and hostname methods.

The next step is to configure any additional parameters you want to set for your client. Go to the Oracle Names tab. See Figure 6.4. On this screen, you can set values for the following:

```
Default Domain
Resolution Persistence
        Maximum Wait Each Attempt
        Attempts Per Names Server
Performance
        Maximum Open Connections
        Initial Preallocated Requests
```

On a Unix server, the Default Domain value will be blank (null). For an NT server, it will be set to world. This can be changed to whatever domain you are using.

The Resolution Persistence parameter has to do with the connection behavior of the client. The Maximum Wait Each Attempt value is set in seconds, and the default is to wait for 15 seconds. This sets the **NAMES.INITIAL_ RETRY_TIMEOUT** parameter in the sqlnet.ora file.

This is also where you set the Attempts Per Names Server value, which is the number of connection attempts that will be made. The default setting is 1.

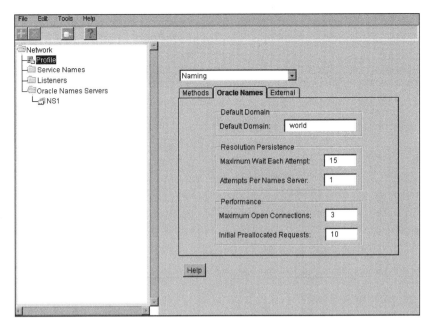

Figure 6.4   Net8 Assistant Oracle Names client configuration for a Names server.

This value configures the **NAMES.REQUEST_RETRIES** in the sqlnet.ora parameter file.

The Performance section of the screen is where you set the values relating to the connections allowed. The Maximum Open Connections value is the number of connections the Names server may have open at one time. The default is 10 connections. This value configures the **NAMES.MAX_OPEN_ CONNECTIONS** parameter in the sqlnet.ora file.

On this screen, you can also set the Initial Preallocated Requests value, which determines the number of messages in the message pool on the client. These messages are used for future requests to the Names server. By default, this is set to 10 messages. This value configures the **NAMES.MESSAGE_ POOL_START_SIZE** in the sqlnet.ora file.

The final Net8 screen when configuring the client designates the Names server that is to be used first. Select Preferrered Oracle Names Server from the pull-down menu, and select the network protocol from the pull-down menu. Depending upon the protocol you choose, this you will be prompted for the appropriate values. For TCP, you need to fill in the host and port number. By clicking on the New button, you can add additional Names servers to your preference list. Use the Delete button to remove Names servers from your preference list. This configures the sqlnet.ora **NAMES.PREFERRED_SERVERS** parameter.

To update or create the client sqlnet.ora file, you need to save your configuration. Choose Save Network Configuration from the Edit menu on the toolbar.

To test the configuration of your Names server, you need to eliminate other connection methods and test the connection using a front-end application, such as SQL*Plus. Select the Profile icon. Choose Naming from the pull-down menu and select the Methods tab. Remove all the other connection methods except ONAMES. Select Save Network Configuration from the File menu item on the toolbar. Now test your connection using SQL*Plus (e.g., sqlplus scott/tiger@prod1) or another front-end application. If the connection works, you know that the Oracle Names Server configuration is correct.

Review the basic steps in configuring the client when using a Names server:

1. Highlight the Profile icon.

2. Choose the Naming option from the pull-down menu.

3. Go to the Methods tab and select ONAMES as the naming method.

4. Go to the Oracle Names tab to configure additional parameters.

5. Choose Preferred Oracle Names Servers from the pull-down menu and provide the address information for the preferred Names server.

6. Select Save Network Configuration from the Edit menu item on the toolbar.

7. Review the sqlnet.ora file to ensure it is correct.

Client-Side Cache

When you are using an Oracle Names Server, the connect descriptor information for all the service names is stored in a central location. While this increases the ease of maintenance, it could become a performance bottleneck. In order to speed up the requests for service name resolution, a client-side cache is created. A client-side cache daemon is started on the Names server to send information to a client cache. If the information is available in the local client cache, there is no need for the client to send a request to the Names server.

When a client connects to a Names server, the address information is sent down to the client. Then, subsequent connection requests first check the local client cache before connecting to the Names server. If the information is found in the client cache, the time-to-live (TTL) value is checked. The TTL value is the amount of time that the cache is allowed to be used for connection information. If the TTL value shows this time has expired, then the connection information is requested from the Names server and the client-side cache is repopulated with new information and a new TTL value. The following is an example of the TTL parameter setting:

```
NAMES.DOMAINS =
      (DOMAIN_LIST =
            (DOMAIN =
                  (NAME = WORLD) (MIN_TTL = 86400)
            )
            (DOMAIN =
                  (NAME = WORLD2) (MIN_TTL = 86400)
            )
      )
```

Controlling And Monitoring The Oracle Names Server

You can control and monitor the Oracle Names Server in two ways: with the Names Control utility or Net8 Assistant.

Names Control Utility (namesctl)

The Names Control Utility (namesctl) is the command-line interface for starting, stopping, and controlling the Oracle Names Server processes. You can type in the full command at the operating-system prompt, execute commands from within namesctl, and include namesctl commands in batch programs. On a Unix server, namesctl is used for the command. For an NT server, the command is namesctl80. See Table 6.1.

Table 6.1 Names Control Utility (namesctl) commands.	
Command	**Action**
DELEGATE_DOMAIN	Defines a domain to be the start for the subregion of a domain.
DOMAIN_HINT	Provides name and address of Names server in another region to Names servers in the current region.
EXIT	Closes namesctl utility.
flush	Drops all nonauthoritative data from Names server cache.

(continued)

Table 6.1   Names Control Utility (namesctl) commands (continued).

Command	Action
FLUSH_NAME	Drops nonauthoritative data for a specified Names server or Names servers from the cache.
HELP	Provides a list of commands or a brief explanation of the specified command.
LOG_STATS	Sends the current statistics for the Names server to the log file.
PASSWORD	Registers password for privileged operations.
PING	Tests connectivity.
QUERY	Tests or retrieves contents of a Names server object.
QUIT	Closes namesctl utility.
REGISTER	Registers a network option to the Names server.
RELOAD	Checks for data changes and reread files.
REPEAT	Repeats certain commands.
REORDER_NS	Tests connections and sets order of Names servers in the list.
RESET_STATS	Resets the statistics to original values.
RESTART	Resets Names server to values at original startup without stopping the processes.
SET	Dynamically changes a parameter.
SHOW	Displays parameter setting.
SHUTDOWN	Stops the Names server process.
START	Starts the Names server process.
STARTUP	Starts the Names server process.
START_CLIENT_CACHE	Starts the client-side cache process.
STATUS	Displays information on the Names server process.
STOP	Shut downs the Names server process.
TIMED_QUERY	Shows all registered data in the Names server cache.
UNREGISTER	Deletes a network object from the Names server.
VERSION	Display current version and name.

The most commonly used commands are **START, STOP,** and **STATUS.** The **START** command starts up the Names server processes. The **STOP** command performs a shutdown of these processes. The **STATUS** command provides information on the settings and actions taken by the Names server.

The **STATUS** command can be issued by itself or with the command **SHOW STATUS.** The following code is an example of output.

```
Server Name:   ns1.acme.com
Server has been running for:   10 hours 20 minutes 10.11 seconds
Request processing enabled:   yes
Request forwarding enabled:   yes
Requests recveived:    8
Requests forwarded:    0
Foreign data items cached:    0
Region data next checked for reload in:      not set
Region data reload check failures:    0
Cache next checkpointed in:    not set
Cache checkpoint interval:    not set
Cache checkpoint file name:    C:\ORANT\NET80\names\ckpcch.ora
Statistic counters next reset in:   not set
Statistic counter reset interval:   not set
Statistic counters next logged in:    not set
Statistic counter logging interval:    not set
Trace level:    0
Trace file name:        C:\ORANT\NET80\trace\names.trc
Log file name: C:\ORANT\NET80\log\names.log
System parameter file name:    C:\ORANT\NET80\admin\names.ora
Command line parameter file name:      ""
Administrative region name:      ""
Administrative region description:      ""
ApplTable Index:        0
Contact:      ""
Operational Status:    0
Save Config on Stop:    no
```

The concept of the client-side cache was explained in the section on configuring the client. In order to start the process of caching information on the client, it is necessary to have a daemon running on the Names server. The command within namesctl to start this daemon is **START_CLIENT_CACHE.** This command has two requirements:

➤ The client cache daemon process must be stopped.

➤ A Names server list must exist.

To test if a Names server is operational, you can use the **namesctl PING** command with the name of the Oracle Names Server to send a test out to that server. The response is the roundtrip time in seconds.

The **REORDER_NS** command performs the discovery function. This command is used to test the connections and set the order these connections should be tried from the fastest to the slowest response time. This command is used both for the clients and servers. In order to determine the connection time, it first must perform a discovery action to identify all the Names servers on the network, contacting them with the specified address, which is obtained from one of the following methods:

➤ Including it in the command

➤ The preferred Names server parameter in the sqlnet.ora file on the client

➤ An existing list of Names servers

➤ The well-known Names server on the network

For each Names server that is found, the namesctl utility will send out a query to determine all the Names servers in that region. Once all the Names servers have been identified, a **ping** command is sent to each Names server. The speed of the response to the **ping** commands determines the order of each in the Names server list. If no Names server list is available, a new list is created. If a list already exists, that list is replaced. The following is an example of using the **ping** command from inside the Names Control Utility:

```
NAMESCTRL> ping server1.world
round trip time is 0.02 sconds.
```

> *Note: If a Names server list does not exist, you can create it with the REORDER_NS command.*

The **PASSWORD** command must be used inside the namectl utility. The **SET** command is used to register the password within the namectl utility. The password is set in the **NAMES.SERVER_PASSWORD** parameter in the sqlnet.ora file for the client running namesctl and the **NAMES.PASSWORD** password in the names.ora file on the Names server. The passwords in the sqlnet.ora and names.ora files must match. When a password is included, it is necessary to execute the following commands:

➤ **FLUSH**

➤ **FLUSH_NAME**

➤ **LOG_STATS**

➤ RELOAD

➤ RESET_STATS

➤ RESTART

➤ SET FORWARDING_AVAILABLE

➤ SET LOG_FILE_NAME

➤ SET LOG_STATS_INTERVAL

➤ SET NAMESCTL_TRACE_LEVEL

➤ SET REQUESTS_ENABLED

➤ SET RESET_STATS_INTERVAL

➤ SET TRACE_LEVEL

➤ SHUTDOWN

➤ STOP

The **RELOAD** command is used to immediately bring new information into the Names server without stopping the Names server processes. This command checks for any changes in its administrative region that relate to service names, global database links, and/or aliases.

The delegated domain in each region has authority over all the subdomains within the region. The **DELEGATE_DOMAIN** command allows you to create a new region and assign the servers in the current region to be under the authority of that region.

The **DOMAIN_HINT** command provides a method to define a path to other regions. This command is used as the way to make subregions aware of regions that are within another root region. You can use this command to provide the Names server with the name and address of Names servers in other regions.

The **FLUSH** command removes all foreign or nonauthoritative data from the cache. This command should be issued after a large number of changes have been made to the Names servers or when numerous errors have been encountered with connection requests. This command forces the next connection request from the client to go to the Names server instead of the server cache for the address.

The **REPEAT** command is used when statistics are gathered for the Names server. This command performs **QUERY, REGISTER, TIMED_QUERY,** or **UNREGISTER** multiple times and computes the average return rates.

The **QUERY** command is used to test an object or retrieve information about an object. It is useful in finding information such as the address for an alias.

The **REGISTER** command registers a network object to a Names server, which is useful for manually registering an object. The registered object can be a hostname, listener name, or address. Once registered with one Names server, this information is then propagated to the other Names servers. The **UNREGISTER** command can be used to remove the network object.

To dynamically change parameters for a Names server, use the **SET** command. See Table 6.2.

To display current parameter settings, use the **SHOW** command. See Table 6.3.

Table 6.2	Parameters modifiable with the namesctl SET command.
Command	**Action**
CACHE_CHECKPOINT_INTERVAL	Sets the frequency, in seconds, for collection of information about foreign regions that is saved in the Names server cache.
DEFAULT_DOMAIN	Changes the default domain for the client.
FORWARDING_AVAILABLE	Turns name request forwarding on and off.
LOG_FILE_NAME	Changes the log file name.
LOG_STATS_INTERVAL	Changes the frequency, in seconds, for logging statistics.
NAMESCTL_TRACE_LEVEL	Changes the level for tracing.
REQUESTS_ENABLED	Determines if the Names server will respond to requests.
RESET_STATS_INTERVAL	Changes the time interval, specified in seconds or days, for resetting statistics to zero or the initial values.
SERVER	Changes the current Names server for which commands are being issued within namesctl.
TRACE_FILE_NAME	Changes the destination trace file name.
TRACE_LEVEL	Changes the level of tracing.

Table 6.3 Parameters displayed with the namesctl SHOW command.	
Command	**Action**
CACHE_CHECKPOINT_INTERVAL	Displays the frequency for collection of information about foreign regions that is saved in the Names server cache.
DEFAULT_DOMAIN	Displays the default domain for the client.
FORWARDING_AVAILABLE	Shows whether request forwarding is on or off.
LOG_FILE_NAME	Displays the name of the file used for logging.
LOG_STATS_INTERVAL	Displays the frequency for logging statistics.
NAMESCTL_TRACE_LEVEL	Displays the level for tracing.
REQUESTS_ENABLED	Shows whether or not the Names server will respond to requests.
RESET_STATS_INTERVAL	Displays the time interval for resetting statistics to zero or the initial values.
SERVER	Shows the name of the Names server for which commands are being executed within namesctl.
STATUS	Shows general information about the Names server.
SYSTEM_QUERIES	Displays the next occurrence of all system queries.
TRACE_FILE_NAME	Displays the name of the trace file.
TRACE_LEVEL	Displays the level for tracing.
VERSION	Displays the current version and name of the Names server.

Controlling And Monitoring With Net8 Assistant

Instead of manually configuring the parameters for your Names server, you can use Net8 Assistant to perform these tasks. Start Net8 Assistant, and highlight the Names Server icon. Choose the Manage Server option from the pull-down menu to access six controls:

➤ Monitor

➤ Control

➤ Tuning

➤ Logging

➤ Cache

➤ Advanced

The Monitor tab is used to report on the statistical information for the server and schedule options such as statistics gathering and cache parameters. See Figure 6.5.

The Control tab provides the options associated with starting and stopping the Names server. It also controls statistical operations such as writing the statistics to a log file and resetting statistics. See Figure 6.6.

The Tuning tab provides the options for setting parameters that are associated with time. The number of days, hours, minutes, and seconds can be set using this screen, and the changes can be dynamically applied. See Figure 6.7.

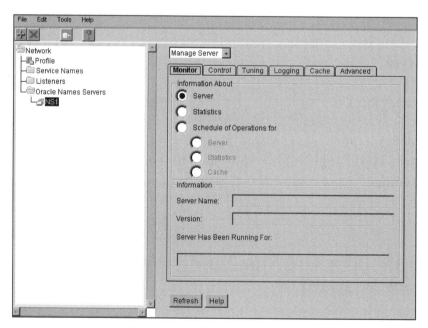

Figure 6.5 Net8 Assistant screen for monitoring the Names server.

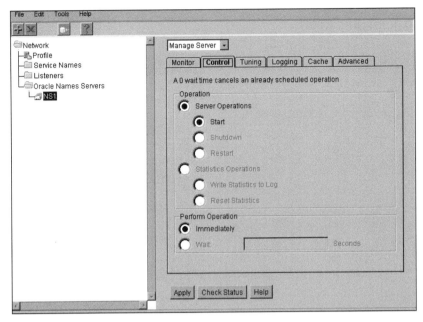

Figure 6.6   Net8 Assistant screen for controlling the Names server.

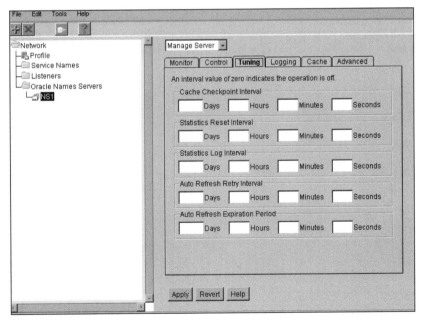

Figure 6.7   Net8 Assistant screen for tuning the Names server.

Figure showing the Net8 Assistant application window. The menu bar reads File, Edit, Tools, Help. The left panel shows a tree: Network, Profile, Service Names, Listeners, Oracle Names Servers, NS1. The right panel shows "Manage Server" dropdown with tabs Monitor, Control, Tuning, Logging (selected), Cache, Advanced. Under Logging: Log Directory, Log File. Under Tracing: Trace Level (OFF), Trace Directory, Trace File. Buttons at bottom: Apply, Revert, Help.

Figure 6.8 Net8 Assistant screen to set logging parameters for the Names server.

The Logging tab is where the directory and file names are specified for logging and tracing. In addition, the trace level can be set using this screen. See Figure 6.8. The levels for tracing are:

➤ Off

➤ User

➤ Admin

➤ Support

The same trace levels are used wherever tracing can be set.

The Cache tab provides a place to set the cache operations and when they should be performed. See Figure 6.9.

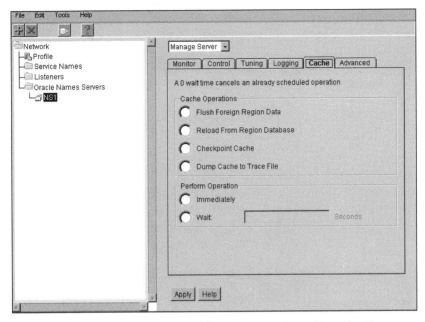

Figure 6.9   Net8 Assistant screen for setting cache options for the
Names server.

The Advanced tab is used for setting the following options:

➤ Authority Required

➤ Default Forwards Only

➤ Forwarding Desired

➤ Forwarding Available

➤ Modify Requests

The Advanced tab provides a place to control the settings related to forwarding requests. See Figure 6.10.

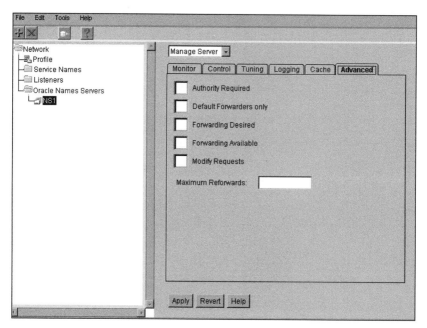

Figure 6.10 Net8 Assistant screen used to set forwarding options for the Names server.

Practice Questions

Question 1

> The utility used to configure and control the Names server is _____.
>
> ○ a. lsnrctl
>
> ○ b. namesctl
>
> ○ c. Names Wizard
>
> ○ d. Oracle Service Name Wizard
>
> ○ e. sqlnetctl

The correct answer is b. The lsnrctl utility is used to control the listener process. The Names Wizard is used in the configuration of Names servers, and
the Oracle Service Name Wizard is used in the configuration of Service Names.
There is no such utility as the sqlnetctl. The Names control Utility (namesch)
is used for controlling (for example STOP and STARTUP) and configuring
(with the SET commands) the Oracle Names Server.

Question 2

> The Names server can be configured by which two methods? [Choose the
> two best answers]
>
> ❑ a. Manually create or edit he names.ora file
>
> ❑ b. Manually edit the tnsnames.ora file
>
> ❑ c. Net8 Assistant
>
> ❑ d. Names Wizard

The correct answers are a and c. While you can configure the Names server
manually, using Net8 Assistant will ensure against syntax errors in the names.ora
file. The tnsnames.ora file is not used for the Oracle Names Server method.
The Names Wizard is called from within Net8 Assistant.

Question 3

> The command used to discover all Names servers on the network is _____.
>
> ○ a. **DISCOVER**
>
> ○ b. **SET**
>
> ○ c. **REORDER_NS**
>
> ○ d. **START**
>
> ○ e. **STATUS**

The correct answer is c. The **REORDER_NS** command will discover all the Names servers, perform a PING against each, and then order them from fastest response to slowest. It will then update the names service list. If there is no name service list, it will create one.

Question 4

> Which of the following files is configured when setting up the Oracle Names Server? [Choose the two best answers]
>
> ❑ a. listener.ora
>
> ❑ b. tnsnames.ora
>
> ❑ c. names.ora
>
> ❑ d. sqlnet.ora
>
> ❑ e. namesctl

The correct answers are c and d. The names.ora file is configured on the Names server and the sqlnet.ora file is configured on the client. The listener.ora is the parameter file for the listener on the server. While you can use the tnsnames.ora file to load service names into the Names server, it is not configured when setting up the Oracle Names Server.

Question 5

What is a regional database?

○ a. The repository of service names stored by the Names server

○ b. The repository of parameters for the sqlnet.ora file

○ c. The daemon that controls the client cache process

○ d. The regional Names server for the network

The correct answer is a. The regional database stores information for the Names servers and is used for the replication of information to other Names servers.

Question 6

What are the two methods of replication for Names servers? [Choose the two best answers]

❑ a. Client-side cache

❑ b. Regional database

❑ c. Cache replication

❑ d. Advanced replication

❑ e. Regional replication

The correct answers are b and c. Cache replication is used by default and when there is no regional database configured. The client-side cache is used to store address information on the client for better performance. Answers d and e are not replication methods for Names servers.

Question 7

You are configuring your first Names server using Net8 Assistant. What is the first step?

○ a. Choose the Discover Oracle Names Server from the Tools menu on the toolbar.

○ b. Enter a name for your Names server.

○ c. Indicate if the Names server is the first in the region.

○ d. Select the protocol from the pull-down list and fill in the relevant values.

○ e. Highlight the Oracle Names Server icon and then select Create from the Edit menu list on the toolbar.

The correct answer is e. The first step is to choose the Oracle Names Server icon and then select Create from the Edit menu list on the toolbar. Take a close look at the figures (screenshots from Net8 Assistant). Use these to become familiar with what is an icon, what is a pull-down, etc.

Question 8

You are configuring your first Names server using Net8 Assistant. You have selected TCP for your protocol and have filled in the host and port information. What is the next step?

○ a. Choose the Discover Oracle Names Server from the Tools menu on the toolbar.

○ b. Enter a name for your Names server.

○ c. Indicate if the Names server is the first in the region.

○ d. Indicate if the Names server is in the root region.

○ e. Highlight the Oracle Names Server icon and then select Create from the Edit menu list on the toolbar.

The correct answer is c. The next step is to indicate if the Names server is the first in the region. You may wish to review the section on configuration using Net8 Assistant. Take a close look at the figures (screenshots from the Net8 Assistant).

Question 9

You are using the namesctl utility to monitor your Names server. What command will provide you with detailed information on your Names server?

○ a. **SET TRACE_LEVEL**

○ b. **VERSION**

○ c. **RELOAD**

○ d. **STATUS**

○ e. **REORDER_NS**

The correct answer is d. **STATUS**. Review the sample listing of the information provided by a **STATUS** command. Review of the table on the namesctl utility commands and become familiar with the ones covered in the text.

Question 10

You are using the namesctl utility. What commands will close the utility and return you to the operating-system command line? [Choose the two best answers]

❑ a. **STOP**

❑ b. **SHUTDOWN**

❑ c. **EXIT**

❑ d. **QUIT**

❑ e. **CLOSE**

The correct answers are c and d. The **EXIT** and **QUIT** commands will close the namesctl utility. The **STOP** and **SHUTDOWN** commands are used to stop the Names server process. **CLOSE** is not a namesctl command.

Need To Know More?

 The first place to look for more information is the *Oracle Net8 Administrator's Guide* Release 8.0. Chapter 6 "Oracle Names," Appendix A. "Oracle Names Control Utility (NAMESCTL)," B "Oracle Names Parameters (NAMES.ORA)."

 Toledo, Hugo. *Oracle Networking*. Oracle Press, 1996. Chapter 4 "TNS Applications: Oracle Names, MPI, SNS, and SNMP." While somewhat out of date, this continues to have some valuable information.

 RevealNet Oracle Administration Knowledge Base. Network Management.

MTS Usage And Configuration

Terms you'll need to understand:

√ Multithreaded server (MTS)

√ Dispatcher

√ Shared server

√ Request queue

√ Response queue

√ Connection pooling

Techniques you'll need to master:

√ Understanding MTS and when to use it

√ Configuring the MTS option

√ Monitoring the MTS option

√ Understanding connection pooling

To control the number of processes on a server and therefore the type of connection established, you can use three types of configurations:

➤ Single-task

➤ Two-task

➤ Multithreaded

With Oracle's emphasis on supporting larger user communities, the multithreaded server (MTS) option has become an important part of the Oracle Net8 architecture. Thus, for the Oracle8 Network Administration OCP exam, you'll need to understand how MTS works and how it is configured. This chapter provides an overview of the MTS option, explains how it works, and covers:

➤ What database initialization parameters are used with MTS

➤ How to monitor and alter your MTS parameters

➤ How to use the connection pooling feature

Overview Of MTS

In a single-task server architecture, the user and server processes are combined into a single process. For single-tasking, one process executes both the front-end application code and the Oracle code while keeping both separated. The single-task server architecture requires that the operating system be capable of executing both processes while maintaining the integrity of each. The Open VMS operating system supports the single-task server architecture, whereas Unix does not support it.

 The single task architecture will be discontinued in a future version of Oracle. For this exam, you will need to know that the supported server configurations are single task, two task, and MTS.

In a two-task server architecture, the application code is handled by one process and the Oracle code by another. Each database connection (Oracle code) is handled on the server with either a dedicated or a shared process. A client/server environment uses two-tasking with the client handling the application process (or user process) and the server handling the Oracle code.

With the typical two-task server architecture, the client can be a workstation or another server. Two-task means that a separate process for the application code and Oracle code are maintained even if the client is on the same server.

When dedicated server connections are used, a process is required even if the client application is idle. This connection is referred to as a *shadow process* because it is working with one client application process.

With multithreaded connections, each server process is shared by multiple user processes, in a variation of the two-task server architecture. In this type of configuration, one Oracle process can handle multiple connections for multiple clients. The multithreaded server (MTS) option is a very efficient method to maintain multiple connections, especially in an On-Line Transaction Processing (OLTP) environment. In an OLTP environment—where users are entering information or performing queries—the idle time is very high. Rather than having processes sitting idle, these processes can be shared by other users. Thus, the MTS server can support many more processes.

> *Note: In an NT environment, only TCP/IP can be used for an MTS configuration.*

MTS Configuration

With the MTS configuration, multiple users are sharing the same connection to the database, which reduces the number of processes required. Because each database connection requires some memory on the part of the server, having fewer connections reduces the amount of memory needed on the server.

Let's assume that you have a Unix server that can typically support 50 processes, but the actual number of users far exceeds the capacity of your server. By configuring MTS, you can create shared processes that each handle multiple connections, allowing you to support a larger user population within your 50-process maximum.

Using an MTS configuration does not preclude dedicated connections from being established. Even with the MTS configuration, some Oracle processes will require a dedicated connection—for example, starting and stopping the database requires a dedicated connection. The same is also true for any situation that requires a connection as internal. Also, some processes may just work better with a dedicated connection. For example, if a large batch job is to be performed, a dedicated connection may be desired because there is very little idle time.

The listener's role has been previously covered in detail. Basically, the listener will either spawn a dedicated connection process or redirect the connection to a process that already exists. Configuring the database for MTS requires that the database register with the listener and that the listener process be on the same server as the database. Both the dispatcher processes and the database instance register information with the listener process. Because of this registration process, the listener should be started before the MTS-configured database is started.

The listener will be aware of the MTS processes that can be used for shared connections. The listener can redirect connections to those processes (called *dispatchers*) and maintain information on the dispatcher processes and their workload. The listener can perform load balancing of connection requests. See Figure 7.1.

When the initialization parameter file for the database includes the MTS Configuration parameters, Oracle will automatically configure the SGA to handle dispatches and shared servers at startup time. Within the System Global Area (SGA), a single-request queue and multiple dispatcher response queues are created. The single-request queue handles all incoming requests, and the response queue is created for each dispatcher and assigned to it for the life of the dispatcher process. See Figure 7.2.

The dispatcher places the SQL commands from the client into the request queue in the database SGA. The shared server processes monitor the request queue. As a request comes in and a shared server process is available, the request is picked up by the available shared server process. The shared server process executes the command and places the results into the response queue

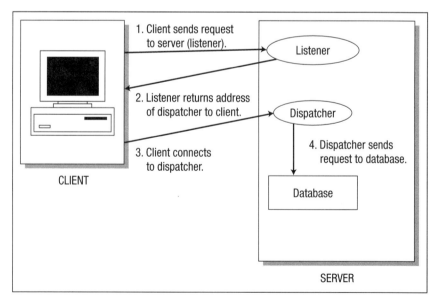

Figure 7.1 Listener and the MTS option.

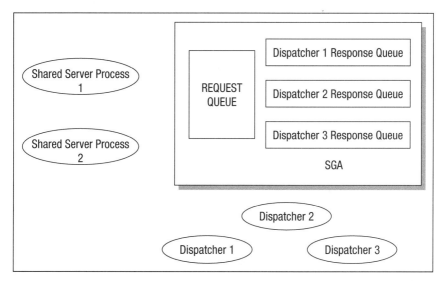

Figure 7.2   MTS processes and the SGA.

for the dispatcher that is handling that client (the calling dispatcher). See Figure 7.3.

The dispatcher retrieves the response from its queue and returns this to the client. This connection between the client and the dispatcher is maintained for the entire session, even when the client is idle. However, each dispatcher request may be handled by any available shared server. Each SQL command from a client is processed on a first-in/first-out basis.

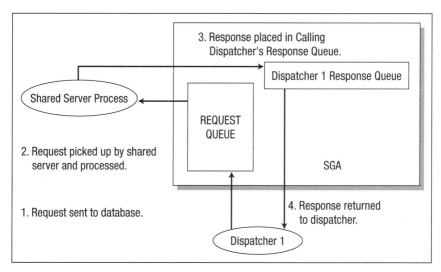

Figure 7.3   MTS connection process.

Follow the steps below to review the connection process for MTS.

1. MTS database registers with the listener at database startup.

2. Listener awaits connection requests.

3. Connection request is redirected to dispatcher process.

4. SQL commands from the client are placed in the request queue.

5. A shared server process picks up and processes the request.

6. Response to SQL command is placed in the response queue for the calling dispatcher.

7. The dispatcher picks up the response and returns it to the client.

Initialization Parameters For MTS

In order for the listener process on the server to be aware of the MTS option for a database, the dispatchers must be registered with the listener process. This requires you to configure specific initialization parameters that are used when the database is started. The MTS option requires the request queue and dispatcher response queues to be contained within the SGA. If additional dispatchers are created, then additional response queues will be created for them.

 When using the MTS option, some additional processes must be configured within the SGA. In addition, session information is also placed in the SGA for each user. Always compensate by configuring a larger SGA.

The SGA and Program Global Area (PGA) in a dedicated server environment is different than in a database that uses MTS. In the dedicated server environment, the following information resides in the PGA at the operating-system level:

➤ Stack space is composed of information on local variables used by the process or runtime area.

➤ User session data includes both the security and resource usage information.

➤ Cursor state contains runtime memory values for the SQL commands.

The configuration that uses MTS differs in that only the stack space is placed in an operating-system level PGA. The SGA will hold all the user session data and cursor-state information. This user area is referred to as the User Program Area (UGA).

The following database-initialization parameters are used when setting up the database to use MTS:

➤ LOCAL_LISTENER

➤ MTS_SERVICE

➤ MTS_DISPATCHERS

➤ MTS_MAX_DISPATCHERS

➤ MTS_SERVERS

➤ MTS_MAX_SERVERS

In order for the database connections to use MTS, they must be directed to the database using the listener process. MTS requires a Net8 (or SQL*Net) connection. If the client is signed onto the database server and connects directly to the database using SQL*Plus or another front-end application that sets the local variables, the connection will be a dedicated connection. In addition, if the client is configured in the local sqlnet.ora parameter file to use dedicated processes, this will override the use of MTS shared processes.

LOCAL_LISTENER

The **LOCAL_LISTENER** parameter is used to specify the service name for the listener or listeners with which the dispatcher processes must register. This can be a single address or a list of addresses for Net8 listeners. You must place this service name in a tnsnames.ora file on the server, and it is very important that the spacing and keywords be exact in the tnsnames.ora file. The following is an example of the tnsnames.ora entry for a **LOCAL_LISTENER**:

```
mts1 =
(DESCRIPTION =
      (ADDRESS =
             (PROTOCOL = TCP)
             (HOST = prodsvr1)
             (PORT = 1710)
      )
      (CONNECT_DATA = (SID=prod1) ) )
```

This entry in the tnsnames.ora file would match the following entry in the initialization parameter file for the database:

```
LOCAL_LISTENER = mts1
```

The **LOCAL_LISTENER** initialization parameter is static and cannot be altered with an **ALTER SYSTEM** command. In order to alter the **LOCAL_LISTENER** parameter, you must stop and restart the database.

If there is no **LOCAL_LISTENER** parameter in the database-initialization parameter file for a SID that is otherwise configured to use MTS, the defaults will be used. The default for the **LOCAL_LISTENER** parameter is to first look for a plug-and-play listener process. If it does not find one, it will look for a default TCP/IP listener on port 1521. Finally, it will default to the **ORACLE_SID** parameter.

> *Note: In some versions of Oracle8, there is a bug with the use of the LOCAL_LISTENER parameter. Instead, you should use the MTS_LISTENER_ADDRESS parameter. But, for the Oracle8 Network Administration exam, you should answer LOCAL_LISTENER and not MTS_LISTENER_ADDRESS.*

MTS_SERVICE

The **MTS_SERVICE** initialization parameter is used to specify the name of the service with which the dispatchers are associated. The name specified for the **MTS_SERVICE** must be unique in your environment and should not include quotation marks or special characters. This value is defined in the database initialization parameter file as follows:

```
MTS_SERVICE = prod1
```

The **MTS_SERVICE** parameter cannot be dynamically changed with the **ALTER SYSTEM** command. If this value is not specified in the database-initialization parameter file and the SID is configured to use MTS, then the default value will be used. The default value for this parameter is the same value that is specified for the **DB_NAME** parameter.

Oracle will always check for this service before making the Net8 connection. Oracle recommends that this name be the same as the instance name (SID). If both names are the same, the connection request will make a successful database connection even if the MTS dispatchers are unavailable.

MTS_DISPATCHERS

The **MTS_DISPATCHERS** database-initialization parameter specifies the number of dispatchers that will be initially started when the database is started. The **MTS_DISPATCHERS** parameter defaults to null. Dispatchers can be configured to use various network protocols, and each network specification includes the number of dispatchers to be started for that network protocol.

For each dispatcher, only one of the following specifications is used to indicate the network protocol:

➤ PROTOCOL

➤ ADDRESS

➤ DESCRIPTION

PROTOCOL, which can be abbreviated to **PRO** or **PROT**, indicates the network protocol for which the dispatcher will generate a listening endpoint. The **ADDRESS** keyword can be abbreviated to **ADD** or **ADDR**. If an address is specified, this indicates the actual network address to listen on. The **DESCRIPTION** keyword can be abbreviated as **DES** or **DESC**. If a description is specified, this will be the endpoint for the dispatchers to listen on. Both the **ADDRESS** and **DESCRIPTION** specifications include the network protocol.

The keyword **DISPATCHERS** can be abbreviated as **DIS** or **DISP**. This is the initial number of dispatchers to start. If the **MTS_DISPATCHERS** parameter is specified without the number of dispatchers listed, then it will default to one dispatcher per protocol.

In addition to the protocol specification and **DISPATCHERS** keyword, you can include additional parameters in the **MTS_DISPATCHERS** parameter. You can include the keyword **SESSIONS** (abbreviated **SES** or **SESS**) to set a maximum number of network sessions to be supported by each dispatcher. The **LISTENER** parameter (abbreviated **LIS** or **LIST**) can be included to specify the network name of an address for a Net8 listener. This can also be an address list. The **SERVICE** parameter (abbreviated **SER** or **SERV**) can be included to specify the service name for the dispatcher to register with. If the **SERVICE** parameter is included in the **MTS_DISPATCHERS** parameter, this will override the **MTS_SERVICE** parameter.

It is very important to have the keywords in the correct position (protocol first and number of dispatchers second) in the specification of the **MTS_DISPATCHERS** parameter. This specification must be a double-quoted string and is defined in the database-initialization parameter file as follows:

```
MTS_DISPATCHERS = "(PROTOCOL=TCP)(DISPATCHERS=3)"
```

For multiple network protocols, the parameter would include the protocol and number of dispatchers for each—for example:

```
MTS_DISPATCHERS = "(PROTOCOL=TCP)(DISPATCHERS=3) \
                  (PROTOCOL=IPC)(DISPATCHERS=2)"
```

The Oracle7 specification did not include the keywords. (The position of the value determined whether it was the protocol or the number of dispatchers.) Oracle8 will still accept the Oracle 7 specification, and the previous specification for multiple network protocols would look like:

```
MTS_DISPATCHERS = "TCP,3'
MTS_DISPATCHERS = "IPC,2"
```

The MTS_DISPATCHERS initialization parameter must be specified in order to configure the database for MTS. If there is not at least one **MTS_DISPATCHERS** configured, then the NULL default will mean that MTS won't be used.

When the database is started, the specified number of dispatcher processes are started for each network protocol. The **MTS_DISPATCHERS** parameter sets the number of dispatchers that will be created for each protocol. For each dispatcher process, there will be an operating system process created. Each of the dispatcher processes will be named with a *d* (for "dispatcher"), a number, and the database SID. For example, if the SID *prod1* has three TCP dispatchers, the following processes will be created:

```
ora_d001_prod1
ora_d002_prod1
ora_d003_prod1
```

The following formula is used to calculate the number of dispatchers that should be started initially per network protocol for your MTS configuration:

number of dispatchers =
    CEIL(Maximum number of concurrent sessions/Connections per dispatcher)

The database administrator can monitor the activity of dispatchers using the V$CIRCUT and V$DISPATCHER data dictionary views (covered later in this chapter). If the load on the dispatchers is consistently high, the user requests will experience delays. You can increase the number of dispatchers using the **ALTER SYSTEM** command. However, you can not increase the number of dispatchers beyond the **MTS_MAX_DISPATCHERS** parameter value. If the load on the dispatchers is consistently low, you can decrease the number of dispatchers to less than the **MTS_DISPATCHERS** parameter value.

It is very important to include an **MTS_DISPATCHERS** protocol specification for every network protocol that you want to support with MTS. To add additional network protocols, you must change the **MTS_DISPATCHERS** parameter and then stop and restart the database.

MTS_MAX_DISPATCHERS

The **MTS_MAX_DISPATCHERS** parameter is used to specify the maximum number of additional dispatchers that can be created. If this parameter is omitted from the MTS specifications, then the default is used. (The default is 5 or the value of **MTS_DISPATCHERS**, whichever is higher.) The actual maximum number of dispatchers supported simultaneously is dependent upon the operating system.

Following is an example of an **MTS_MAX_DISPATCHERS** initialization parameter setting:

```
MTS_MAX_DISPATCHERS = 2
```

This parameter cannot be changed interactively with any alter commands. Therefore, it is important that you set this parameter to the maximum number of dispatchers you will need at the peak time. Use the following formula to estimate the maximum number of dispatchers you should configure for MTS:

MTS_MAX_DISPATCHERS =
   Maximum number of concurrent sessions/Connections per dispatcher

MTS_SERVERS

The **MTS_SERVERS** database-initialization parameter determines the number of shared server processes that will be started at the operating-system level when the database is started. Following is an example of an **MTS_SERVERS** initialization parameter setting:

```
MTS_SERVERS = 3
```

Each of the shared server processes will be named with an *s* (for "shared server"), a number, and the database SID. For example, if you start three shared servers for the *prod1* instance, you will have the following processes:

```
ora_s001_prod1
ora_s002_prod1
ora_s003_prod1
```

The default setting for **MTS_SERVERS** is 0, meaning that you will not have any shared servers when the database is started. If you set **MTS_SERVERS** to 0, the MTS option is disabled. You can change this setting using the **ALTER SYSTEM** command. You must set **MTS_SERVERS** to 1 or higher in order to start the database with the MTS option.

The number of shared servers that will be needed is based on the number of users and the processing performed by them. If user processes include a large amount of idle time, then a single shared server can easily process requests for 10 to 20 users. However, if the user application has very little idle time, then the number of users per shared server should be set much lower.

Oracle recommends that you initially configure a small number of shared server processes. Oracle will automatically increase the number of shared servers that it needs to handle requests, up to the **MTS_MAX_SERVERS** parameter. Shared servers are automatically deallocated as the idle time is increased. However, the number of shared servers configured with the **MTS_SERVERS** parameter will always remain active, even if they are not needed. Setting a high **MTS_SERVERS** parameter value can cause your server to experience unnecessary overhead, which affects performance.

MTS_MAX_SERVERS

The **MTS_MAX_SERVERS** database-initialization parameter setting specifies the maximum number of shared server processes that will be created. The default for this parameter is 20 or 2 times the value of **MTS_SERVERS**, whichever is higher. (The range of values supported is dependent on the operating system.) Following is an example of an **MTS_SERVERS** initialization parameter setting:

```
MTS_MAX_SERVERS = 2
```

The MTS_MAX_SERVERS parameter should be set to support the maximum activity level of your environment. This parameter cannot be changed interactively with any alter command.

Monitoring And Altering Parameters For MTS

When you are configuring the MTS option, it may be necessary to experiment with several parameters until you determine the best settings for your environment. To initially determine if MTS is configured for a database, check the listener control utility (lsnrctl). Execute the **SERVICES** command for the listener process. (Refer to the earlier chapter on configuration of the server for more information about using the lsnrctl utility.)

You should be familiar with six data dictionary views for monitoring your MTS configuration:

➤ **V$CIRCUIT**

➤ **V$DISPATCHER**

➤ **V$SHARED_SERVER**

➤ **V$MTS**

➤ **V$QUEUE**

➤ **V$SESSION**

V$CIRCUIT

You can use the **V$CIRCUIT** view to determine if you are using the MTS option. This **V$CIRCUIT** view shows one entry per MTS connection and is used to show information about virtual circuits. Virtual circuits are user connections to the database that use the dispatcher and shared server processes. See Table 7.1.

If there is a problem with a specific process in the database, you can use the **V$CIRCUIT** view to obtain information on the specific user. The saddr column of the **V$CIRCUIT** view provides the session address that corresponds to the saddr column in the **V$SESSION** view.

V$DISPATCHER

You can use the **V$DISPATCHER** view to monitor your dispatchers. Table 7.2 describes the **V$DISPATCHER** view, and Table 7.3 lists the possible values for the status column of the **V$DISPATCHER** view and the meaning for each. The dispatcher's idle and busy times are the most important aspects to monitor. Use the following query to determine the total busy rate for the dispatcher for each network:

```
SELECT network,
       sum(busy) / (sum(busy) + sum(idle)  )
FROM V$DISPATCHER
GROUP BY network;
```

If the load on the dispatchers is consistently low, you may want to reduce the number of dispatchers that are maintained. If the load on the dispatcher processes is too great, user connection requests will have to wait. Therefore, if the

Table 7.1 V$CIRCUIT data dictionary view.

Column	Description
Circuit	Circuit address
Dispatcher	Current dispatcher process address
Server	Current server address
Waiter	Address of server process waiting for an available circuit
Saddr	Address of session
Status	BREAK for interrupted; EOF for about to be removed; OUTBOUND for outward link to a remote database; NORMAL
Queue	COMMON if waiting to be picked up by a shared server; SERVER if currently being serviced; OUTBOUND if waiting to establish a connection; DISPATCHER if waiting for a dispatcher; NONE if idle
Message0	Size in bytes of first message buffer
Message1	Size in bytes of second message buffer
Messages	Total number of messages that have gone through this circuit
Bytes	Total number of bytes that have gone through this circuit
Breaks	Total number of interruptions for this circuit

Table 7.2 V$DISPATCHER data dictionary view.

Column	Description
Name	Name of this dispatcher process
Network	Network protocol (i.e., TCP or DECnet)
Paddr	Process address
Status	Status of the dispatcher
Accept	YES to indicate that this dispatcher is accepting new connections; NO to indicate that this dispatcher is not accepting new connections
Messages	Number of messages processed by this dispatcher
Bytes	Total number of bytes for the messages processed by this dispatcher
Breaks	Number of breaks that have occurred in this connection
Owned	Number of circuits owned by this dispatcher
Created	Number of circuits created by this dispatcher
Idle	Total idle time (hundreds of a second)

(continued)

Table 7.2 V$DISPATCHER data dictionary view (continued).	
Column	**Description**
Busy	Total busy time (hundreds of a second)
Listener	The last error number received from the listener process

Table 7.3 STATUS column values for the V$DISPATCHER view.	
Status	**Meaning**
WAIT	Idle
SENT	Currently sending a message
RECEIVE	Currently receiving a message
CONNECT	Establishing a connection
DISCONNECT	Processing a request to disconnect
BREAK	Processing a break
OUTBOUND	Establishing an outbound connection

total busy rate is greater than 50 percent, you should add additional dispatcher processes. You can increase the number of dispatchers for use by new connections. It will not increase the number of dispatchers available to users already logged into the database. For example, the following command can be used to increase the number of dispatchers from an initial setting of three TCP to six TCP dispatchers:

```
ALTER SYSTEM
SET MTS_DISPATCHERS = '(PROTOCOL=TCP)(DISPATCHERS=6)';
```

You cannot decrease the number of dispatchers to less than the original **MTS_DISPATCHERS** setting, and you cannot increase the number of dispatchers to exceed the **MTS_MAX_DISPATCHERS**. Nor can you dynamically add dispatchers for a protocol that has not been specified in the database initialization parameter **MTS_DISPATCHERS**.

If you dynamically change the number of dispatchers but do not change the database-initialization parameter file, the parameter will revert to the original setting when the database is shut down and restarted. If you determine the best settings for **MTS_DISPATCHERS** should be increased, change this interactively with the **ALTER SYSTEM** command and immediately change your database initialization parameter file setting.

V$SHARED_SERVER

To monitor information on the shared server processes, use the **V$SHARED_ SERVER** view. See Table 7.4. You should monitor the load on the shared servers to determine the correct setting for the **MTS_SERVERS** parameter. The number of shared servers can be changed with the **ALTER SYSTEM** command. For example, to change the **MTS_SERVERS** from three to six, type in the following command:

```
ALTER SYSTEM
set MTS_SERVERS = 6;
```

> *Note: Anyone with the **ALTER SYSTEM** privilege can interactively change the MTS configuration settings.*

Table 7.4 describes the columns in the **V$SHARED_SERVER** view. Table 7.5 lists the possible values for the status column of the **V$SHARED_SERVER** view and the meaning for each. You can determine the number of shared servers that are currently running with the following query:

```
SELECT COUNT(*) FROM V$SHARED_SERVER
WHERE status != 'QUIT';
```

Since the number of shared servers is dynamically increased and decreased as needed, Oracle recommends starting with a low number of servers (1 per 100

Table 7.4 V$SHARED_SERVER data dictionary view.	
Column	**Description**
Name	Name of this server process
Paddr	Process address
Status	Status of this shared server
Messages	Number of messages processed by this server
Bytes	Total number of bytes in all the messages
Breaks	Number of breaks
Circuit	Address for the current circuit being served
Idle	Total idle time (hundreds of a second)
Busy	Total busy time (hundreds of a second)
Requests	Total number of requests serviced from the common queue since this server was created

Table 7.5	STATUS information for the V$SHARED_SERVER view.
Status	**Meaning**
EXEC	Executing a SQL statement
WAIT(ENQ)	Waiting for a lock
WAIT(SEND)	Waiting to send data to a user
WAIT(COMMON)	Waiting for a user request to service
WAIT(RESET)	Waiting for a circuit to reset after a break
QUIT	Terminating

users) and increasing the number of shared servers as necessary. If you set the initial number of shared servers too high, this will result in too much overhead and cause an unnecessary load on the server.

If you decide to temporarily disable the MTS option, you can dynamically change the **MTS_SERVERS** parameter to 0. If you do this, current shared server processes will become inactive as they become idle and no new shared server processes will be started. To enable MTS again, alter the **MTS_SERVERS** parameter to one or higher to once again create shared server processes.

V$MTS

The **V$MTS** view is used to monitor the maximum number of MTS shared servers started for tuning purposes. This number should be monitored to determine the highest activity level for your shared servers. This will help you determine the ideal setting for the **MTS_MAX_SERVERS** database-initialization parameter setting. See Table 7.6.

Table 7.6	V$MTS data dictionary view.
Column	**Description**
maximum_connections	Maximum number of connections that each dispatcher can support (based on the operating system)
servers_started	Total number of additional shared servers started since the database started (excluding those specified during startup)
servers_terminated	Total number of shared servers stopped since instance startup
servers_highwater	The highest number of servers at any time

V$QUEUE

V$QUEUE provides information on the MTS queues for the dispatcher and shared servers. Table 7.7 describes the **V$QUEUE** view. The following query can be used to determine the average wait time for a connection waiting in the response queue for a dispatcher process:

```
SELECT network
       DECODE (SUM(totalq), 0, 'NO RESPONSES',
       SUM(wait)/SUM(totalq) )
FROM V$QUEUE, V$DISPATCHER
WHERE v$queue.type = 'DISPATCHER'
AND   v$queue.paddr = v$dispatcher.paddr
GROUP BY network;
```

To determine the average wait time for each shared server request, you can execute the following query:

```
SELECT DECODE( totalq, 0, , 'NO RESPONSES',
       wait/totalq)
FROM V$QUEUE
WHERE type = 'COMMON';
```

V$SESSION

It is vital when using the MTS option that, if it becomes necessary to kill a user session, that session be killed using the Oracle database command and not with an operating system command. Since the Dispatchers and Shared Servers are handling multiple connections, killing a Dispatcher or Shared Server at the operating system level will affect more that one user. To view information on individual sessions, use the **V$SESSION** view. The information of most interest to you in the **V$SESSION** view is the SID, SERIAL#, USERNAME, and SERVER. If the SERVER is set to SHARED, then it is using the MTS

Table 7.7	**V$QUEUE data dictionary view.**
V$QUEUE	
Column	**Description**
Paddr	Address of the process that owns the queue
Type	COMMON for processed by servers; OUTBOUND for queues used by remote servers DISPATCHER
Queued	Number of items in the queue
Wait	Total time that all items have been queued
Totalq	Total number of items that have been in the queue

shared server. If it is set to DEDICATED, there will be a dedicated process at the operating system level.

Connection Pooling With MTS

Connection pooling is a new feature with Oracle8 that allows you to support an even larger user population. Connection pooling maximizes utilization of your resources by minimizing the number of physical connections to an MTS-configured database. The dispatcher connections are shared among multiple client processes, which is very useful in environments where the dispatchers have a very high idle/search time. This is usually the situation in OLAP and messaging systems.

Connections are made to dispatchers as described previously in this chapter. As long as dispatcher processes are available to respond to a request, a session will be connected immediately. Without connection pooling, when the maximum number of connections is reached for a dispatcher, additional sessions must wait for a session to disconnect before a connection can be established. With connection pooling enabled, instead of waiting for a session to disconnect, the incoming session only needs to wait until a session becomes idle. When a session becomes idle, Oracle will temporarily disconnect the idle session and allow the new session to use that connection.

In order to enable connection pooling, the **MTS_DISPATCHERS** database-initialization parameter must be configured with additional information. The following parameters control connection pooling:

➤ POOL

➤ CONNECTION

➤ TICKS

For example, the database-initialization parameter specification for connection pooling with TCP would look like the following:

```
MTS_DISPATCHERS =
"(PRO=TCP)(CON=20)(DIS=4)(POO=ON)(TIC=3)(SESS=25)"
```

POOL

The **POOL** parameter can be abbreviated to **POO**. The default is to disable connection pooling. The **POOL** parameter must be included in the **MTS_DISPATCHERS** database-initialization parameter to enable connection pooling. The following values will enable connection pooling for both incoming and outgoing network connections:

➤ On

➤ Yes

➤ True

➤ Both

In order to perform connection pooling only for incoming network connections, this can be set to IN. To use connection pooling only for outgoing connections, this value is set to OUT. To set a timeout value for incoming and/ or outgoing connections, you can specify a numeric value with the IN and/or OUT parameter. If the timeout is set to 0, the default will be used. This numeric value is in ticks. Following is an example of a setting for 5 ticks on incoming connections and 10 ticks for outgoing connections:

```
(IN=5)(OUT=10)
```

You can specify any of the following to disable connection pooling, or simply omit the associated parameters from your database-initialization file:

➤ No

➤ Off

➤ False

CONNECTION

The **CONNECTION** parameter can be abbreviated as **CON** or **CONN**. This parameter specifies the maximum number of network connections that can be established for each dispatcher process. The default is operating-system specific.

Earlier in this chapter, we covered the **SESSION** parameter, which specifies the maximum number of user processes that can be associated with a dispatcher (both active and idle combined). If the **CONNECTION** parameter is set higher than the **SESSION** parameter, then connection pooling cannot take place. Therefore, the **CONNECTION** parameter must be set lower than the **SESSION** parameter. The following formula is used to determine the number of waiting sessions that can be handled by connection pooling:

SESSION – CONNECTION = maximum number of waiting sessions

TICKS

The **TICKS** parameter can be abbreviated as **TIC** or **TICK**. It specifies the number of 10-second intervals for waiting to establish a connection. The default wait timeout for a connection when all dispatchers are busy is 10 ticks (100 seconds).

Practice Questions

Question 1

> Which of the following is not a benefit provided by MTS?
>
> ○ a. Increased maximum number of users per server
>
> ○ b. Reduces system overhead (memory requirements)
>
> ○ c. Automatic load balancing
>
> ○ d. Supports connection pooling
>
> ○ e. Increased performance for batch jobs

The correct answer is e. The MTS option is most useful when there is a high idle time, such as with OLTP applications, not batch jobs. Note that the question is phrased in the negative. All but e are benefits of MTS.

Question 2

> Which of the following is moved into the SGA in an MTS configuration? [Choose the two best answers]
>
> ❑ a. Stack space
>
> ❑ b. Cursor state
>
> ❑ c. User session data
>
> ❑ d. Shared pool

The correct answers are b and c. The shared pool is always in the SGA, regardless of whether or not an MTS configuration is used. The stack space is always in the operating-system PGA.

Question 3

> Which of the following picks up a connection request in an MTS configuration?
>
> ○ a. Dispatcher
>
> ○ b. Shared server
>
> ○ c. Response queue
>
> ○ d. Request queue
>
> ○ e. Dedicated process

The correct answer is a. The dispatcher picks up the request and places it in the request queue. The shared server picks up the request, executes it, and places the response in the calling dispatcher's response queue. If you could not answer this question, review the connection process in the chapter text.

Question 4

> Which of the following parameters is an example of a configuration for connection pooling?
>
> ○ a. **MTS_DISPATCHERS =**
>   "(PRO=TCP)(CONN=20)(POO=ON)(SESS=15)"
>
> ○ b. **MTS_DISPATCHERS =**
>   "(PRO=TCP)(CONN=20)(POOLING=ON)(SESS=30)"
>
> ○ c. **MTS_DISPATCHERS =**
>   "(PRO=TCP)(CONN=20)(POO=ON)(SESS=30)"
>
> ○ d. **MTS_DISPATCHERS** = '(PROTOCOL=TCP)(DISPATCHERS=2)"

The correct answer is c. Since connection pooling defaults to disabled, answer d is wrong. In answer a, the number of connections is lower than the number of sessions, which will in effect disable connection pooling. In answer b, "POOLING" is not an accepted parameter.

Question 5

> If you set the **TIC** parameter to 10 for connection pooling, how long will the connection wait?
>
> ○ a. 100 seconds
>
> ○ b. 10 seconds
>
> ○ c. 10 minutes
>
> ○ d. 60 seconds

The correct answer is a, 100 seconds. Each tick is equivalent to 10 seconds.

Question 6

> Which view will help you determine the highest number of shared servers used since system startup?
>
> ○ a. **V$DISPATCHERS**
>
> ○ b. **V$SESSION**
>
> ○ c. **V$MTS**
>
> ○ d. **V$DISPATCHER**

The correct answer is c. The servers_highwater column in the **v$mts** view is the highest number of servers. The **v$session** and **v$dispatchers** are not used for views this information. The **v$dispatchers** does not exist. Review the section on monitoring MTS.

Question 7

> In an MTS configuration, the role of the shared server is to _____:
>
> ○ a. Accept connection requests from the client
>
> ○ b. Redirect connection requests to a dispatcher
>
> ○ c. Pick up a request from the request queue and process the request
>
> ○ d. Pick up a request from a dispatcher and resolve the request
>
> ○ e. Return the response to the client

The correct answer is c. The results of the request are placed in the calling dispatcher's response queue. The dispatcher returns the response to the client. See Figure 7.3 to review this process.

Question 8

If the mts_dispatchers = 3 and mts_max_dispatchers = 12, which of the following commands will succeed?

- O a. **ALTER SYSTEM SET MTS_DISPATCHERS =
  '(protocol=tcp)(dispatchers=10)';**
- O b. **ALTER DATABASE SET MTS_DISPATCHERS =
  '(protocol=tcp)(dispatchers=10)';**
- O c. **ALTER SYSTEM SET MTS_DISPATCHERS =
  '(protocol=tcp)(dispatchers=20)';**
- O d. **ALTER SYSTEM SET MTS_MAX_DISPATCHERS =
  '(protocol=tcp)(dispatchers=20)';**
- O e. **ALTER SYSTEM SET MTS_MAX_DISPATCHERS =
  '(dispatchers=10)(protocol=tcp)';**

The correct answer is a. Answer b is incorrect because the **ALTER SYSTEM** command is used to dynamically change the number of dispatchers. Answer c is incorrect because the number of dispatchers cannot be set to exceed the number of maximum dispatchers set in the **MTS_MAX_DISPATCHERS** parameter. Answer d is incorrect because the **MTS_MAX_DISPATCHERS** parameter cannot be interactively altered. Answer e is incorrect because of the positioning of the parameters.

Question 9

What is the result of the following command?

```
Alter system set mts_servers = 0;
```

- O a. All connections using MTS are immediately disconnected.
- O b. MTS is temporarily disabled.
- O c. No dedicated connections will be allowed.
- O d. You will receive an error message.
- O e. Dispatcher processes are terminated as they become active.

The correct answer is b. This will temporarily disable the MTS option until the number of shared servers is increased. Connections will not be terminated. The shared servers will be terminated as they become idle.

Question 10

How can you change the **MTS_SERVICE** parameter?

○ a. Stop the database, change the **MTS_SERVICE** parameter in the init.ora file and restart the database.

○ b. Use the **ALTER SYSTEM** command to change the value.

○ c. Use the **ALTER DATABASE** command to change the value.

○ d. Change the listener.ora file and reload the listener.

○ e. None of the above.

The correct answer is a. The **MTS_SERVICE** parameter can not be changed unless the database is stopped, the init.ora parameter is changed and the database is restarted. Changing the listener.ora or issuing an **ALTER** command will not change the MTS_SERVICE setting.

Need To Know More?

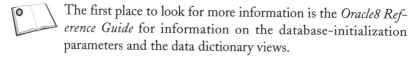

The first place to look for more information is the *Oracle8 Reference Guide* for information on the database-initialization parameters and the data dictionary views.

Ault, Michael. *Oracle8 Administration and Management*. Wiley, 1998. Chapter 16 "Managing in a Distributed Environment," section 16.8 addresses using the multithreaded server.

Burleson, Don. *High Performance Oracle8 Tuning*. Coriolis, 1998. Chapter 9 "Performance and Tuning for Oracle Database Connectivity Tools" addresses performance-tuning the MTS option.

Corey, Michael J., et al. *Oracle8 Tuning*. Oracle Press, 1998. Chapter 2 "Memory/CPU" addresses the Multithreaded Server.

Niemiec, Richard J. *Oracle Performance Tuning Tips & Techniques*. Oracle Press, 1999. Chapter 4 "Tuning the init.ora" discusses techniques for tuning MTS.

"Configuring MTS for Listener Load Balancing" in RevealNet Oracle Administration Knowledge Base.

Connection Manager Usage And Administration

8

. . . .

Terms you'll need to understand:

√ Connection concentration

√ Multiprotocol

√ cman.ora

√ CMAN_PROFILE

√ CMGW

√ CMADM

√ MULTIPLEX

√ CMAN_RULES

√ CMCTL

Techniques you'll need to master:

√ Understanding what Connection Manager is and how it works

√ Configuring connection concentration

√ Understanding multiprotocol configuration and functionality

In this chapter, I'll cover Connection Manager (CMAN), a networking service included as part of Net8. CMAN is aimed at database environments that need to support more than 1,000 users in a three-tier environment. While you can install CMAN on any node that has Net8 installed, it is recommended that CMAN be configured on the middle tier of a three-tier architecture to take full advantage of the features provided. See Figure 8.1 for an example of the three-tier environment with CMAN.

The following topics will be covered in this chapter:

➤ Overview of CMAN

➤ cman.ora file

➤ Configuration of CMAN

➤ Controlling and monitoring CMAN

Overview Of CMAN

The Oracle Connection Manager (CMAN) is a new Net8 option that provides the following features:

➤ Connection concentration

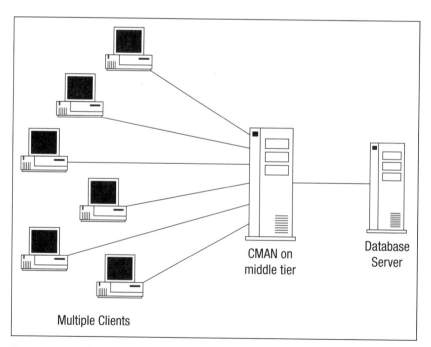

Figure 8.1 Three-tier environment with CMAN.

➤ Multiprotocol connectivity

➤ Secure network access

Connection Concentration

CMAN can be used to increase scalability and make better use of your resources, and a key feature is that it allows you to do this without changing existing applications. CMAN supports both Oracle7 and Oracle8 client connections.

> *Note: Connection Manager supports out-of-band breaks. It will pass the break signal on to the server. For more on out-of-band breaks see Chapter 3, Exception Handling Operations.*

CMAN works in conjunction with the Multithreaded Server (MTS) option to provide support for large populations. With Connection Manager, you can multiplex (or channel) many logical client sessions through one transport connection to a database that is configured to use MTS.

To scale even further, you can use a configuration with multiple connection managers. Using multiple connection managers allows you to partition your network and maximize your existing server and network environment to support thousands of concurrent client connections. Using multiple connection managers also provides automatic fault tolerance for your connections. If the primary connection manager server is not available, connections will automatically switch to another connection manager.

Multiprotocol Connectivity

The Connection Manager service replaces the MultiP rotocol Interchange (MPI) that Oracle previously used as an interface between network protocols. This aspect of CMAN allows you to have a client with one network protocol transparently communicate with a server that uses a different protocol. The following protocol conversions are provided by CMAN:

➤ APPC (LU6.2)

➤ DECnet

➤ Named pipes

➤ SPX/IPX

➤ TCP/IP

This conversion between the network protocols is bidirectional between the client and server and can be performed between clients and servers of any size, from small workstations to large mainframes. See Figure 8.2.

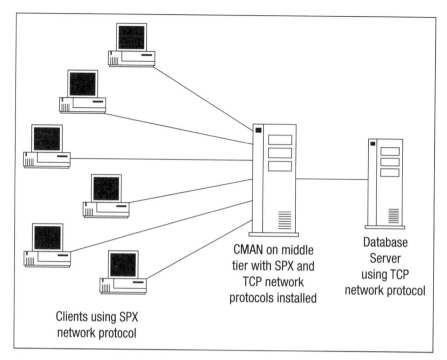

Figure 8.2   A multiprotocol environment with CMAN on the middle tier.

CMAN also provides logging and tracing to identify errors and resolve problems in a multiprotocol environment.

Secure Network Access

CMAN can be used to set up connection rules that filter connection requests. If CMAN is implemented along with the Advanced Networking option, it can enhance the access restrictions that the Advanced Networking option provides. In addition, CMAN can be used to obtain statistics for auditing purposes and can serve as a firewall for incoming connections. It can be configured to accept or reject connections based on the following criteria:

➤ Origin

➤ Destination

➤ SID

cman.ora File

On the middle tier, Connection Manager must be defined before the connection manager process can be started. The parameter file, cman.ora, is used to configure CMAN. (See Figure 8.3. See Appendix E for a sample cman.ora file.)

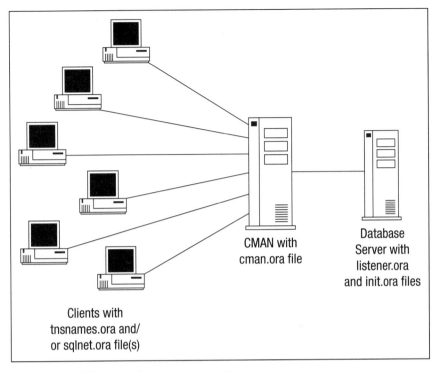

Figure 8.3   Files used by Connection Manager.

This file actually consists of three sections:

➤ CMAN

➤ CMAN_PROFILE

➤ CMAN_RULES

CMAN

The CMAN entry contains the address information for the connection manager. This entry can be omitted only if the default configuration is used. Following is an example of the CMAN entry in a cman.ora file:

```
CMAN =
        (ADDRESS_LIST =
            (ADDRESS =
                (PROTOCOL = TCP)
                (HOST = appsvr1)
                (PORT = 1610)
            )
        )
```

CMAN_PROFILE

The CMAN_PROFILE entry contains the general configuration parameters for CMAN. These parameters are used to determine the behavior of the CMAN backup processes. If the defaults are used, this section may be omitted.

The following parameters are configured in the CMAN_PROFILE:

➤ MAXIMUM_RELAYS

➤ LOG_LEVEL

➤ TRACING

➤ RELAY_STATISTICS

➤ SHOW_TNS_INFO

➤ USE_ASYNC_CALL

➤ AUTHENTICATION_LEVEL

➤ MAXIMUM_CONNECT_DATA

➤ ANSWER_TIMEOUT

The **MAXIMUM_RELAYS** parameter specifies the number of concurrent connections that will be allowed. The default is 8 and the maximum is 1,024.

The **LOG_LEVEL** is used to determine the level for logging. The default is 0 for no logging. The values supported for logging are 1 to 4, with 4 being the most detailed.

The **TRACING** parameter can be set to YES or NO (the default). If tracing is set to YES, a trace file will be created. This trace file can only be read using Oracle Trace. With CMAN you cannot configure as many levels for tracing as you can in other Net8 utilities. You are limited to either USER or ADMIN.

The **RELAY_STATISTICS** parameter can be set to either YES or NO (the default). If this parameter is set to YES, then CMAN will maintain statistics on network activity. These statistics will provide information on I/O activities, such as:

➤ Number of bytes in

➤ Number of bytes out

➤ Number of packets in

➤ Number of packets out

The **SHOW_TNS_INFO** parameter can be specified as either YES or NO (the default). If this is set to YES, then information on TNS events will be placed in the log file.

The **USE_ASYNC_CALL** parameter can be specified as either YES or NO (the default). If this parameter is set to YES, CMAN will use all asynchronous functions in answering, accepting, and calling phases of the connection process.

The **AUTHENTICATION_LEVEL** can be specified as either 0 or 1. The default is 0, which is not to use authentication. If this parameter is set to 1, CMAN will reject any connection requests that do not use Secure Network Services (part of the Advanced Networking option).

The **MAXIMUM_CONNECT_DATA** parameter is used to specify the maximum number of bytes to be transferred in the data portion of a TNS packet. This parameter can range from 257 to 4,096.

The **ANSWER_TIMEOUT** parameter specifies the maximum number of seconds to wait for a response. This must be greater than zero.

Following is an example of the CMAN_PROFILE section of the cman.ora file:

```
CMAN_PROFILE =
       (PARAMETER_LIST =
              (MAXIMUM_RELAYS = 206)
              (LOG_LEVEL = 1)
              (TRACING = YES)
              (RELAY_STATISTICS = YES)
              (SHOW_TNS_INFO = YES)
              (USE_ASYNC_CALL = YES)
              (AUTHENTICATION_LEVEL = 0)
              (MAXIMUM_CONNECT_DATA = 4096)
              (ANSWER_TIMEOUT = 30)
       )
```

CMAN_RULES

The CMAN_RULES section contains the rules to be used for security filtering of incoming connection requests. The CMAN rules will be covered later in this chapter.

Configuration Of Connection Manager

You can configure CMAN to make use of any of the features available in any combination. However, certain general requirements must be met to use any of the features provided by CMAN. Depending upon the features you decide to implement, the configuration will have certain additional requirements.

This section will cover the following:

➤ General requirements for configuration of CMAN

➤ CMAN requirements for connection concentration

➤ CMAN requirements for multiprotocol connectivity

➤ CMAN configuration for security

➤ CMAN and Oracle Names

General Requirements

In order to use CMAN, you must have the following background processes:

➤ CMGW

➤ CMADM

The CMGW and CMADM processes communicate with each other using interprocess communication (IPC). These background processes are controlled using the control utilities (CMCTL or CMCTL80) that are covered later in this chapter.

 On an NT server, the background processes include the version number (CMGW80 and CMADM80).

CMGW

The background process that acts as the hub for CMAN is the Connection Manager Gateway, known as CMGW in a Unix environment and CMGW80 in Windows NT. The CMGW must be assigned to listen on a port, and the default port assignment is either 1610 or 1600, depending upon the operating system.

The CMGW registers with the CMADM background process for connection concentration. It listens for incoming requests for Oracle7's SQL*Net 2 and Oracle8's Net8 clients. It sends the connection requests to the Oracle8 listener process, which was covered in an earlier chapter. The CMGW process relays the commands from the client application to the database on the server. It also relays the data, which is returned from the database on the server, to the client. CMAN processes connection request in the following manner:

1. CMGW is started on the middle-tier server.

2. Request is sent from the client to the middle tier and is picked up by CMAN.

3. CMAN may reject the request or send it on to the listener on the database server.

4. If the request is forwarded to the listener, the listener process will either spawn a dedicated connection or redirect the connection to an existing process.

In addition, the CMGW answers requests from the Connection Manager control utility (CMCTL or CMCTL80).

CMADM

Configurations that use both CMAN and an Oracle names server must have a special background process called CMADM in a Unix environment (CMADM80 for NT).

CMADM is a multithreaded process that handles the administrative issues for the CMAN. It maintains address information for the Oracle names server on behalf of the SQL*Net 2 and Net8 clients. It also provides the following services for CMAN:

➤ Process registration of CMGW (or CMGW80)

➤ Locate the local Oracle names server

➤ Identify the listener processes

➤ Register address information on the CMGW (or CMGW80) and the listener processes with CMAN

➤ Monitor changes in the network and update the names server

➤ Answer requests from CMCTL (or CMCTL80)

CMAN Requirements For Connection Concentration

When configuring the client to make use of CMAN, the local tnsnames.ora file must contain entries for both the CMAN server and the destination server. It must also contain the following parameter:

```
SOURCE_ROUTE = YES
```

Following is an example of a service name definition in a tnsnames.ora file that makes use of Connection Manager:

```
PROD1 =
     (DESCRIPTION =
          (ADDRESS_LIST =
               (ADDRESS =
                    (PROTOCOL = TCP)
                    (HOST = appsvr1)
                    (PORT = 1610)
               )
               (ADDRESS =
                    (PROTOCOL = TCP)
                    (HOST = server1)
                    (PORT = 1521)
               )
          )
          (CONNECT_DATA =
               (SID = PROD1)
               (SOURCE_ROUTE = YES)
          )
     )
```

The first address in this example is for CMAN. The second address is for the listener on the database server (destination node). The entry for the **CONNECT_DATA** includes the SID and the **SOURCE_ROUTE** parameters. Without the **SOURCE_ROUTE = YES** line, the default would cause the address entries to be treated as separate listener processes on the database server. The CMAN will act as a routing device between the client and the listener process.

On the server, the initialization parameter file for the SID must be configured to use the Multithreaded Server (MTS) option, which was covered in a previous Chapter 7. The following parameter must be included in the **MTS_DISPATCHERS** definition:

```
MULTIPLEX
```

Following is an example of an **MTS_DISPATCHERS** parameter setting for connection concentration:

```
MTS_DISPATCHERS = "(PROTOCOL = TCP)(DIS = 2) (MULT = ON)"
```

Note: Connection concentration and connection pooling are not compatible. You can configure either; but, not both. Use connection pooling to share connections at the database server level. Use connection concentration to share connections at the middle-tier level.

The **MULTIPLEX** parameter may be abbreviated either **MUL** or **MULT**. If this parameter is not included, the default is for **MULTIPLEX** to be disabled (which means that connection concentration is not used). In addition to omitting this parameter, you can disable connection concentration with the following settings:

➤ 0

➤ NO

➤ OFF

➤ FALSE

The following settings can be used to enable connection concentration for both incoming and outgoing connections:

➤ 1

➤ ON

➤ YES

➤ TRUE

➤ BOTH

If **MULTIPLEX** is set to IN, then connection concentration is enabled only for incoming network connections. If it is set to OUT, then only outgoing network connections will use connection concentration.

CMAN Configuration For Multiprotocol Connectivity

In order to connect between two nodes that support different network protocols, you can configure two addresses with different protocols in the tnsnames.ora file on the client. The node where CMAN is installed will need to have both network protocols installed. This is the functionality that was previously provided with the MultiProtocol Interchange (MPI) product in Oracle7. See Figure 8.2.

Following is an example of a tnsnames.ora specification for connectivity between a server with the TCP protocol and a client with the SPX protocol:

```
prod1 =
        (DESCRIPTION =
                (ADDRESS =
                        (PROTOCOL = SPX)
                        (SERVICE = appsvr1)
                )
                (ADDRESS =
                        (PROTOCOL = TCP)
                        (HOST = server1)
                        (PORT = 1521)
                )
            (CONNECT_DATA =
                (SID = prod1)
                (SOURCE_ROUTE = YES)
            )
        )
```

In this example, the client will send a connection using the SPX protocal to CMAN on the middle tier server (appsvr1). At the CMAN node, the network conversion will take place, and the connection will be sent to the server (server1) using TCP. Notice that the example has two addresses but that the normal tnsnames.ora file parameter **ADDRESS_LIST** is not included. The **SOURCE_ROUTE=YES** parameter is included to indicate that this connection is to be routed through the Connection Manager process.

CMAN Configuration For Security

The security features of CMAN are configured in the cman.ora file. The **CMAN_RULES** section of the cman.ora file contains the access control rules to be enforced by Connection Manager. Four parameters can be configured for each rule:

➤ **SRC** (used to specify the source)

➤ **DST** (used to specify the destination)

➤ **SRV** (the SID of the target database)

➤ **ACT** (can be set to either accept (**ACCEPT** or **ACC**) or reject (**REJECT** or **REJ**) the connection based on the rule defined)

The source and destination can be either the hostname or IP address of the database server. (You can use wildcards in the IP address specification, as in 110.x.x.x.) The rules can be any combination of source, destination, and SID specifications.

Each rule is defined separately in the **RULES_LIST**, and the default action for each rule is to accept the request. You can define multiple rules, but, if two rules conflict, the earlier one determines the action. If no rules are defined, the default is to permit the connection request. Following is an example of setting up the **CMAN_RULES** parameters in the cman.ora file:

```
CMAN_RULES =
        (RULES_LIST =
            (RULE =
                    (SRC = hrwk1)
                    (DST = server2)
                    (SRV = prod2)
                    (ACT = REJ)
            )
            (RULE =
                    (SRC = finwk2)
                    (DST = server1)
                    (SRV = prod1)
                    (ACT = ACC)
            )
            (RULE =
                    (SRC = server2)
                    (DST = server1)
                    (SRV = prod1)
                    (ACT = REJ)
            )
        )
```

In this example, the **hrwk1** client requests that are going to the database server (**server2**) to connect to SID **prod2** will be rejected. Requests from the **finwk2** client to the database server **server1** for SID **prod1** will be accepted. Remember that database servers can act as clients to databases on other servers. The third example will not allow any users from **server2** to connect to the database **prod1** that resides on **server1**.

 Carefully review how rules are configured and the four values that can be configured. Remember that each rule is defined with a separate entry in the **RULES_LIST**.

CMAN And Oracle Names

When you are using CMAN with an Oracle names server, the CMAN process will automatically update the Names server with the CMAN address. In order to configure CMAN to work with Oracle Names, it is necessary to add the following parameter to the sqlnet.ora file on the client:

```
USE_CMAN = TRUE
```

If the **USE_CMAN** parameter is not in the sqlnet.ora file, the default is to choose a connection path at random (which is also the result if **USE_CMAN** is set to FALSE).

If the **USE_CMAN** parameter is included and set to TRUE, the client is forced to use Connection Manager. The path used for CMAN is chosen randomly from the ADDRESS_LIST service names that include **SOURCE_ROUTE=YES** in the description. If the description contains no indirect paths, then a path to CMAN is picked at random.

Controlling And Monitoring CMAN

Chapter 4 discussed the lsnrctl utility that is used to control and monitor the listener process. Connection Manager has an equivalent utility to monitor and control the Connection Manager processes (CMGW and CMADM). In a Unix environment, it is CMCTL and in NT it is CMCTL80. Commands starting with the CMCTL and followed by the command can be issued at the command line. The alternative method is to start the CMCTL utility and issue commands at the prompt.

The syntax for the CMCTL utility is:

```
CMCTL <command> <process_name> {argument}
```

The **<command>** is equivalent to one of the commands listed in Table 8.1. The **<process_name>** is one of the following:

➤ CMAN for both CMGW and CMADM

➤ CM for CMGW

➤ ADM for CMADM

The most commonly used commands are

➤ START

➤ STOP

➤ STATUS

➤ VERSION

Table 8.1 CMAN commands.	
Command	**Action**
EXIT	Quit the CMCTL program.
LOG_OFF	Turn logging off.
LOG_ON	Turn logging on.
START	Start up CMAN processes.
START	Provide statistics on the CMAN process.
STOP	Shut down CMAN processes.
TRACE_OFF	Turn off tracing.
TRACE_ON	Turn on tracing.
VERSION	Display version of CMGW and CMADM.

The **START** command is used to startup the CMGW and CMADM background processes, and it can be used in conjunction with the following arguments:

➤ CMAN

➤ CM

➤ ADM

 This is a case of Oracle including information on the OCP test that is directly from a class and may not be true in your experience. I agree that the **START**, **STOP**, and **STATUS** commands are commonly used. But, I would not consider the **VERSION** command as used more than the commands for turning, logging, and tracing on and off, or even the **EXIT** command.

The **START** command issued alone or with the CMAN argument will start up both the CMGW and CMADM background processes. The **START CM** command will start only the gateway process (CMGW), whereas the **START ADM** command starts only the administration process (CMADM).

The **STOP** command alone or **STOP CM** shuts down both the CMGW and CMADM background processes. When the CMGW process stops, the CMADM process will also stop. The CMADM process cannot run without the CMGW process. The Connection Manager processes cannot be stopped if current connections are using these processes.

The **STATUS** command provides status information on the Connection Manager processes. The **STATUS** command alone, **STATUS CMAN** or **STATUS CM**, will provide status information on the CMGW process. For status on the CMADM process, you must use the command **STATUS ADM**.

The **VERSION** command shows the version number for the Connection Manager control program. (This provides the version numbers of both CMGW and CMADM.)

The only command that requires an argument is the **TRACE_ON** command. For the **TRACE_ON** command, you must supply the level for tracing. Only USER and ADMIN levels are available with the CMAN utility.

Tracing is used to gather information to troublshoot problems with CMAN. The commands **LOG_ON** and **LOG_OFF** allow you to turn logging on and off. Chapter 10 includes information on the differences between logging and tracing.

Practice Questions

Question 1

Which of the following are background processes for Connection Manager? [Choose the two best answers]

- ❑ a. CMGW
- ❑ b. CMCTL
- ❑ c. CMADM
- ❑ d. LSNRCTL
- ❑ e. NAMESCTL

The correct answers are a and c. The CMGW is the Connection Manager Gateway process. The CMADM is the Connection Manager Administration process. The CMCTL is the Connection Manager control utility. You should recognize lsnrctl as the listener control utility and namesctl as the names control utility.

Question 2

What is the parameter that is required in the tnsnames.ora file to use CMAN for connection concentration?

- ○ a. **CMAN_RULES**
- ○ b. **CMAN_PROFILE**
- ○ c. **MULTIPLEX**
- ○ d. **SOURCE_ROUTE**

The correct answer is d. The **SOURCE_ROUTE** parameter must be set to YES to enable connection concentration with Connection Manager. The **MULTIPLEX** parameter is set on the server in the database initialization parameter file. The **CMAN_RULES** and **CMAN_PROFILE** are part of the cman.ora file.

Question 3

> What are the sections of the cman.ora file?
>
> ○ a. CMAN, CONNECTION_DATA, CMAN_RULES
>
> ○ b. CMAN, CMAN_PROFILE, CMAN_RULES
>
> ○ c. CMAN, CMAN_PROFILE, CMAN_SECURITY
>
> ○ d. ADDRESS, CMAN, CMAN_RULES

The correct answer is b. The CMAN section contains the address information and is always required in the cman.ora file. The CMAN_PROFILE section sets the general parameters. The CMAN_RULES section is used for definition of security rules.

Question 4

> Which of the following does the SRC parameter define?
>
> ○ a. SID
>
> ○ b. Destination
>
> ○ c. Source
>
> ○ d. Action
>
> ○ e. Service

The correct answer is c. The **SRC** parameter defines the source of the request. The **SRV** defines the target SID. The **DST** parameter defines the destination server. The parameter **ACT** is used for the action to be taken (accept or reject) for the requested connection. You should recognize that Service is not a parameter for CMAN rules.

Question 5

> When using Connection Manager to translate between two network proto-
> cols, where must these protocols be installed?
>
> ○ a. Only on the client
>
> ○ b. Only on the server
>
> ○ c. On both the client and server
>
> ○ d. On the Connection Manager middle tier
>
> ○ e. On the client, server, and Connection Manager middle tier

The correct answer is d. The Connection Manager is installed on the middle tier
of a three-tier architecture to provide translation between different network protocols on the client and server. This replaces the functionality of the Oracle 7
MultiProtocol Interchange. Read the question carefully; it asks "where must these
protocols be installed"—with "protocols" being plural. The client and server each
have one of these protocols installed. But, only the CMAN middle tier requires
both protocols be installed in a multiprotocol environment.

Question 6

> What will be the result of the following Connection Manager rule?
>
> `(RULE = (SRC=svr1)(DST=svr2)(SRV=prod1)(ACT=REJ) )`
>
> ○ a. Connection requests from **svr2** will not be allowed to connect
> to **svr1** databases.
>
> ○ b. Connection requests from **svr2** will be allowed to connect to **svr1**
> databases.
>
> ○ c. Connection requests from **svr1** will not be allowed to connect to
> **prod1** on **svr2**.
>
> ○ d. Connection requests from **prod1** will not be allowed to connect
> to **svr1**.

The correct answer is c. Answers a and b are incorrect because this rule does
not accept or reject connection requests from **svr1** to connect to other SIDs on
svr2. Answer d is incorrect because **SRC** is for the source and **SRV** is for the
SID. This rule does not allow svr1 (the source server) connection requests to
connect to the specified SID (prod1) on the destination server (svr2); the action is set to REJ (rejection).

Question 7

> What is the result of the following command?
>
> ```
> cmctl stop cm
> ```
>
> ○ a. Only the CMGW process will shut down.
> ○ b. Only the CMADM process will shut down.
> ○ c. Both the CMGW and CMADM processes will stop.
> ○ d. Both the CMGW and CMADM processes will stop if there are no current connections using CMAN.
> ○ e. No action; this is an invalid command.

The correct answer is d. Answer c is only partially true because this command will not stop the Connection Manager processes if any current connections use CMAN. The administration process cannot be running if the gateway process is stopped. Therefore, the administration process will automatically terminate when the CMGW process is stopped.

Question 8

> What are the most common commands used with the CMCTL utility?
>
> ○ a. **START, STOP, TRACE_ON, TRACE_OFF**
> ○ b. **TRACE_ON, TRACE_OFF, VERSION, STATUS**
> ○ c. **LOG_ON, LOG_OFF, START, STOP**
> ○ d. **START, STOP, STATUS**
> ○ e. **START, STOP, STATUS, VERSION**

The correct answer is e. The **LOG_ON** and **LOG_OFF** are used only to gather logging information. The **TRACE_ON** and **TRACE_OFF** are used only for information on problems. This answer relies solely on material presented in the class. Oracle says that the most common commands are **START, STOP, STATUS,** and **VERSION**; therefore, that is the correct answer.

Question 9

Which of the following is used to configure the client to use Connection Manager in an environment that uses an Oracle Names server?

○ a. **SOURCE_ROUTE=YES** in the tnsnames.ora file

○ b. **SOURCE_ROUTE=TRUE** in the sqlnet.ora file

○ c. **USE_CMAN=TRUE** in the sqlnet.ora file

○ d. **USE_CMAN=YES** in the sqlnet.ora file

○ e. **USER_CMAN=TRUE** in the tnsnames.ora file

The correct answer is c. This parameter setting will force the client to connect to the Oracle database using CMAN in the environment that uses Oracle Names. The tnsnames.ora file is used for local naming, not for Oracle Names. The **USE_CMAN** parameter must be set to TRUE not YES. If you answered "a", read the question again and note the reference to Oracle Names.

Question 10

Which of the following is not a feature provided by CMAN?

○ a. Support for a large user population

○ b. Enhanced security for connections

○ c. Multiprotocol connectivity

○ d. Easy configuration in a simple tier architecture

The correct answer is d. CMAN configuration should be used in a three-tier architecture with CMAN installed on the middle tier. Note that this question is worded in the negative Easy configuration in a simple tier architecture is an advantage of host naming.

Need To Know More?

 The first place to look for more information is the *Oracle8 Reference Guide,* Chapter 7 on Connection Manager, and Appendices A.3 and B.6.

 Corey, Michael J. et al. *Oracle8 Tuning.* Oracle Press, 1998. Chapter 10 contains a brief discussion of Connection Manager.

 Loney, Kevin. *Oracle8 DBA Handbook.* Oracle Press, 1998. Chapter 13 discusses the MultiProtocol Interchange and includes a brief paragraph on using Connection Manager.

 RevealNet Oracle Administration Knowledge Base. Connection Manager parameters.

Intelligent Agent Usage And Administration

. . . .

Terms you'll need to understand:

√ Intelligent Agent

√ Oracle Enterprise Manager

√ Communications Daemon

√ Repository

√ snmp_ro.ora

√ snmp_rw.ora

√ services.ora

√ catsnmp.sql

Techniques you'll need to master:

√ Understanding the purpose of the Intelligent Agent software

√ Configuring Intelligent Agent

√ Controlling Intelligent Agent

The Intelligent Agent software runs on a server and performs a variety of tasks and monitoring actions. The Oracle Enterprise Manager (OEMGR or OEM) uses intelligent agents to run jobs and monitor events on remote servers.

The Intelligent Agent process executes independently of the Oracle database; therefore, it can be running even if the database is shut down. Intelligent Agent runs on each Oracle database server and performs the following tasks:

➤ Monitors events and performs actions based on these events

➤ Accepts jobs or events

➤ Cancels jobs or events

➤ Executes and queues jobs for execution

➤ Collects the results of jobs

➤ Checks events and jobs

➤ Generates a report of the results of events and jobs

➤ Returns job and event reports to the user

➤ Handles SNMP requests

➤ Discovers services on the nodes where the agents reside

In this chapter, I'll cover how to configure and control Intelligent Agent

Configuration Of Intelligent Agent

The Intelligent Agent software is installed on each Oracle database server where jobs and events will be executed. The two methods to communicate with Intelligent Agent are the Oracle Enterprise Manager (OEMGR or OEM) and the listener control utility (lsnrctl). (This is the same lsnrctl utility that is used to control the listener process, as discussed in Chapter 4.)

The OEMGR is installed on all nodes that will act as the console. A communications daemon on the OEMGR console handles communications from OEMGR to Intelligent Agent. The daemon communicates with Intelligent Agent on the servers using Oracle Remote Operations, which is a remote procedure call mechanism based on the transparent network substrate (TNS) layer. (The TNS network protocol stack layer is covered in Chapter 3.) By default, the following listening address is used for the communications daemon:

```
(ADDRESS = (HOST=iaconsole)(PROTOCOL=tcp)(PORT=7770) )
```

The communications daemon is a multithreaded process that handles multiple activities simultaneously; as such, it performs efficiently in a large, distributed environment with multiple servers. This daemon must be operational on every console (client workstation) that is to be used by the OEMGR to communicate with Intelligent Agent.

In order to use the Intelligent Agent software with the OEMGR, you must create a repository, a set of Oracle tables that store information on job and event status, tasks performed, and messages from the communications daemon. You can create this repository on any server in your network. If you do not already have a repository created, the OEMGR will create one the first time it attempts to connect to a server that has Intelligent Agent running. Each database administrator using the OEMGR must have a repository, and you can designate one userid to be the OEMGR database administrator for all the databases on your network as long as that userid is created in all the databases and has DBA privileges in each database. See Figure 9.1.

You can configure and use the Oracle Enterprise Manager (OEMGR) without the Intelligent Agent. However, this exam is only looking at OEMGR from the point of view of how it is used with the Intelligent Agent.

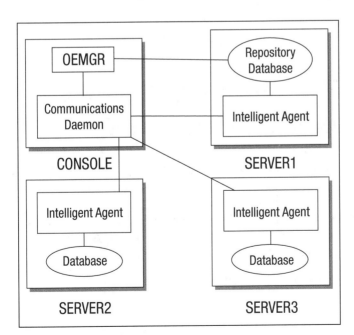

Figure 9.1   Intelligent Agent configuration.

The repository is created by the OEMGR Repository Manager. In addition to initially creating the repository, the Repository Manager will upgrade the repository automatically if it determines that the repository is out of date. If the Performance Pack is used, the Repository Manager will also create and upgrade the repository for each tool that is used.

> *Note: The Performance Pack is a separate product and is not included with the Oracle RDBMS. It works with Oracle Enterprise Manager for advanced performance monitoring and tuning of the Oracle databases.*

The console does not have to be available for Intelligent Agent to perform actions. If the console is unavailable, Intelligent Agent will queue any messages and store them on the server, delivering them to the administrator the next time the administrator logs onto the console. Queued messages are stored in the $ORACLE_HOME/network/agent directory on Unix systems and the $ORACLE_HOME\net80\agent directory on NT. The messages can be identified by the ".q" extension appended to each file name. The maximum number of queued messages is 500, after which the oldest messages are deleted as newer messages are generated.

In order to configure Intelligent Agent on the Oracle database server, you must perform three actions:

➤ Create the configuration control files.

➤ Create a user (or designate a current user) to run the jobs.

➤ Grant the necessary roles to the designated user.

Intelligent Agent Configuration Files

Intelligent Agent files should *never* be created manually. When you start Intelligent Agent for the first time, it will create the files it needs and determine what services are available on the server. If the files become corrupted or you accidentally modify any of the files, you should remove them and restart Intelligent Agent. When you restart Intelligent Agent, it will recreate the missing files. When you add new services, you must restart Intelligent Agent so that it can modify the configuration files to include the new services.

The following files are required on the Oracle database server:

➤ services.ora

➤ snmp_ro.ora

➤ snmp_rw.ora

The snmp_ro.ora and snmp_rw.ora files are placed in the TNS_ADMIN directory. If no TNS_ADMIN variable is set explicitly, Intelligent Agent will use the default, which is the same as that used for other Net8 administration files (for example, listener.ora, tnsnames.ora, and sqlnet.ora) on both the client and server: $ORACLE_HOME/network/admin (for Unix) or $ORACLE_HOME\net80\admin (for NT). The third Intelligent Agent file, services.ora, is placed in the agent subdirectory under the $ORACLE_HOME/network/agent directory (for Unix) or $ORACLE_HOME\net80\agent directory (for NT).

The snmp_ro.ora File

The snmp_ro.ora file is the primary configuration file for Intelligent Agent. The "RO" in the file name stands for *read only*. Following is an example of an snmp_ro.ora file:

```
snmp.visibleservices=(LISTENER,svr1.us.abc.com)
snmp.shortname.LISTENER=LISTENER
snmp.longname.LISTENER=LISTENER_svr1
snmp.configfile.LISTENER=/sqlhome/oracle/8.0.5/admin/listener.ora
snmp.SID.svr1.us.abc.com = prod1
snmp.oraclehome.svr1.us.abc.com = /sqlhome/oracle/8.0.5
snmp.address.svr1.us.abc.com =
        (DESCRIPTION=(ADDRESS_LIST=
            (ADDRESS=(PROTOCOL=TCP)(HOST=svr1)(PORT=1521) ) )
            (CONNECT_DATA=(SID=prod1) ) )
ifile=/sqlhome/oracle/8.0.5/admin/snmp_rw.ora
```

The snmp_rw.ora File

The second configuration file used by Intelligent Agent is the snmp_rw.ora file. This file is referenced in the snmp_ro.ora file. (See the *ifile* reference in the snmp_ro.ora file example.) Following is an example of an snmp_rw.ora file:

```
snmp.contact.LISTENER = ""
snmp.index.LISTENER = 1
snmp.contact.svr1.us.abc.com = " "
snmp.index.svr1.us.abc.com = 2
```

The services.ora File

The third file used by Intelligent Agent is the services.ora file, which contains the services discovered by the listener process. Following is an example of a services.ora file:

```
LISTENER_svr1=
        (ORACLE_LISTENER, svr1, (ADDRESS_LIST =
            (ADDRESS = (PROTOCOL=TCP)(HOST=svr1)(PORT=1521) ) ) )
```

```
svr1.us.abc.com=
        (ORACLE_DATABASE, svr1, (DESCRIPTION = (ADDRESS_LIST =
        (ADDRESS=(PROTOCOL=TCP)(HOST=svr1)(PORT=1521) ) )
        (CONNECT_DATA=(SID=prod1) ) ), LISTENER_svr1)
```

Intelligent Agent User And Role

You must create an Oracle user (or designate a current user) to become the owner of the Intelligent Agent tables. This Oracle user must have DBA privileges and a Unix (or NT) account with permissions to write to the directory that contains the services.ora file (typically the $ORACLE_HOME/network/agent directory on Unix and $ORACLE_HOME\net80\agent on NT).

> Note: If you are using one Oracle userid as your database administrator
> for the OEMGR, that userid must be created in each database on your
> network that will be accessed by OEMGR and intelligent agent.

If you are setting up the Intelligent Agent user on an NT server, you need to perform the following actions:

1. Select User Manager from the Administrative Tools program group.

2. Select New User from the User menu.

3. Enter the user and password. (Do not use *sys* or *system* as the username.)

4. Be sure that the "User Must Change Password At The Next Logon" option is not selected.

5. Select the User Rights option from the Policies menu.

6. Select the "Show Advanced User Rights" checkbox.

7. Select "Logon As A Batch Job" from the privileges list.

8. Add the advanced user right to the user you have created.

This user will be responsible for managing the jobs and events that are executed on that server and must be granted the Oracle SNMPAGENT role. To create this role, you must run the catsnmp.sql script, which is executed as part of the database creation process and is called by the catalog.sql script. The script is located in the $ORACLE_HOME/rdbms/admin directory.

Controlling And Monitoring Intelligent Agent

The listener control utility (lsnrctl) is used to start, stop, and monitor the intelligent agent. The lsnrctl utility can be used either in command-line mode or by first starting the lsnrctl utility and then issuing commands from inside lsnrctl.

The **DBSNMP_START** command is used to start Intelligent Agent and the **DBSNMP_STOP** command is used to stop it. The **DBSNMP_STATUS** command provides general information on Intelligent Agent.

For NT, the lsnrctl utility is started with the **LSNRCTL80** command. This is also used for command-line actions (for example, **LSNRCTL80 DBSNMP_START**).

Note: The prompt within the lsnrctl utility on NT is lsnrctl and not lsnrctl80.

Two additional methods can be used instead of the **LSNRCTL80** commands on NT. This is the NT services panel and the net commands at the DOS level. The DOS net commands on an NT platform are:

➤ NET START OracleAgent

➤ NET STOP OracleAgent

➤ NET STATUS

It is important to know there are various methods for starting and stopping and obtaining status information for Intelligent Agent on an NT platform. It is not necessary to know how to do this using the NT services panel, but you should know that this is an option.

The Oracle Enterprise Manager (OEMGR) communicates with Intelligent Agent to execute jobs and monitor events. The communication daemon works with Intelligent Agent to gather information and perform a variety of tasks. Information gathered by Intelligent Agent is displayed to the user via OEMGR.

The Job Scheduling and Event Management windows in the OEMGR are used to interface with Intelligent Agent. Job and event requests are sent to Intelligent Agent via the communications daemon. Reports and messages are returned to the OEMGR.

Configuration and usage of the Oracle Enterprise Manager are not included in the Oracle8 Network Administration exam.

Practice Questions

Question 1

Which of the following are configuration files for the Oracle Intelligent Agent? [Choose the three best answers]

❑ a. services.ora

❑ b. names.ora

❑ c. listener.ora

❑ d. snmp_ro.ora

❑ e. snmp.ora

❑ f. snmp_rw.ora

The correct answers are a, d, and f. The snmp_ro.ora is the main configuration file for Intelligent Agent, and the snmp_rw.ora is referenced in the snmp_ro.ora file. The services.ora file contains the services discovered by the listener. The names.ora file is used for Oracle Names, and the listener.ora file is used to configure the listener process. There is no snmp.ora file.

Question 2

Your assistant mistakenly edits the snmp_rw.ora file. What should you do?

○ a. Nothing. Intelligent Agent will re-create this file the next time it is started.

○ b. Nothing. Oracle Enterprise Manager will re-create this file the next time it is started.

○ c. Reinstall Intelligent Agent and re-create this file using the lsnrctl utility.

○ d. Remove the files and restart Intelligent Agent.

○ e. Call Oracle support immediately.

The correct answer is d. You should never edit or try to manually create the Intelligent Agent configuration files. If any of the files becomes corrupted, you should remove all three files and then restart Intelligent Agent. If the files are not there, then Intelligent Agent will re-create them. If you do not remove the files, Intelligent Agent will not re-create them and will not be able to function properly.

Question 3

How is the repository for the Oracle Enterprise Manager created?

- ○ a. It is created by running the catsnmp.sql script.
- ○ b. It is created automatically by OEMGR when it connects to a server running Intelligent Agent.
- ○ c. It is created automatically under the sys user when you create your database.
- ○ d. It is created automatically under the system user when you create your database.
- ○ e. It is created automatically for the sys user when OEMGR connects to the database on a server running Intelligent Agent.

The correct answer is b. When the database administrator logs on to a server where Intelligent Agent is running, the OEMGR will automatically create the repository if none exists on the network. The repository should never be created under the sys or system Oracle ID. The catsnmp.sql script is used to create the SNMPAGENT role. I consider this a trick question because you can use OEMGR with a repository even if you are not using the Intelligent Agent.

Question 4

Which of the following is performed by Intelligent Agent?

- ○ a. Creating agents
- ○ b. Executing a job and monitoring an event
- ○ c. Reporting on the status of the listener
- ○ d. Reporting the status of the communications daemon

The correct answer is b. Intelligent Agent is used to execute jobs and monitor events. It can return a report or execute other actions based on the results of the job or event. I have marked this as a trick question because you could easily read more into it than it actually states, especially if you are an experienced user. An experienced user might want to consider c as being correct because you could write a job to be executed by Intelligent Agent to perform this action. Be careful to read the question exactly as it is stated and pick the most appropriate answer. Don't add your experiences into the question and answers.

Question 5

> What methods can be used to start Intelligent Agent on an NT server?
>
> ○ a. lsnrctl start, NT services panel, net start OracleAgent
>
> ○ b. lsnrctl80 dbsnmp_start, NT services panel, net start OracleAgent
>
> ○ c. lsnrctl80 dbsnmp_start, net start OracleAgent
>
> ○ d. lsnrctl 80 dbsnmp_start, NT services panel
>
> ○ e. lsnrctl80 start, net start OracleAgent

The correct answer is b. Three methods can start and stop Intelligent Agent for an NT platform: the **LSNRCTL80** command (remember the version is part of the command on NT), the NT services panel, and the **NET START OracleAgent** at the DOS prompt. This type of question can be the hardest because there are multiple items in each answer. You need to look closely and eliminate any answer that is not complete. While answers c and d are partially correct, they are not complete. You need to choose the best answer.

Question 6

> Which of the following is not true when creating a user on the NT server for the repository manager?
>
> ○ a. You can use the User Manager tool.
>
> ○ b. The user name must not be *sys* or *system.*
>
> ○ c. The user should be given the "Logon As A Batch Job" privilege.
>
> ○ d. The user should have the "User Must Change Password At The Next Logon" option checked.

The correct answer is d. Look carefully at the question and note that this is asking which is *not* true. The user should *not* have the "User Must Change Password At The Next Logon" option checked; therefore, this is the correct answer.

Question 7

> What component is used to discover services on the server?
>
> ○ a. Intelligent Agent
>
> ○ b. Net8 Assistant
>
> ○ c. Names Server
>
> ○ d. Connection Manager

The correct answer is a. Intelligent Agent performs a discovery process to determine the services that are available on the node or server on which it is operating.

Question 8

> In which file can you see the services discovered by Intelligent Agent?
>
> ○ a. services.ora
>
> ○ b. snmp_ro.ora
>
> ○ c. snmp_rw.ora
>
> ○ d. listener.ora

The correct answer is a. While you should never edit the SERVICES.ORA file, you can view this file to see the services discovered by Intelligent Agent. The snmp_ro.ora and snmp_rw.ora are Intelligent Agent configuration files. The listener.ora file is the configuration file for the listener process.

Question 9

> What role is created for Intelligent Agent?
>
> ○ a. DBSNMP_AGENT
>
> ○ b. DBSNMP_ADMIN
>
> ○ c. ADMINISTRATOR
>
> ○ d. SNMPAGENT

The correct answer is d. The SNMPAGENT role is created by the catsnmp.sql script when the database is created and the catalog script is executed.

Need To Know More?

 The first place to look for more information is the *Oracle Enterprise Manager Administrator's Guide* Release 1.6.0. Chapter 6, "Agents and Communications Daemons."

 Austin, David. *Using Oracle8*. QUE, 1998. Chapter 4, "Managing with Oracle Enterprise Manger (OEM)," contains screenprints and excellent diagrams on both OEM and Intelligent Agent.

Troubleshooting Net8

Terms you'll need to understand:

√ Logging

√ sqlnet.log

√ listener.log

√ names.log

√ Tracing

√ trcasst

Techniques you'll need to master:

√ Analyzing and resolving problems with Net8

√ Configuring and using logging

√ Configuring and using tracing

√ Using the Oracle Trace Assistant

This chapter covers how to obtain information concerning a Net8 problem, analyze the situation, and resolve the problem. The Oracle tools for trouble-shooting networking problems are logging, tracing, and the Oracle Trace Assistant.

Troubleshooting Overview

Before you begin the process of troubleshooting the Net8 problem, you should verify that the problem is not with the network functionality or the database. It is also important to find out if the problem is with a single workstation or program or if the problem is widespread.

Check that you can connect from the workstation to the server. If you cannot make a connection between the client and the server, you should look for a network problem. You can use the operating system **ping** command (*ping host*) to test for network connectivity. Also check to be sure that the network protocol and the Oracle network protocol adapter have been installed on both the client and the server.

Use either the tnsping utility or Net8 Assistant to check for connectivity to the service name. The **tnsping** command can be issued at the operating-system level (*tnsping service_name*); it returns an estimate of the number of millisec-onds for a roundtrip connection to the specified service name. If the connection fails, the **tnsping** command returns an error message. Because the tnsping util-ity does not actually make a connection to the database, it does not require an Oracle username and password.

To test connectivity using Net8 Assistant, highlight the Service Names icon and then select Test Service Names Connectivity from the Tools item on the toolbar. See Figure 10.1.

Next, you should connect to the server and check that both the listener and the database are operational. You can perform a listener control utility (**lsnrctl**) com-mand to check the status of the listener and ensure it is listening for that database SID. Use the **LSNRCTL services** command to check to see if the listener is refusing any connections. (See Chapter 4 for examples of the information pro-vided by the **LSNRCTL status** and **LSNRCTL services** commands.) You can check that the database is operational by logging directly into the database on the server. You can check the Net8 listener on the server by forcing a connection to connect via Net8 (for example, *sqlplus scott@prod1*).

If you need additional information to analyze and resolve the problem, you should enable tracing and logging. Oracle recommends that you start with the client side. If the problem is still unresolved, then enable logging and/or tracing

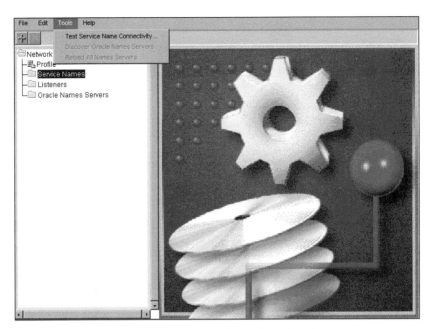

Figure 10.1   Testing Connectivity with Net8 Assistant.

on the middle tier, and finally on the server. It may be necessary to enable logging and/or tracing at all levels if the problem is complex and Oracle support is needed. (By obtaining information at all levels, Oracle support will be able to get a detailed report of the problem.)

Oracle log and trace files are used to obtain information on the interaction between the various network components. You can evaluate the information in the log and trace files to determine the cause of the error message. Three tiers can be configured to obtain log and trace information: client, middle tier, and Oracle database server. The sqlnet.ora file can be configured on any of these levels to obtain logging and tracing information on the connection.

If you are using Connection Manager on the middle tier, you can configure the cman.ora file to obtain additional information. If you are using an Oracle names server, you can configure the logging and tracing parameters of the names.ora configuration file. At the Oracle database level, a listener.ora file configures logging and tracing for the listener process. See Figure 10.2.

Use the checklist below as a guide to resolving Net8 problems.

Troubleshooting Checklist

1. Is the problem widespread or related to one workstation or program?

2. Can you make a connection from the client to the server?

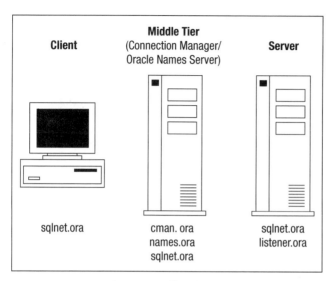

Figure 10.2 Configuration files for troubleshooting networking problems.

3. Are the network protocol and Oracle network protocol adapters installed on both the client and server?

4. Is the listener operational and listening for that database?

5. Is the database operational?

6. If necessary, enable logging and/or tracing to obtain more information.

Logging In Net8

Logs provide helpful information on the status of network components. When errors are encountered in Net8, the error message is placed in the log file. The database administrator or network administrator can use this information to review the error message and error stack.

When using the log file to analyze an error, you first need to go down the file until you reach the error code and message that matches the error you received from the application. This error message is usually near the end of the log file. At this point, start reading up the file until your find the first nonzero entry. This is usually the actual cause of the error. If this error message does not provide sufficient information, review the error messages continuing to read up the file. If the log file does not provide sufficient information, you will need to enable tracing to obtain more detailed information.

Logging On The Client

In order to ensure that all errors are recorded, logging cannot be disabled on the client. The log file for the client can be redirected to another directory or renamed by setting parameters in the sqlnet.ora file. The sqlnet.ora file can either be edited manually or by using Net8 Assistant. Because manual configuration increases the possibility for configuration errors, Oracle recommends using Net8 Assistant to create or change the sqlnet.ora file.

To configure the sqlnet.ora file using Net8 Assistant, highlight the Profile icon and then chose General from the pull-down list, and click on the Logging tab. This screen allows you to specify the directory and file for the client. When you have completed filling in the information, remember to save your configuration by selecting Save Network Configuration from the File menu on the toolbar. See Figure 10.3.

The parameters configured for logging on the client are **LOG_ DIRECTORY_CLIENT** and **LOG_FILE_CLIENT**. The default for the **LOG_FILE_CLIENT** is sqlnet.log, and the default for the **LOG_ DIRECTORY_CLIENT** is the directory from which the executable is started.

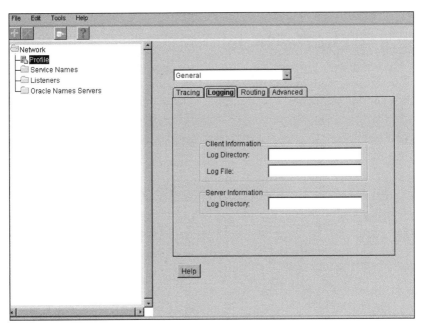

Figure 10.3   Net8 Assistant logging configuration screen.

The following is an example of the information that is provided in a sqlnet.log file on a client workstation:

```
Fatal NI connect error 12545, connecting to:
 (DESCRIPTION=(ADDRESS=(PROTOCOL=TCP)(HOST=default_host)
   (PORT=1521))(CONNECT_DATA=(SID=ORCL)(CID=(PROGRAM=C:\ORANT\
   JRE11\BIN\JAVA.EXE)(HOST=DEFAULT)(USER=barbara))))

  VERSION INFORMATION:
       TNS for 32-bit Windows: Version 8.0.4.0.0 - Production
       Windows NT TCP/IP NT Protocol Adapter for 32-bit Windows:
         Version 8.0.5.0.0 - Production
  Time: 09-OCT-99 17:35:37
  Tracing to file: c:\orant\net80\trace\sqlnet.trc
  Tns error struct:
    nr err code: 12206
    TNS-12206: TNS:received a TNS error during navigation
    ns main err code: 12545
    TNS-12545: Connect failed because target host or object does
      not exist
    ns secondary err code: 12560
    nt main err code: 515
```

Logging On The Server

The server has two types of log files: one for incoming connection requests (configured according to the parameters in the sqlnet.ora file) and another for the listener process (configured according to the parameters in the listener.ora file). If there is no sqlnet.ora file, the default of "no logging" is used. The default for the listener process is to enable logging.

The sqlnet.ora file is configured to log information on the networking operation at the server side for incoming requests. Net8 Assistant can be used to configure only the **LOG_DIRECTORY_SERVER** parameter; the default of sqlnet.log is used for the file name. The parameters configured for logging on the client are **LOG_DIRECTORY_SERVER** and **LOG_FILE_SERVER**. The defaults for these parameters are the same as for the corresponding client entries. See Figure 10.3.

The parameters for logging the listener process are logging_<listener_name>, **LOG_DIRECTORY_**<listener_name> and LOG_FILE_<listener_name>, all of which are configured in the listener.ora file. The listener log file includes audit trail information about each client connection request and most of the listener control utility commands. Also included in the listener log file is when the listener was started and stopped. Unlike logging on the client side, you can

. . . .

disable the logging of the listener process. The default for **LOGGING_**
<listener_name> is for it be enabled. To turn logging off, this parameter must
be explicitly included in the listener.ora file and must be defined as OFF.

Following is an example of the information provided in a listener.log file:

```
TNSLSNR for IBM/AIX RISC System/6000: Version 8.0.5.0.0 -
   Production on 10-OCT-99 08:09:21

Copyright (c) Oracle Corporation 1994. All rights reserved.

System parameter file is /orax5/oracle/8.0.5/network/admin/
   listener.ora
Log messages written to /orax5/oracle/8.0.5/network/log/
   listener.log
Trace information written to /orax5/oracle/8.0.5/network/trace/
   listener.trc
Trace level is currently 0

Listening on: (ADDRESS=(PROTOCOL=tcp)(DEV=6)(HOST=120.1.1.1)
   (PORT=1521))
TIMESTAMP * CONNECT DATA [* PROTOCOL INFO] * EVENT [* SID] *
   RETURN CODE
10-OCT-99 08:09:21 * (CONNECT_DATA=(CID=(PROGRAM=)(HOST=svr1)
   (USER=oracle))(COMMAND=status)(ARGUMENTS=64)(SERVICE=LISTENER)
   (VERSION=134238208)) * status * 0
10-OCT-99 08:09:48 * (CONNECT_DATA=(SID=T80RA)(CID=(PROGRAM=)
   (HOST=svr1)(USER=oracle))) * (ADDRESS=(PROTOCOL=tcp)
   (HOST=120.1.1.1)(PORT=1190)) * establish * T80RA * 0
System parameter file is /orax5/oracle/8.0.5/network/admin/
   listener.ora
Log messages written to /orax5/oracle/8.0.5/network/log/
   listener.log
Trace information written to /orax5/oracle/8.0.5/network/trace/
   listener.trc
Trace level is currently 0
10-OCT-99 08:10:33 * (CONNECT_DATA=(CID=(PROGRAM=)(HOST=svr1)
   (USER=oracle))(COMMAND=reload)(ARGUMENTS=64)
   (SERVICE=LISTENER)(VERSION=134238208)) * reload * 0
10-OCT-99 08:10:38 * (CONNECT_DATA=(CID=(PROGRAM=)(HOST=svr1)
   (USER=oracle))(COMMAND=stop)(ARGUMENTS=64)(SERVICE=LISTENER)
   (VERSION=134238208)) * stop * 0

TNSLSNR for IBM/AIX RISC System/6000: Version 8.0.5.0.0 -
   Production on 10-OCT-99 08:10:45

Copyright (c) Oracle Corporation 1994. All rights reserved.
```

```
System parameter file is /orax5/oracle/8.0.5/network/admin/
   listener.ora
Log messages written to /orax5/oracle/8.0.5/network/log/
   listener.log
Trace information written to /orax5/oracle/8.0.5/network/trace/
listener.trc
Trace level is currently 0

Listening on: (ADDRESS=(PROTOCOL=tcp)(DEV=6)(HOST=120.1.1.1)
   (PORT=1521))
TIMESTAMP * CONNECT DATA [* PROTOCOL INFO] * EVENT [* SID] *
   RETURN CODE
10-OCT-99 08:10:45 * (CONNECT_DATA=(CID=(PROGRAM=)(HOST=svr1)
   (USER=oracle))(COMMAND=status)(ARGUMENTS=64)(SERVICE=LISTENER)
   (VERSION=134238208)) * status * 0
```

Logging For The Oracle Names Server

Although logging is mandatory for the Oracle names server, you can control several aspects of the logging process with parameters in the names.ora file.

The directory for the log file is operating-system specific. You can override this by setting the **NAMES.LOG_DIRECTORY** parameter in the names.ora configuration file. The log file will always have a .log extension with the default name of names.log. You can override the log file name (but not the .log extension) using the names.log_file parameter in the names.ora configuration file. In addition, you can set the names.log_unique parameter to True if you want to maintain copies of your log files.

Logging For Connection Manager

The log file for Connection Manager is controlled by parameters in the **CMAN_PROFILE** section of the cman.ora configuration file. Connection Manager provides logging at levels 0 to 4, with 4 providing the most-detailed information. (The default is to set the logging level to 0.) If you want to include logging for the TNS network protocol stack layer, you must explicitly set **SHOW_TNS_INFO** to YES.

The following is an example of the **CMAN_PROFILE** section of the cman.ora file with an entry for logging.

You cna turn logging on with the **LOG_ON** command inthe cmctl utility. The cmctl command **LOG_OFF** will turn loggin off. See Chapter 8 for more information on the cmctl utility.

```
cman_profile =
    (parameter_list =
        (maximum_relays = 512)
        (log_level = 1)
        (show_tns_info = yes)
        (tracing = no)
        (use_async_call = yes)
        (authentication_level = 0)
    )
```

Tracing In Net8

If the log file does not provide sufficient information, then the trace file—which contains information on the internal operation of the various components of Net8—is used to obtain detailed information for analyzing a connection problem. The trace files include the information on the network protocol stack layer with details on the routines used within each of the layers. Because not all layers of the protocol stack are used for each connection, do not expect to see entries in the trace file for every layer. To review the various protocol stack layers and their functions, see Chapter 3. Each of the layers may have multiple routines, and each routine is prefixed with the alias for that layer. Each layer may call routines in other layers one or more times during the connection process. See Table 10.1.

Depending upon the level of tracing configured, this file may contain very detailed statements of each event as it is executed. Tracing is disabled by default. Because tracing writes detailed information to a file, it can have an impact on performance and should be used only when this information is needed to resolve a problem. You should enable tracing only for the time that it takes to reproduce the error. You should also remember that, because extensive information is being written to a log file, the targeted directory should have sufficient space for the trace files.

Table 10.1   Protocol Stack TNS Layer Components.

Alias	Layer
NI	Net8 Interface Layer
NR	Network Routing
NN	Network Naming (Oracle Names)
NS	Network Session (main and secondary layers)
NA	Network Authentication (NAU) and Network Encryption (NAE)
NT	Network Transport (main, secondary, and operating system layers)

The common levels for tracing are **OFF**, **USER**, **ADMIN**, and **SUPPORT**. The exceptions to this are for Intelligent Agent which does not suppoort tracing and Connection Manager which, according to Oracle, does not have the **SUPPORT** level. If you are asked about obtaining detailed information, the answer will usually be to set tracing to **SUPPORT**.

Tracing On The Client

In order to configure tracing on the client, you can manually create or edit the sqlnet.ora file or you can use Net8 Assistant. (Oracle recommends using Net8 Assistant in order to avoid syntax errors.) To use Net8 Assistant, highlight the Profile icon, chose General from the pull-down list, and click on the Tracing tab. This screen allows you to specify the level, directory, file, and whether each trace file should have a unique name. The trace level is selectable from a pull-down menu. The setting for a unique trace file name is a checkbox. The file and directory names need to be filled in with a valid directory name and a file name of your choice. When you have completed filling in this information, remember to save your configuration by selecting Save Network Configuration from the File menu on the toolbar. See Figure 10.4.

The parameters used to configure tracing on the client are **TRACE_ LEVEL_CLIENT**, **TRACE_DIRECTORY_CLIENT**, **TRACE_FILE_ CLIENT**, and **TRACE_UNIQUE_CLIENT**. The default for the

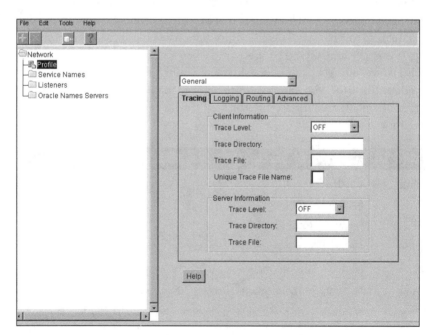

Figure 10.4 Net8 Assistant tracing configuration screen.

TRACE_FILE_CLIENT is SQLNET.TRC, and the default for the **TRACE_DIRECTORY_CLIENT** is the $ORACLE_HOME/network/ trace (or ORACLE_HOME\net80\trace for NT). The trace level is set to OFF by default. The trace level can also be set to USER, ADMIN, or SUPPORT. (The maximum information is obtained by setting the trace level to SUPPORT.) By default, the trace file will be overwritten each time. In order to save the trace files for analysis, you need to set the **TRACE_UNIQUE_ CLIENT** to ON. This will append the process ID (PID) to the end of each file name.

The following is a partial example of a client trace file.

```
-- TRACE CONFIGURATION INFORMATION FOLLOWS --
New trace stream is "c:\orant\net80\trace\sqlnet.trc.trc"
New trace level is 16
-- TRACE CONFIGURATION INFORMATION ENDS --
nigini: entry
nigini: Count in NI global area now: 1
nigini: Count in NI global area now: 1
nrigbi: entry
nrigbni: entry
nrigbni: Unable to get data from navigation file tnsnav.ora
nrigbni: exit
nrigbi: exit
nigini: exit
niqname: Hst is already an NVstring.
niqname: Inserting CID.
niotns: entry
niotns: niotns: setting up interrupt handler...
niotns: Not trying to enable dead connection detection.
niotns: Calling address: (DESCRIPTION=(ADDRESS_LIST=(ADDRESS=
  (PROTOCOL=BEQ)(PROGRAM=oracle80)(ARGV0=oracle80orcl)
  (ARGS='(DESCRIPTION=(LOCAL=YES)(ADDRESS=(PROTOCOL=beq)))')))
  (CONNECT_DATA=(SID=orcl)(CID=(PROGRAM=C:\ORANT\BIN\OSTART80.EXE)
  (HOST=DEFAULT)(USER=barbara))))
nricall: entry
nric2a: entry
nric2a: Getting local community information
nriglp: entry
nriglp: Looking for local addresses setup by nrigla
nriglp: No addresses in the preferred address list
nriglp: exit
nric2a: TNSNAV.ORA is not present. No local communities entry.
nrigla: entry
nrigla: Getting local address information
nrigla: Address list being processed.
nrigla: No community information so all addresses are local
```

```
nrigla: exit
nridst: entry
nridst: Resolving address to use to call destination or next hop
nridst: Processing address list.
nridst: No community entries so iterate over address list
nridst: exit
nric2a: This is a local community access
nric2a: exit
nricall: Got routable address information.
nricall: Making call with following address information:
  (DESCRIPTION=(CONNECT_DATA=(SID=orcl)(CID=(PROGRAM=C:\ORANT\
  BIN\OSTART80.EXE)(HOST=DEFAULT)(USER=barbara)))
  (ADDRESS=(PROTOCOL=BEQ)(PROGRAM=oracle80)(ARGV0=oracle80orcl)
  (ARGS='(DESCRIPTION=(LOCAL=YES)(ADDRESS=(PROTOCOL=beq)))'))).
nricdt: entry
nricdt: Calling with outgoing connect data:
  (DESCRIPTION=(ADDRESS_LIST=(ADDRESS=(PROTOCOL=BEQ)
  (PROGRAM=oracle80)(ARGV0=oracle80orcl)(ARGS='(DESCRIPTION=
  (LOCAL=YES)(ADDRESS=(PROTOCOL=beq)))'))))(CONNECT_DATA=(SID=orcl)
  (CID=(PROGRAM=C:\ORANT\BIN\OSTART80.EXE)(HOST=DEFAULT)
  (USER=barbara)))).
nscall: entry
nscall: connecting...
nsc2addr: entry
```

A trace file from the Support setting can easily be 12 pages or longer. Due to space limitations, it is not possible to include a complete sample trace file. For the purposes of the exam, you will not be required to analyze a trace file and diagnosis the problem.

Tracing On The Server

Tracing the Net8 process at the server side is set using the following sqlnet.ora parameters: **TRACE_DIRECTORY_SERVER, TRACE_FILE_SERVER,** and **TRACE_LEVEL_SERVER.** These sqlnet.ora parameters correlate to the client trace parameters and perform the same actions.

In order to perform diagnostics on the listener process, you must set the tracing parameters in the listener.ora file. The following parameters set the listener tracing process: **TRACE_DIRECTORY_<listener_name>, TRACE_FILE_ <listener_name>,** and **TRACE_LEVEL_<listener_name>.** These parameters work the same as the corresponding sqlnet.ora parameters. The trace levels are also the same (OFF, USER, ADMIN, and SUPPORT). The default is for tracing to be OFF.

The following is a partial example of a listener trace file:

```
TNSLSNR for IBM/AIX RISC System/6000: Version 8.0.5.0.0 -
  Production on 04-APR-99 14:04:21

Copyright (c) Oracle Corporation 1994. All rights reserved.


-- TRACE CONFIGURATION INFORMATION FOLLOWS --
New trace stream is "/orax5/oracle/8.0.5/network/trace/
  listener.trc"
New trace level is 16
-- TRACE CONFIGURATION INFORMATION ENDS --
nscontrol: entry
nttctl: entry
ntvlin: entry
ntvllt: entry
ntvllt: No PROTOCOL.ORA file is found
ntvllt: exit
ntvlin: exit
nscontrol: cmd=10, lcl=0x0
nscontrol: normal exit
tnslsnr: Resolved "CONNECT_TIMEOUT_LISTENER" to: 60
tnslsnr: Resolved "STARTUP_WAIT_TIME_LISTENER" to: 0
........
sntseltst: FOUND: connection request on socket 6
sntseltst: Events on 1 cxds
nsevwait: 1 newly-posted event(s)
nsevwait: event is 0x1, on 1
nsevwait: 1 posted event(s)
nsevwait: exit (0)
tnslsnr: Event on cxd 0x20018078.
tnslsnr: Allocating cxd 0x20015a18
nsanswer: entry
nsopen: entry
nsmal: entry
nsmal: 472 bytes at 0x20015ab8
nsmal: normal exit
nsopen: opening transport...
....
nttcon: NT layer TCP/IP connection has been established.
nttcon: exit
nsopen: transport is open
nsnainit: entry
nsnainit: answer
nsnadct: entry
nsnadct: normal exit
```

```
nsnasvnainfo: entry
nsnasvnainfo: NA disabled for this connection
nsnasvnainfo: normal exit
nainit: entry
nagblini: entry
nau_gin: entry
nau_gparams: entry
nam_gbp: Reading parameter "sqlnet.authentication_required" from
  parameter file
nam_gbp: Parameter not found
nau_gparams: Using default value "FALSE"
nau_gslf: entry
nam_gic: entry
nam_gic: Counting # of items in "sqlnet.authentication_services"
  parameter
nam_gic: Parameter not found
nam_gic: Found 0 items
nam_gic: exit
nau_gslf: Using default value "all available adapters"
```

Tracing On The Oracle Names Server

The names.ora configuration file is used to control tracing for the Oracle names server. By default, tracing is set to OFF. The names.ora file supports configuration of the same trace levels as the sqlnet.ora and listener.ora files (OFF, USER, ADMIN, SUPPORT) and the ability to make the trace files unique (**NAMES.TRACE_UNIQUE**). In order to enable tracing, you must set the **NAMES.TRACE_LEVEL** to one of the supported levels.

The directory used for the trace file is operating-system specific, but this default can be overridden using the **NAMES.TRACE_DIRECTORY** parameter. The default name for the trace file is NAMES.TRC. By setting the **NAMES.TRACE_FILE**, you can specify a different file name; but, you cannot change the .trc file extension.

An additional parameter is available for enabling an internal mechanism to control tracing by function name (**NAMES.TRACE_FUNC**). The default for this parameter is False. Unless you are familiar with the various function calls, this parameter may not provide any information that you will find useful. However, it may be useful when you are working with Oracle Support to resolve a problem.

Tracing For Connection Manager

Two parameters can be used to set tracing for Connection Manager: **TRACING** and **TRACE_DIRECTORY**. These parameters are set in the

CMAN_PROFILE section of the cman.ora file. In the cman.ora file you can only set TRACING to YES or NO, with No the default. The level of tracing for CMAN is limited to USER and ADMIN. You can issue the cmctl command TRACE_ON <level> to start tracing. The TRACE_OFF command in cmctl will turn tracing off. See Chapter 8 for more information on cmctl.

Following is an example of the CMAN_PROFILE section of the cman.ora file with an entry for tracing.

```
cman_profile =
    (parameter_list = =
        (maximum_relays = 512)
        (log_level = 1)
        (show_tns_info = yes)
        (tracing = yes)
        (trace_directory = /orax1/oracle/admin/cman)
        (use_async_call = yes)
        (authentication_level = 0)
    )
```

Trace Assistant

Trace Assistant is used to format the output from trace files. It will help you analyze the trace file by providing a more understandable view of the flow of the packets with an indication of which Net8 component is generating an error and related error codes. Before using Trace Assistant, obtaint he most detailed trace file possible. If you set the trace level to SUPPORT. This level will include the contents of each Net8 packet.

Trace Assistant analyzes the events in the trace file at the Transparent Network Substrate (TNS) network protocol stack layer and at the Two Task Common (TTC) layer. By providing statistical information on both of these layers, you can identify potential bottlenecks and performance issues.

The amount and type of information provided by the Trace Assistant is selectable by the user. The Trace Assistant can be invoked at the command line with the **TRCASST** command. The syntax for this command is:

```
trcasst [options] <filename>
```

The default options for Trace Assistant are -odt -e -s which provides a detailed display of the Net layer and TTC layer information with error and statistical information displayed. For a listing of the available options, see Table 10.2.

Table 10.2	Trace Assistant options.
Option	**Display**
-o	Display SQL*Net and TTC information
c	Combined with -o for summary SQL*Net information
d	Combined with -o for detailed SQL*Net information
u	Combined with -o for summary TTC information
t	Combined with -o for detailed TTC information
-p	Display performance measurements (internal use only)
-s	Display statistical information
-e	Display error information
0	Combined with -e for NS error number translation
1	Combined with -e for NS error translation plus all other errors
2	Combined with -e for NS error number without translations

Following is an example of the output from a **TRCSST** command using the default options:

```
****************************************************************
*                  Trace  Assistant  Tool                     *
*                       TRCASST                                *
****************************************************************
Error found. Error Stack follows:
id: 00000
Operation code: 00065
NS Error 1: 12541
NT Generic Error: 00511
OS Error: 00000
NS & NT Errors Translation
12541, 00000, "TNS:no listener"
//*Cause: The connection request could not be completed because the
// listener is not running.
//*Action: Ensure that the supplied destination address matches one
// of the addresses used by the listener - compare the TNSNAMES.ORA
// entry with the appropriate LISTENER.ORA file (or TNSNAV.ORA if
// the connection is to go by way of an Interchange). Start the
// listener on the remote machine.
/
```

```
================================================================
Trace File Statistics:
- - - - - - - - - - - - - - - - - - - - - - - - - - - - - - - - - - - - - - - - - - - - - - - - - - - - - - - -

DATABASE:
Operation Counts: 0 opens, 0 parses, 0 executes, 0 fetches.
Operation Counts: 0 opens, 0 parses, 0 executes, 0 fetches.

SQL*Net:
      Total Calls:  0 sent,   0 received,   0 upi
      Total Bytes:  0 sent,   0 received
    Maximum Bytes:  0 sent,   0 received


****************************************************************
*              Trace Assistant has completed                  *
*                        TRCASST                              *
****************************************************************
```

The following is an example of the Trace Assistant output using the -s option to obtain statistical information:

```
****************************************************************
*              Trace   Assistant   Tool                       *
*                        TRCASST                              *
****************************************************************



================================================================
Trace File Statistics:
- - - - - - - - - - - - - - - - - - - - - - - - - - - - - - - - - - - - - - - - - - - - - - - - - - - - - - - -


SQL*Net:
      Total Calls:     48 sent,    47 received,   42 upi
      Total Bytes:   4674 sent,  1499 received,
    Average Bytes:     97 sent,    31 received,
    Maximum Bytes:    271 sent,   139 received
GRAND TOTAL PACKETS    48 sent,    47 received


****************************************************************
*              Trace Assistant has completed                  *
*                        TRCASST                              *
****************************************************************
```

Common Problems With Net8

You'll find that the most common cause of problems with Oracle networking is syntax errors in the configuration files. Of these errors, the most common is to omit a keyword or a parenthesis. The only character set values that can be used are A-Z, a-z, and 0-9. Some symbols are reserved and should not be used for any of the values in the configuration files for Net8. They are ( ) \ " ' #. In addition, you should not use <space>, <tab>, <carriage return>, or <newline>within a connect descriptor. Oracle recommends using Net8 Assistant as much as possible for generating configuration files in order to avoid common syntax errors.

It is important to understand common Net8 error messages and how to resolve them. This section will provide the error code, error message, and the corrective action to resolve the common errors.

 Most of the Oracle errors for Net8 will have numbers in the 12000 range. You can assume that there is a problem related to Net8 if a user calls with an error number in that range.

Common Client Errors

The most common error messages at the client side are 12154, 12198, 12203, 12533, and 12545.

Error 12154 "TNS: could not resolve service name" can mean different things depending upon whether it is being received consistently on one client or in an intermittent fashion by various clients. If it is consistent with one client, the problem is usually a tnsnames.ora problem. The corrective action is to check the tnsnames.ora file to make sure that it is accessible and correct. The service name must not have any punctuation or other special characters and must begin with a character, not a number. This error could also be caused by duplicate sqlnet.ora files on the client or if the client has incorrectly specified the connect string. If the problem is actually related to the listener process on the server, then a different corrective action is required. (See the following section on servers.)

Error 12198 "TNS: could not find path to destination" and Error 12203 "TNS: unable to connect to destination" are both indicative of the same problem. The corrective action would be the same for both: you should check the tnsnames.ora address parameters for syntax and values. You should also check to see if this file is in the correct directory. If the tnsnames.ora file is correct and in the proper place, the listener process may not be operational on the server or the user may be logging in with an incorrect connect string.

Error 12533 "TNS: illegal ADDRESS parameter" means that the parameters required for a specific protocol are incorrect. The tnsnames.ora file is very sensitive to any errors and requires different parameters for different network protocols. By using Net8 Assistant to configure your tnsnames.ora file, you will avoid incorrect parameter specifications.

Error 12545 "TNS: name lookup failure" means that the listener on the specified server cannot be contacted. You should first verify that the address information in the tnsnames.ora file on the client and the listener.ora file on the server are correct. Another cause may be that the listener process has not been started on the server. The listener process can be checked with the **lsnrctl STATUS** command. If this is the problem, it can be easily resolved by starting the listener.

Common Server Errors

The most common problems with the listener process are error codes 01169, 12154, 12224, and 12500.

Error 01169 "The listener has not recognized the password" is self-explanatory: Either the wrong (or no) password was provided when a command requiring a password was issued. This can be easily resolved by starting the lsnrctl utility and issuing the statement **SET PASSWORD** <password>. Once the password is set, reissue the failed command within the lsnrctl utility.

Error 12154 "No listener" may be caused when so many connection requests are sent to the listener that it cannot handle them all. The solution is to increase the **QUEUESIZE**. Set a larger **QUEUESIZE** in the listener.ora file and then either stop and start the listener or issue the reload command.

Error 12224 "TNS: no listener" is usually received because the listener process is not operational on the database server. The corrective action is to start the listener process. You should be aware of two other causes of this error. If the destination address on the client does not match (e.g., host and port for tCP) the address on the server, the connection will not find a listener and will assume that the listener is not operational. The corrective action is to change the incorrect address so that they match. This error can also be the result of a compatibility issue, if the SQL*Net version running on the client is newer than the version on the server. The corrective action is to bring the versions into synch by installing a newer (or older) version on the server (or client).

Error 12500 "TNS: listener failed to start a dedicated server process" means that the listener process was unable to connect the request with the database instance

(SID) as listed in the connection request. This can be the result of an incorrect SID in the CONNECT_DATA section on the client tnsnames.ora file. You may also get this message if the user does not have adequate privileges to connect to the specified database.

If your database is configured for the Multithreaded Server (MTS) option, you should regularly check v$sysstat, v$session_wait, and v$session_event. If these show high waits, this could be an indication that there is a network problem.

Connection Manager

The most common error associated with Connection Manager is 12202 "TNS: internal navigation error". You should first check that the CMGW process has been started. If it is not operational, start CMGW. The second corrective action is to check the CMAN_RULES and determine if the connection request was rejected because it violated a CMAN RULE. Finally, check the tnsnames.ora file to be sure that the address has been correctly specified.

Intelligent Agent

If you encounter problems in starting the Oracle Intelligent Agent, the place to look is the $ORACLE_HOME/network/log directory. Error conditions are placed in the dbsnmp*.log file. On an NT operating system, errors can be viewed using the NT Event Viewer by selecting Application from the log menu item.

Practice Questions

Question 1

You have been experiencing problems with the listener refusing connections. Which of the following files is used to configure tracing for the listener process?

○ a. tnsnames.ora

○ b. sqlnet.ora

○ c. listener.ora

○ d. names.ora

○ e. cman.ora

○ f. init.ora

The correct answer is c. Tracing is configured in the listner.ora file for the listener process. The sqlnet.ora process may be used to configure tracing for Net8 connection requests incoming from the client; however, it does not provide trace information on the listener process.

Question 2

You receive a call from a user saying that he cannot connect to the database. Which of the following should be one of the first troubleshooting actions you take?

○ a. Check the basic connectivity between the client and the server.

○ b. Immediately contact Oracle Support.

○ c. Start tracing on the client workstation.

○ d. Start tracing on the server.

The correct answer is a. Before you begin tracing or contact Oracle Support, you should ensure that the issue is not a network problem. Another correct answer would be to check if the problem is localized to that workstation or if it is widespread; however, that is not one of the options listed. If you cannot connect from the client workstation to the server and the problem is not widespread, then it is probably an issue with either the individual workstation or the network. You should not begin tracing until you have checked for basic connectivity.

Question 3

How do you use Net8 Assistant to configure tracing for the client?

○ a. Highlight the Profile icon, select General Parameters from the pull-down menu, and go to the Tracing tab.

○ b. Use the Tools item from the toolbar.

○ c. Highlight the Profile icon, select General from the pull-down menu, and go to the Tracing tab.

○ d. Choose Network from the Tools menu in the toolbar and click on Test Connectivity.

The correct answer is c. You are configuring the profile (sqlnet.ora file) which is one of the icons. Highlight the Profile icon and then select General from the pull-down menu. You will see tabs for logging and tracing. To configure tracing, go to the tab for tracing. If you have not used Net8 Assistant, you should review the figures in this chapter, which show the relevant screens for setting tracing and logging parameters.

Question 4

Which of the following are the options for setting the trace level for the client?

○ a. 0, 1, 2, 3

○ b. USER, ADMIN, 16, ON

○ c. TRUE, FALSE

○ d. USER, ADMIN, SUPPORT, OFF

The correct answer is d. The tracing levels for the client and server are the same: USER, ADMIN, SUPPORT, and OFF. Experienced users may be familiar with the trace level "16" which is equivalent to SUPPORT; however, this is not one of the trace levels that will be included in the exam.

Question 5

You receive the error "ORA-12202: TNS: internal navigation error for the Connection Manager." Which of the following is the probable cause?

○ a. The CMADM process is not operational.

○ b. The CMGW process is not operational.

○ c. The CMAN_RULES parameter is set to Accepted.

○ d. The LISTENER.ORA process is not operational on the server.

The correct answer is b. The most common cause is that the CMGW process has not been started. To resolve the problem, you should start the CMGW process.

Question 6

You are finding it difficult to read and understand the trace file. Which of the following commands will interpret the file into a more readable form?

○ a. **TRCASST**

○ b. **TRACE**

○ c. **TRCFMT**

○ d. **TRCSST**

The correct answer is a. The command to format the trace file using Trace Assistant is TRCASST. This provides a readable file with error codes, messages, and statistical information.

Question 7

Which utility can be used to format the trace file?

○ a. Net8 Assistant

○ b. Net8 Service Names Wizard

○ c. Listener control utility

○ d. Names control utility

○ e. Trace Assistant

The correct answer is e. The Oracle Trace Assistant can be used at the command line to obtain a formatted version of the trace file. Trace Assistant analyzes the net layer and the Two Task Common (TTC) layers.

Question 8

A client is reporting that he is getting the following error message: "ORA-12154 TNS: could not resolve service name." Which of the following could cause this error?

○ a. The service name address is incorrect.

○ b. The service name address has an incorrect character.

○ c. The listener is not operational on the remote server.

○ d. The service name is not correct in the tnsnames.ora file.

The correct answer is d. The most likely problem is that the service name has been incorrectly defined in the tnsnames.ora file. Another possibility, which is not listed, is that the user may have incorrectly typed in the connect string. Many of the Oracle error messages have multiple possible causes. You should use a process of elimination combined with a carefully reading of the error message in order to answer this type of question.

Question 9

You tried to stop the listener and received the following error message: "TNS 01169: The listener has not recognized the password." Which action should you take?

○ a. Type in **lsnrctl STOP <password>**.

○ b. Your listener is already stopped.

○ c. Start the lsnrctl utility, set the password, then issue the **STOP** command.

○ d. You must start the listener using Trace Assistant.

○ e. Type in **lsnrctl STOP <listener_name>**.

The correct answer is c. If a password is required by your listener configuration, the listener cannot be stopped at the command line. You need to start the lsnrctl utility and set the password before you can stop the listener process.

Question 10

Where do you set logging and tracing for Connection Manager?

○ a. names.ora file

○ b. listener.ora file

○ c. **CMAN_PROFILE**

○ d. **CMAN_RULES**

○ e. sqlnet.ora

The correct answer is c. The parameters for setting tracing and logging are in the **CMAN_PROFILE** section of the cman.ora file.

Need To Know More?

 The first place to look for more information is *Oracle's Advanced Networking Option Administrator's Guide*, Release 8.0.

 Another Oracle manual that is helpful for troubleshooting network connection problems is *Net8 Getting Started*, Release 8.0.4 for Windows NT and Windows 95.

 Kreines, David C., and Laskey, Brian. *Oracle Database Administration: The Essential Reference*. O'Reilly, 1999. Chapter 5, "Oracle Network Architecture," pp. 92-96 provides a good general guide for troubleshooting Net8 problems.

 "Network Management," RevealNet Oracle Administration Knowledge Base, provides an excellent guide for troubleshooting Net8 problems, including how to set the required parameters.

Security In Net8

Terms you'll need to understand:

√ Data privacy

√ Data integrity

√ Authentication

√ Authorization

√ Data encryption

√ Cryptographic checksumming

√ Authentication services

Techniques you'll need to master:

√ Understand network security risks

√ Understand the features available with the Advanced Networking Option

√ Understand how to configure the Advanced Networking Option

Data is a very important asset to your company and should be well protected; the weakest link in securing your company data is often the network component. This chapter focuses on network security risks, how these risks can be addressed using the Oracle Advanced Networking Option, and how to configure the Oracle Advanced Networking Options.

Network Security Risks

Your environment has four major elements of risk: data privacy, data integrity, authentication, and authorization. Each must be secured to ensure a secure network. To know how to use the features of Net8 and the Advanced Networking Option (ANO) to create a secure network environment, you first need to understand what these security risks entail.

With the increase of e-commerce, unscrupulous parties have developed new methods to take advantage of unwary people and businesses. I'm sure you've seen in your local newspaper and on television the many examples of the types of problems that unsecured networks can create. And network security will continue to be a very important issue for businesses that are increasingly dependent upon new technology.

Examples using Scott (the client) and Jackel, the data thief, will be used to illustrate each type of security violation.

Data Privacy

Data privacy is ensuring that the data is not disclosed or stolen during transmission. The theft of data during transmission is applicable to both actual data and passwords. See Figure 11.1.

It is extremely easy for an intruder to tap into any type of network. By placing a tap on the network, a data thief can obtain vital information by viewing the transmissions between the client workstation and the Oracle database server.

The Oracle database stores user passwords in an encrypted form to protect them. However, during normal login operations, Net8 transmits the user password unencrypted and this is when it could be obtained by a tap on the network connection.

To ensure data privacy, data encryption is supported by the Advanced Networking option.

EXAMPLE:

Scott is using the Internet to research information to prepare a bid for a construction job. Scott then submits his bid using the client's application (which is

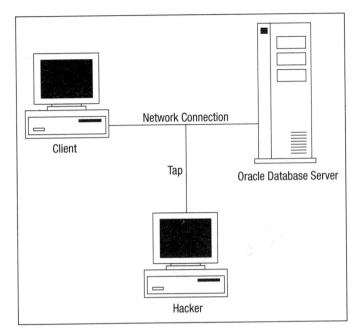

Figure 11.1   Risk to data privacy.

using an Oracle database). His rival, Jackel, had placed a tap on the network to see the information that Scott is accessing, as well as the final bid that Scott transmitted. Jackel created his own bid for the construction job, making it slightly lower than Scott's. If the data were transmitted in encrypted format, Jackel would not have been able to obtain this information.

Data Integrity

Data integrity is ensuring that data is not modified or disrupted during transmission. See Figure 11.2.

By intercepting the transmissions between the client workstation and the Oracle database server, unscrupulous parties can intercept the data. Once intercepted, this data can be rerouted to another site without the client being aware of it. This is known as *data disruption*. The data could also be intercepted, modified, and then placed back to continue through the network in a process called *data modification*.

To ensure data integrity, cryptographic checksumming is supported with the Advanced Networking Option.

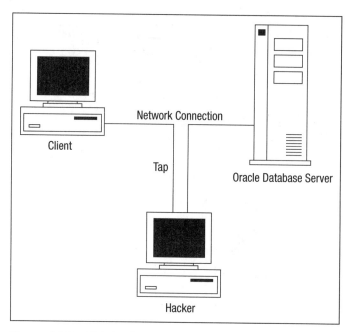

Figure 11.2 Risk to data integrity.

EXAMPLE:

Scott logs on to his Internet provider and goes to his bank account. He decides to pay his bills online. Jackel intercepts the transmissions. Instead of paying the bills Scott has indicated, Jackel transmits an order to place the money into his own account. If cryptographic checksumming had been in place, the bank would have realized that the data was modified during transmission.

Authentication

Data authentication is the process of verifying that the identities of the clients, hosts, and devices are correctly identified as a prerequisite to access the database or computer system.

Security within the database can be defined using Oracle grants, roles, and profiles. However, no matter how well the security within the database is designed, a security risk always remains unless the actual user can be identified. Some mechanism must be set in place to authenticate that the clients logging into the Oracle database are actually who they claim to be.

To authenticate the client, the Advanced Networking Option supports authentication mechanisms.

EXAMPLE:
Scott is interested in ordering books on gardening via the internet. Scott logs into his Internet provider and goes to his favorite site for purchasing books. Jackel has placed a tap on the line. When Scott provides information on his credit card for the order, Jackel records this information. Jackel later places his own orders while claiming to be Scott.

Authorization

Data authorization is the permission given to a user, program, or process to access an object or objects. Oracle uses grants and roles to determine who can access what objects and perform what actions. In order to ensure that both the clients and servers are who they claim to be (and with the necessary permissions to access an object), the Oracle Advanced Networking Option supports authentication mechanisms.

EXAMPLE:
Jackel wants to know the salary of the CEO, but he is not authorized to see this information. However, he knows that Scott is. So Jackel logs into the server claiming to be Scott and accesses this information.

Advanced Networking Option Features

As you can see from the above examples, security is a very important issue in our technology-driven world. Oracle's solution is to offer a separate product called the Advanced Networking Option (ANO), which enhances security at the network level with data encryption, cryptographic checksumming, and authentication mechanisms. These features can be used separately or in any combination.

ANO works with Connection Manager to reduce the overhead of encryption and decryption of data by passing the encrypted data between network protocols.

Data Encryption

Data encryption is a technique whereby the data is scrambled according to a specified key. Without the key, the data cannot be unscrambled. Special hardware is used to perform the encryption. ANO supports two encryption algorithms: Data Encryption Standard (DES) and RC4 by RSA Data Security, Inc. (RSA RC4).

The longer the encryption key, the more difficult it is to break the code. Oracle data encryption supports the following encryption key options:

➤ 40-bit RSA RC4 algorithm (RC4_40)

➤ 56-bit RSA RC4 (RC4_56)

➤ 128-bit data encryption RSA RC4 algorithm (RC4_128)

➤ 40-bit DES algorithm (DES40)

➤ 56-bit DES algorithm (DES)

The data is encrypted at the sending side and is unencrypted at the receiving side. Both the sender and receiver must have the same key and the same encryption algorithm to be able to encrypt and unencrypt the data. If a tap is placed on the line, the only information that will be obtained is a meaningless string of characters.

Crytographic Checksumming

Oracle's cryptographic checksumming uses MD5 (message digest) algorithm from RSA Data Security, Inc. that computes a hash value for each message packet, based on the data that the packet contains. This value is recorded at the end of the packet. At the receiving end, the same hash calculation is applied to the data to determine if it is unchanged. Without knowing the hash key, it's extremely unlikely that anyone could intercept and modify the data in such a way as to still have a valid checksum.

In addition, sequencing is used in the transmission of the packets. Each packet is labeled (e.g. A B C) before transmission. When the data packets arrive, the receiving end checks to see if the packets are in order. Using checksumming on the data that is passed ensures data integrity.

Authentication Mechanisms

Oracle's ANO provides authentication through authentication adapters that support third-party products. These third-party mechanisms are used to ensure that the user, client, and server are correctly identified. These devices fall into three types:

➤ Network authentication services such as ACE/Server, Kerberos, and CyberSAFE Challenger

➤ Token cards such as Security Dynamics' SecurID

➤ Biometric devices such as Identix TouchNet II

Network Authentication Services

Users of many different systems will often decide on a single password that is used to access all of their accounts on various servers. Although convenient for the user, this practice poses a serious security problem. If a password is compromised, then all the accounts for that user are accessible. Another common password error is to vary the password on each system by some pattern such as a number. A data thief can easily guess any logical pattern. Yet another common password problem is that the user may write down complex passwords in order to remember them. Once they are written down, they are capable of being found and used by someone else.

Network authentication services provide a secure, centralized method of authentication. It eliminates the need to rely on clients and hosts to verify identities to each other. It also reduces the risks inherent to using passwords.

Using a network authentication service provides the benefit of having a single sign-on that requires a user to memorize only one password. It also provides a centralized place for administration of users and passwords. The following list explains the process of identification using network authentication services:

1. The client requests identification from the authentication server.

2. The authentication server issues a digital certificate (also called a *ticket* or *credentials*) to the client.

3. The client passes this digital certificate to the Oracle database server when requesting a connection to the database.

4. The Oracle database server sends the digital certificate to the authentication server for verification.

5. The authentication server verifies the digital certificate and notifies the Oracle database server whether the connection request is valid. If the connection request is valid, the Oracle database server grants the client connection request. If the connection request is not valid, the Oracle database server refuses the request.

This process is also known as *mutual authentication* or *shared secrets*, because both the client and Oracle database server are obtaining validation from the same authentication server. If a user tries to access the database without first obtaining a digital certificate, the connection will be refused even if the password is correct. See Figure 11.3.

Oracle provides support for authentication servers with authentication adapters that are similar to network protocol adapters. The biggest advantage to this type of implementation is that it is transparent to both the user and the application.

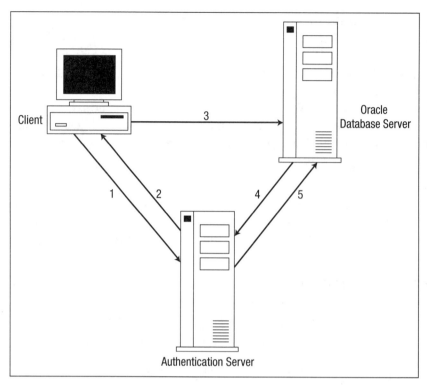

Figure 11.3 Network Authentication Services process.

No changes are required in the application code. Authentication services such as Kerberos provide the advantages of a single sign-on, centralized password storage, database link authentication, and enhanced workstation security; all of which reduce the burden of security administration.

Token Cards

Token Cards provide a one-time password method. The client is issued an access card and a personal identification number (PIN). Instead of memorizing multiple passwords, the user needs to remember only a single PIN. Security is enhanced because both the security card and the PIN are required for access. Token cards use single-use access codes that change every 60 seconds, and no two security cards can ever have the same encoded number at the same time. See Figure 11.4.

Biometric Authentication

Biometric authentication adapters provide support for devices that are linked to something that will individually identify a person, such as a fingerprint. The

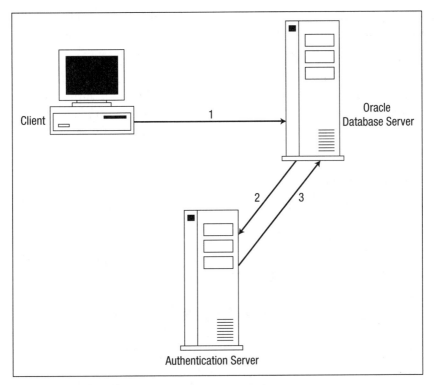

Figure 11.4   Token Card Authentication process.

biometric authentication adapters must be installed on both the client and Oracle database server, because biometric authentication data is passed between the two.

In order to use the Identix Touchsafe II biometric device, the fingerprint for each user must be enrolled in the security system. In order to log in, the user places a finger on the Touchsafe II fingerprint reader. The fingerprint is scanned and compared to the previously stored (enrolled) fingerprint. If the fingerprints match, then the user is authenticated for access.

Configuration Of ANO

In order to use features of Oracle's Advanced Networking option (ANO), it must be installed on both the client workstation and the Oracle database server. In addition, the same algorithm must be available on both the client and server. Data encryption, cryptographic checksumming, and authentication mechanisms may be used together or separately. (The options are configured using the sqlnet.ora file on both the client and server.) As we covered previously, a server may also be a client, which is true whenever you are using database links.

The sqlnet.ora file entries for the client may be included in the sqlnet.ora file configured for the server and vise versa. Net8 will use the entries in the sqlnet.ora file as appropriate.

The next sections cover the sqlnet.ora parameters that are required to configure data encryption, cryptographic checksumming, and authentication mechanisms. The following four options are configured in the sqlnet.ora file for data encryption and cryptographic checksumming:

➤ Client encryption

➤ Server encryption

➤ Client checksum

➤ Server checksum

In order to use authentication devices, only the **SQLNET. AUTHENTICATION_SERVICES** parameter is required.

Data Encryption sqlnet.ora parameters

The client sqlnet.ora parameters for data encryption are **SQLNET. ENCRYPTION_TYPES_CLIENT** and **SQLNET.ENCRYPTION_ CLIENT**. The corresponding entries on the server are **SQLNET. ENCRYPTION_TYPES_SERVER** and **SQLNET.ENCRYPTION_ SERVER**. The encryption types parameter specifies the encryption algorithm to be used (for example, DES40 for DES 40-bit).

The encryption algorithm to be used is determined by both the sqlnet.ora parameters (encryption types) and what algorithms are installed on both the client and server. The first algorithm listed in the sqlnet.ora file on the server that is also listed in the client's sqlnet.ora file is used. For example, if the client is configured with the following:

```
sqlnet.encryption_types_client = (DES40, RC4_40)
```

and the server is configured with:

```
sqlnet.encryption_types_server = (RC4_40, DES40)
```

then the RC4_40 algorithm will be used. Remember the server side will determine the method based on the order of the algorithms listed in the server sqlnet.ora file. If neither the client nor the server sqlnet.ora files lists any algorithms to be used, then any algorithm installed on both could be used.

Table 11.1	Data encryption and cryptographic checksum meaning of modes.
Accepted	On if the other side wants it turned on
Rejected	Do not turn on security
Requested	Turn on security if the other side allows it
Required	Turn on security or do not make the connection

The **SQLNET.ENCRYPTION_CLIENT** and **SQLNET.ENCRYPTION_ SERVER** parameters specify one of the following modes: Accepted, Rejected, Requested, and Required. See Table 11.1.

The Accepted parameter means the security service becomes active if that service (data encryption or cryptographic checksumming) is either requested or required by both the sending and receiving sides. The default for **CRYPTO_CHECKSUM** and encryption is Accepted. The Rejected parameter deactivates the service and will cause the connection to fail if the other side of the connection (the partner) requires that service. Requested means the service is active if the partner is set to Accepted, Requested or Required. Required causes the service to be active only if the partner is set to Accepted or Required; the connection will fail if the partner is set to Rejected. In order to better understand the results of setting these modes for connections, study Figure 11.5.

Even if the nodes are configured for security to be enabled, it cannot be enabled unless both the client and server have a common algorithm installed.

		Client			
		Accepted	Rejected	Requested	Required
S e r v e r	Accepted	Off	Off	On	On
	Rejected	Off	Off	Off	Fail
	Requested	On	Off	On	On
	Required	On	Fail	On	On

Figure 11.5 Data encryption and cryptographic checksumming modes results.

If one side is set to Accepted and the other is set to Required—but no common algorithm exists—the following error message will result:

```
ORA-12650  No common encryption or data integrity algorithm
```

In order to use data encryption, you must also specify a **SQLNET .CRYPTO_SEED** entry. This entry is used for encoding and decoding the encrypted data; therefore, it must be the same on both the client and server. (This is commonly called a *single key method*.) The **SQLNET. CRYPTO_SEED** specifies the actual key to be used in encoding and decoding the data. A series of 10 to 70 random characters should be used to form this key.

Cryptographic Checksumming sqlnet.ora Parameters

The client sqlnet.ora parameters for cryptographic checksumming are **SQLNET.CRYPTO_CHECKSUM_TYPES_CLIENT** and **SQLNET .CRYPTO_CHECKSUM_CLIENT**. The corresponding entries on the server are **SQLNET.CRYPTO_CHECKSUM_TYPES_SERVER** and **SQLNET .CRYPTO_CHECKSUM_SERVER**. The crypto_checksum_types parameters specify the algorithm (for example, MD5). The checksum parameters specify one of the following modes: Requested, Required, Accepted, and Rejected. The results of setting the modes for **SQLNET.CRYPTO_CHECKSUM_ CLIENT** and **SQLNET.CRYPTO_CHECKSUM_SERVER** are the same as the results of setting the **SQLNET.ENCRYPTION_CLIENT** and **SQLNET.ENCRYPTION_SERVER** parameters for data encryption. See Table 11.1 and Figure 11.5.

Sample sqlnet.ora File

You can configure one sqlnet.ora file that is then distributed to all the clients and servers on the network. The following is an example of a sqlnet.ora file that is configured for both data encryption and cryptographic checksumming:

```
sqlnet.crypto_seed ="oeurowieruioewrjnerejr"
sqlnet.encryption_types_client = (RC4_40, DES40)
sqlnet.encryption_client = required
sqlnet.crypto_checksum_types_client = MD5
sqlnet.crypto_checksum_client = required
sqlnet.encryption_types_server = (RC4_40, DES40)
sqlnet.encryption_server = required
sqlnet.crypto_checksum_types_server = MD5
sqlnet.crypto_checksum_server = required
```

Configuration Of Authentication Devices

The only parameter to be set in the sqlnet.ora file is the **SQLNET. AUTHENTICATION_SERVICES** parameter, which specifies the authentication adapter to be used. If this is set to NONE, then the connection request will attempt to log into the database using operating-system level security that is controlled by the database-initialization parameters.

The following is an example of a configuration to use Kerberos:

```
sqlnet.authentication_services=(KERBEROS5)
```

In addition to setting the service in the sqlnet.ora file, you should also set two parameters in the database-initialization file: **REMOTE_OS_AUTHENT** and **OS_AUTHENT_PREFIX**. The **REMOTE_OS_AUTHENT** parameter should be set to FALSE. If this is not set to FALSE and the authentication device specified by the client is not supported on the server side, the connection will fail. Setting **REMOTE_OS_AUTHENT** to TRUE will cause a loophole in security because it will allow someone using a nonsecure network protocol (for example, TCP) to log into the Oracle database using operating-system level security. The following is an example of the recommended parameter setting for a database-initialization file:

```
remote_os_authent = FALSE
```

The **OS_AUTHENT_PREFIX** should be set to NULL. Authentication-service names are usually very long; combined with an **OS_AUTHENT_PREFIX**, the authentication_service name could be longer than Oracle's 30-character limit. Following is an example of the recommended database-initialization parameter file setting:

```
os_authent_prefix = ""
```

You will not be expected to know specific requirements, limitations, and configuration information for each type of authentication device. However, if you are interested, this information is available in the *Oracle Advanced Networking Option Administrator's Guide*.

Configuration Of ANO With Net8 Assistant

Net8 Assistant can be used to create a sqlnet.ora file for the client and server. Start Net8 Assistant and highlight the Profile icon. Select Create from the Edit menu and select Advanced Networking Options from the pulldown screen.

The four tabs that can be used to configure ANO are Authentication, Parameter, Integrity, and Encryption.

The Authentication screen lists the available network authentication services. These can be highlighted and moved between the Selected Services and Available Services Screen. Multiple services can be selected and arranged in any order. See Figure 11.6.

The Parameter tab enables you to further configure the authentication services options. First select the Authentication Service from the pull-down menu. This screen will change depending upon the authentication service chosen. You will be prompted for the values required by the selected service. See Figure 11.7.

The Integrity tab is used to configure cryptographic checksumming. You can choose Accepted, Rejected, Required, or Requested for both the client and server. See Figure 11.8.

The Encryption tab is used to configure data encryption. Choose Server or Client from the Encryption pull-down menu. You can choose Accepted, Rejected, Required, or Requested for the encryption type. A box is provided to type in your encryption seed. Finally, the Available Services screen lists the

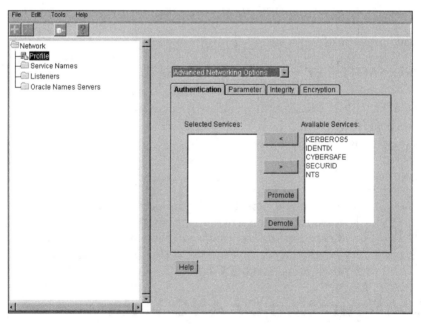

Figure 11.6   Net8 Assistant Authentication Screen.

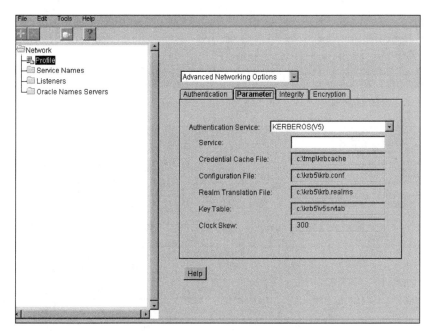

Figure 11.7   Net8 Assistant Parameter Screen.

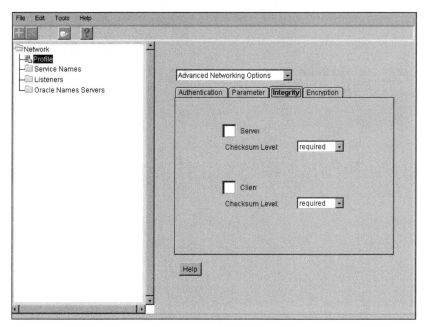

Figure 11.8   Net8 Assistant Integrity Screen.

supported services: DES, RC4_40, DES40, RC4_56, and RC4_128. You can highlight the appropriate service or services and move them to the Selected Services side of the screen. See Figure 11.9.

The sqlnet.ora file is created or changed when you select Save Network Configuration from the File menu item on the toolbar.

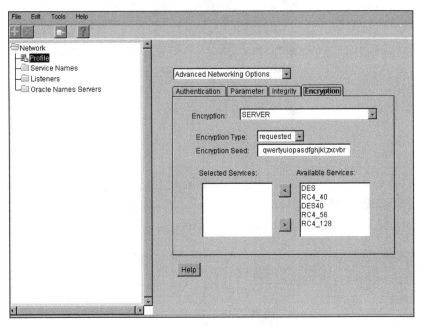

Figure 11.9   Net8 Assistant Encryption Screen.

Practice Questions

Question 1

> Which of the following is a definition of *data privacy*?
>
> ○ a. Ensuring that data is not disclosed or stolen during transmission
>
> ○ b. Ensuring that data is not modified or disrupted during transmission
>
> ○ c. Ensuring that the client identity is known
>
> ○ d. Ensuring that a client is permitted to access an object

The correct answer is a. Data privacy is aimed at keeping the data from being disclosed or stolen during transmission. With current technology, it has become increasingly easy to tap into the network in order to steal information. See Figure 11.1.

Question 2

> Client A logs into his account and transmits a request to transfer $1,000 from his savings account into his checking account. Unknown to him, the transmission is disrupted, and the amount is changed from $1,000 to $100 with the remaining $900 deposited into another account. Which of the following security violations has been encountered?
>
> ○ a. Data privacy
>
> ○ b. Data integrity
>
> ○ c. Authentication
>
> ○ d. Authorization

The correct answer is b. When data is disrupted or modified during transmission, this is known as a violation of data integrity. Securing data integrity is ensuring that the data that has been transmitted is not changed or disrupted during transmission. See Figure 11.2.

Question 3

> Which of the following data-encryption algorithms is supported by Oracle?
> [Choose the two best anwers]
>
> ❑ a. DES
>
> ❑ b. RSA RC4
>
> ❑ c. RCA
>
> ❑ d. MD5
>
> ❑ e. Alpha

The correct answers are a and b. RCA and Alpha are not legitimate algorithms. DES is the Data Encryption Standard, and RSA RC4 is available from RSA Data Security, Inc. MD5 is used for cryptographic checksumming—not data encryption.

Question 4

> Which of the following sqlnet.ora parameters is required on both the client and server for data encryption?
>
> ○ a. **NET8.CRYPTO_SEED**
>
> ○ b. **SQLNET.CRYPTO_CHECKSUM_CLIENT**
>
> ○ c. **SQLNET.CRYPTO_CHECKSUM_SERVER**
>
> ○ d. **SQLNET.CRYPTO_KEY**
>
> ○ e. **SQLNET.CRYPTO_SEED**

The correct answer is e. The **SQLNET.CRYPTO_SEED** provides the key for coding and decoding the encrypted data. It must be identical on both the client and server. The **CRYPTO_CHECKSUM** parameters are used for cryptographic checksumming and not for data encryption. The remaining two are nonexistent parameters.

Question 5

> Which of the following parameters is a correct sqlnet.ora setting for perform-
> ing cryptographic checksumming?
>
> ○ a. **SQLNET.CRYPTO_CHECKSUM_TYPES_SERVER** = MD5
>
> ○ b. **SQLNET.CRYPTO_CHECKSUM_TYPES_SERVER** = DES40
>
> ○ c. **SQLNET.CRYPTO_CHECKSUM_TYPES_SERVER** = RCA
>
> ○ d. **SQLNET.CRYPTO_CHECKSUM_TYPES_SERVER** = MDA
>
> ○ e. **SQLNET.CRYPTO_CHECKSUM_TYPES_SERVER** = RC4_40

The correct answer is a. This type of question is very difficult because the answers are very similar. Both DES40 and RC4_40 are used for data encryp-tion and not for checksumming. MDA and RCA are not valid types of algorithms. Only MD5 is used for cryptographic checksumming.

Question 6

> Which of the following configuration modes will result in a failed connection?
> [Choose the two best answers]
>
> ❑ a. Accepted on the client and rejected on the server
>
> ❑ b. Required on the client and rejected on the server
>
> ❑ c. Rejected on the client and required on the server
>
> ❑ d. Required on the client and requested on the server
>
> ❑ e. Requested on the client and required on the server
>
> ❑ f. Required on the client and accepted on the server

The correct answers are b and c. A combination of Required and Rejected will result in a failed connection. Review Figure 11.5 for the various Accepted/Rejected/Required/Requested combinations and the results of each combina-tion. Also review Table 11.1 which defines the configuration modes.

Question 7

Using fingerprints for identification is an example of _____.

○ a. Network authentication services

○ b. Token cards

○ c. Biometric authentication

○ d. Network protocol adapter

The correct answer is c. Biometric devices are used to identify the client requesting a connection by something personal, such as a fingerprint.

Question 8

Using SecurID and a PIN is an example of _____.

○ a. Network authentication services

○ b. Token cards

○ c. Biometric authentication

○ d. Network protocol adapter

The correct answer is b. A card (SecurID) combined with a personal identification number (PIN) is an example of token card security.

Question 9

Which of the following is used by Network Authentication Services to verify the client ID?

○ a. Digital certificate

○ b. Password encryption

○ c. Fingerprint

○ d. Personal identification number (PIN)

The correct answer is a. The digital certificate (also called a *ticket* or *credentials*) is passed to the Oracle database server with the username and password. The Oracle database server verifies the digital certificate provided by the client with the authentication server. See Figure 11.3.

Question 10

What files are configured when you are setting up the Kerberos Network Authentication Service?

- ○ a. sqlnet.ora on the client, sqlnet.ora on the server, listener.ora on the server
- ○ b. sqlnet.ora on the server, tnsnames.ora on the client, init.ora on the server
- ○ c. names.ora on the client, sqlnet.ora on the server, init.ora on the server
- ○ d. sqlnet.ora on the client, listener.ora on the server, init.ora on the server
- ○ e. sqlnet.ora on the client, sqlnet.ora on the server, init.ora on the server

The correct answer is e. The sqlnet.ora files on both the client and server are used to configure Network Authentication Services. In addition, Oracle strongly recommends that the **REMOTE_OS_AUTHENT** be set to FALSE and **OS_AUTHENT_PREFIX** be set to NULL in the database-initialization file (init.ora). While you can configure Kerberos without setting the initialization parameters, this is not what Oracle recommends. This may seem like an easy question when it is placed in this chapter, because only the sqlnet.ora and init.ora files have been discussed. It is a much harder question when encountered on the test because the test covers all the chapters. Therefore, it is important that you carefully review the various configuration files and understand what is placed in each one.

Need To Know More?

 The first place to look for more information is the *Oracle's Advanced Networking Option Administrator's Guide* Release 8.0.

 Kreines, David C. and Laskey, Brian. *Oracle Database Administration: The Essential Reference.* O'Reilly, 1999. Chapter 5, "Oracle Network Architecture," pp. 81-83, provides a good general overview of ANO.

 "Secure Network Services," RevealNet Oracle Administration Knowledge Base, provides an excellent overview of the Advanced Networking option.

Sample Test

In this chapter, we provide pointers to help you develop a successful test-taking strategy, including how to choose proper answers, how to decode ambiguity, how to work within the Oracle testing framework, how to decide what you need to memorize beforehand, and how to prepare in general for the test. At the end of this chapter, I include a set of 62 questions on subject matter that is pertinent to Exam 1Z0-016, "Oracle8: Network Administration." In Chapter 13, you'll find the answer key to this test. Good luck!

Questions, Questions, Questions

There should be no doubt in your mind that you are facing a test full of specific and pointed questions. The questions belong to one of two basic types: multiple-choice with a single answer and multiple-choice with several answers. The Oracle8: Network Administration test consists of 62 questions that you must complete in 90 minutes.

Always take the time to read a question at least twice before selecting an answer, and always look for an Exhibit button as you examine each question. Exhibits include graphic information that pertains to the question. (An exhibit is usually a screen capture of program output or GUI information that you must examine to analyze the question's scenario and formulate an answer.)

Not every question has only one answer; many questions require multiple answers. Therefore, it's important to read each question carefully—not only to determine how many answers are necessary or possible, but to look for additional hints or instructions when selecting answers. Such instructions often occur in brackets immediately following the question itself (as they do for all multiple-choice questions in which one or more answers are possible).

Picking Proper Answers

Obviously, the only way to pass any exam is to select enough of the right answers to obtain a passing score. However, Oracle's exams are not standardized like the SAT and GRE exams; they are far more diabolical and convoluted. In some cases, questions are strangely worded, and deciphering them can be a real challenge. In those cases, you may need to rely on answer-elimination skills. Almost always, at least one answer out of the possible choices for a question can be eliminated immediately because it matches one of these conditions:

➤ It does not apply to the situation.

➤ It describes a nonexistent issue, an invalid option, or an imaginary state.

➤ It may be eliminated because of the question itself (e.g., the answer contains only one item and the question requires two items).

After you eliminate all answers that are obviously wrong, you can apply your retained knowledge to eliminate further answers. Look for items that sound correct but that refer to actions, commands, or features that are not present or available in the situation that the question describes.

If you're still faced with a blind guess among two or more potentially correct answers, reread the question. Try to picture how each of the possible remaining answers would alter the situation. Be especially sensitive to terminology because sometimes the choice of words (*remove* instead of *disable*) can make the difference between a right answer and a wrong one.

Only when you've exhausted your ability to eliminate answers should you guess at an answer. An unanswered question offers you no points, but guessing gives you at least some chance of getting a question right. Just don't be too hasty when making a blind guess.

 You can wait until the last round of reviewing marked questions (just as you're about to run out of time, or out of unanswered questions) before you start making guesses.

Decoding Ambiguity

Exams are not designed to ensure that everyone passes. They are meant to test knowledge on a given topic, and the scores from a properly designed test will have the classic bell-shaped distribution for the target audience, meaning a certain number will fail. A problem with this exam is that is has been tailored to Oracle's training materials even though some of the material in the training is hearsay, some is old DBA tales, and some is just incorrect. Where obvious errors in the exam questions exist, the previous chapters have attempted to point them out to you.

The only sure way to overcome some of the exam's limitations is to be prepared. You will discover that many of the questions test your knowledge of something that is not directly related to the issues that the questions raise. This means that the answers offered to you, even the incorrect ones, are as much a part of the skill assessment as the questions themselves. If you do not have a thorough grasp of all the aspects of an exam topic (in this case, Oracle8 Network Administration), you will not be able to eliminate answers that are obviously wrong because they relate to a different aspect of the topic than the one the question addresses.

Questions can reveal answers, especially when dealing with commands. So read a question and then evaluate the answers in light of common terms, names, and structure.

Another problem is that Oracle uses some terminology in its training materials that isn't found anywhere else in its documentation sets. Whether this was a deliberate attempt to force you to take its classes to pass the exam or simply a case of sloppy documentation is unknown.

Working Within The Framework

The test questions appear in random order, and many elements or issues that receive mention in one question also crop up in other questions. It's not uncommon to find that an incorrect answer to one question is the correct answer to another question, or vice-versa. Take the time to read every answer to each question, even if you recognize the correct answer to a question immediately. This extra reading may spark a memory or remind you about a feature or function that helps you on another question elsewhere in the exam.

You can revisit any question as many times as you like. If you're uncertain of the answer to a question, check the box that's provided to mark it for easy return later on. You should also mark questions that you think may offer information that you can use to answer other questions. I usually mark somewhere between 25 and 50 percent of the questions. The testing software is designed to let you mark every question if you choose, so use this feature to your advantage. Everything you will want to see again should be marked; the testing software can then help you return to marked questions quickly and easily.

Deciding What To Memorize

The amount you must memorize for an exam depends on how well you remember what you've read, and how well you intuitively know the software. If you are a visual thinker and you can see the drop-down menus and dialog boxes in your head, you won't need to memorize as much as someone who's less visually oriented. Because the tests will stretch your recollection of commands, tools, utilities, and functions related to how Net8 works, you'll want to memorize—at a minimum—the following kinds of information:

➤ Various utilities and the commands associated with them (for example, lsnrctl).

➤ How to configure both the client and server using Net8 Assistant and the parameters in the files created.

➤ The various layers of the protocol stack and what each layer does.

➤ The configuration parameter options for each of the files: tnsnames.ora, sqlnet.ora, listener.ora, cman.ora, names.ora, and relevant init.ora parameters.

If you work your way through this book while sitting at a machine with Oracle8 and Net8 Assistant installed, and you try to manipulate the features and functions of the various commands, tools, and utilities as they're discussed, you should have little or no difficulty mastering this material. Also, don't forget that the Cram Sheet at the front of the book captures the material that is most important to memorize, so don't forget to use it to guide your studies as well.

Preparing For The Test

The best way to prepare for the test—after you've studied—is to take at least one practice exam. We've included one in this chapter for that reason; the test questions are located in the pages that follow. (Unlike the preceding chapters in this book, the answers don't follow the questions immediately; you'll have to flip to Chapter 13 to review the answers.)

Give yourself 90 minutes to take the exam. Keep yourself on the honor system and don't look at earlier text in the book or jump ahead to the answer key. When your time is up or you've finished the questions, you can check your work in Chapter 13. Pay special attention to the explanations for the incorrect answers; these can also help to reinforce your knowledge of the material. Knowing how to recognize correct answers is good, but understanding why incorrect answers are wrong can be equally valuable.

Taking The Test

Relax. Once you're sitting in front of the testing computer, there's nothing more you can do to increase your knowledge or preparation. Take a deep breath, stretch, and start reading that first question.

There's no need to rush; you have plenty of time to complete each question and to return to those questions that you skip or mark for return. If you read a question twice and remain clueless, you can mark it. Both easy and difficult questions are intermixed throughout the test in random order. Don't cheat yourself by spending too much time on a hard question early in the test, which deprives you of the time you need to answer the questions at the end of the test.

You can read through the entire test and, before returning to marked questions for a second visit, figure out how much time you've got per question. As you answer each question, remove its mark. Continue to review the remaining marked questions until you run out of time or you complete the test.

That's it for pointers. Here are some questions for you to practice on.

Sample Test

Question 1

Which file is used to configure the PRESPAWN_MAX parameter?

○ a. sqlnet.ora

○ b. tnsnames.ora

○ c. listener.ora

○ d. names.ora

○ e. cman.ora

Question 2

Which component allows transparent communication with Oracle database servers regardless of the operating system?

○ a. Net8

○ b. ANO

○ c. TCP

○ d. svrmgrl

○ e. CMAN

Question 3

What is the default port for the host naming method?

○ a. 1520

○ b. 1521

○ c. 1526

○ d. 1601

○ e. Any port may be used.

Question 4

Which component of Net8 interprets a network alias into an address?

- ○ a. NI
- ○ b. NA
- ○ c. NR
- ○ d. NN
- ○ e. TCP

Question 5

Which naming method provides a way to centralize the configuration and administration of service names?

- ○ a. Host naming
- ○ b. Local naming
- ○ c. ONAMES
- ○ d. TNSNAMES
- ○ e. Connection pooling

Question 6

In order to use connection pooling, what parameter must be configured in the init.ora file?

- ○ a. LOCAL_LISTENER
- ○ b. MTS_SERVICE
- ○ c. MTS_SERVERS
- ○ d. MTS_DISPATCHERS
- ○ e. MTS_POOL

Question 7

Which utility is used to a start client-side cache?

- ○ a. lsnrctl
- ○ b. namesctl
- ○ c. cmctl
- ○ d. svrmgrl

Question 8

The **SOURCE_ROUTE** parameter is configured in which of the following files?

- ○ a. tnsnames.ora
- ○ b. sqlnet.ora
- ○ c. listener.ora
- ○ d. cman.ora
- ○ e. names.ora

Question 9

Which of the following levels will provide the most information for trouble-shooting a Net8 problem?

- ○ a. Off
- ○ b. User
- ○ c. Admin
- ○ d. Support
- ○ e. 16

Question 10

Which product provides support for connections between multiple protocols for Oracle8?

- ○ a. CMAN
- ○ b. ONAMES
- ○ c. MPI
- ○ d. Intelligent Agent
- ○ e. Two-Task Common

Question 11

Data encryption provides protection against which type of security risk?

- ○ a. Data integrity
- ○ b. Data privacy
- ○ c. Authentication
- ○ d. Authorization

Question 12

Which of the following is used to configure the tnsnames.ora file?

- ○ a. Service Name Wizard
- ○ b. Names Wizard
- ○ c. ANO
- ○ d. ONAMES

Question 13

Which of the following is not a supported data-encryption algorithm?

- ○ a. RC4_40
- ○ b. DES40
- ○ c. DES128
- ○ d. RC4_128
- ○ e. RC4_56

Question 14

What is the last step when configuring Net8 listener.ora parameter files?

○ a. Click on Finish.

○ b. Click on Test Connection.

○ c. Select Save Network Configuration from the File menu.

○ d. Click on the Listener icon.

○ e. Click on the Save Network Configuration button.

Question 15

A client/server configuration is an example of what type of architecture?

○ a. Two-tier

○ b. N-tier

○ c. Three-tier

○ d. Application server

○ e. Middle tier

Question 16

Which of the following parameters for **POOL** will configure connection pooling?

○ a. On

○ b. Yes

○ c. True

○ d. Both

○ e. All of the above

Question 17

What two methods are used by the listener to handle connection requests?
[Choose the two best answers]

❑ a. Create a prespawned server process.

❑ b. Pass the connection request to CMAN.

❑ c. Redirect the connection request to a shared server process.

❑ d. Spawn a dedicated server process for the connection.

❑ e. Redirect connection to an existing process.

Question 18

Which file is used to turn logging off on the client?

○ a. listener.ora

○ b. sqlnet.ora

○ c. cman.ora

○ d. names.ora

○ e. None of the above.

Question 19

The **REORDER_NS** command will list Oracle name servers based on which of
the following?

○ a. Alphabetical

○ b. Physical location

○ c. Results of a ping command

○ d. IP address

○ e. Logs into each and orders them based on the fastest connection

Question 20

You have set up a n-tier architecture and want to install CMAN. Where should the cman.ora file be placed?

- ○ a. On each client
- ○ b. On each server
- ○ c. On the Oracle Names server
- ○ d. On the middle tier

Question 21

You have issued the following command from the operating system prompt:

```
lsnrctl services
```

What will be the result?

- ○ a. A new service will be picked up by Intelligent Agent.
- ○ b. You can now configure a new service_name.
- ○ c. Information on the connections made and refused for the default listener process will be displayed.
- ○ d. General information such as the uptime and services will be displayed.
- ○ e. Information on the connections made and refused for all listener processes will be displayed.

Question 22

If you are configuring the ONAMES connection method, which configuration file and parameter must be on all the clients?

- ○ a. tnsnames.ora, **SOURCE_ROUTE**
- ○ b. sqlnet.ora, **NAMES.DIRECTORY_PATH**
- ○ c. sqlnet.ora, **SQLNET.DIRECTORY_PATH**
- ○ d. listener.ora, **SERVER_ROUTE**
- ○ e. sqlnet.ora, **ONAMES.DIRECTORY_PATH**

Question 23

Which layer of the protocol stack performs character set conversions?

○ a. OCI

○ b. TWO-TASK COMMON

○ c. OPI

○ d. TNS

Question 24

SecurID is an example of what type of security method?

○ a. Data-encryption algorithm

○ b. Cryptographic checksumming

○ c. Token card

○ d. Biometric authentication

○ e. Digital certificate

Question 25

What three files are configured for Intelligent Agent? [Choose the three best answers]

❏ a. services.ora

❏ b. snmp_ro.ora

❏ c. snmp_rw.ora

❏ d. smnp_rw.ora

❏ e. names.ora

❏ f. smnp_ro.ora

Question 26

If you configure six dispatcher processes for MTS, which of the following is also true?

○ a. Six shared servers processes must be configured.

○ b. Six response queues will be created in the SGA.

○ c. Six request queues will be created in the SGA.

○ d. Six pmon processes will be created at the operating system level.

Question 27

A TICK is equivalent to _____?

○ a. 5 seconds

○ b. 10 seconds

○ c. 15 seconds

○ d. 1 minute

○ e. 5 minutes

Question 28

In order to use connection concentration, which of the following configuration file and parameter values is required?

○ a. cman.ora, **MUX**

○ b. sqlnet.ora, **POO**

○ c. listener.ora, **MUX**

○ d. init.ora, **MUX**

Question 29

On an NT server, the default location for the listener.ora file is _____.

○ a. **ORACLE_HOME\network\admin**

○ b. **TNS_ADMIN\net80\admin**

○ c. **ORACLE_HOME\net80\admin**

○ d. **ORACLE_HOME\network\trace**

Question 30

When using client-side caching with Oracle Names, what parameter determines the cache refresh rate?

○ a. **POO**

○ b. **TICKS**

○ c. **CONNECTION**

○ d. **TTL**

○ e. **SESSION**

Question 31

Which formula will determine the number of waiting sessions that can be supported for connection pooling?

○ a. Connections – sessions

○ b. Connections – pool

○ c. Connections + sessions

○ d. mts_max_dispatchers – mts_max_servers

○ e. Sessions - connections

Question 32

The **LOCAL_LISTENER** parameter is found in which file?

○ a. sqlnet.ora

○ b. listener.ora

○ c. names.ora

○ d. tnsnames.ora

○ e. init.ora

Question 33

Which of the following combinations for encryption will always result in a failed connection?

○ a. Requested and rejected

○ b. Requested and required

○ c. Required and rejected

○ d. Requested and accepted

○ e. Accepted and rejected

Question 34

The tnsnames.ora connect descriptor is composed of what two sections? (Choose the two best answers)

❑ a. ADDRESS_LIST

❑ b. SERVICE_NAME

❑ c. HOST

❑ d. PORT

❑ e. CONNECT_DATA

Question 35

You are using Net8 Assistant to load a valid tnsnames.ora file into the regional database. What is the last step?

○ a. Choose the Save Network Configuration from the File menu.

○ b. Click on the SERVICE_NAMES icon to check that the regional database has been configured.

○ c. Choose the Save Network Configuration from the Tools menu.

○ d. Click on the Execute button.

Question 36

For an MTS configuration, which of the following parameters does Oracle recommend setting to your SID?

- O a. **MTS_LISTENER_ADDRESS**
- O b. **LOCAL_LISTENER**
- O c. **HOST**
- O d. **MTS_DISPATCHER_ADDRESS**

Question 37

When configuring a tnsnames.ora file for CMAN, what must be included in this file?

- O a. The specification of 1610 for the CMAN port
- O b. The location for the cman.ora file
- O c. Both the CMAN server and destination server addresses
- O d. The location for the names.ora file

Question 38

Why would you configure a regional database?

- O a. A regional database will act as the central repository for all listener information.
- O b. A regional database will act as a repository for all names server information.
- O c. A regional database can be used to store information for all the root regions.
- O d. A regional database is used with the Oracle Designer tool.

Question 39

Which of the following is a disadvantage of using local naming?

○ a. A tnsnames.ora file must be configured on every client workstation.

○ b. A sqlnet.ora file must be configured on every client.

○ c. A sqlnet.ora file must be configured on every server.

○ d. Only port 1521 can be used for the service_name.

○ e. Multiple listeners are not supported with local naming.

Question 40

How do you start to configure a service name using Net8?

○ a. Select Create Service Name from the Tools menu.

○ b. Click on the Alias icon and then select Create from the File menu.

○ c. Click on the Service Name icon and select Create from the File menu.

○ d. Click on the Profile icon and select Service Name from the pull-down menu that appears on the screen.

Question 41

Which of the following is included in the snmp_ro.ora file?

○ a. snmp.contact.listener

○ b. ifile

○ c. snmp.index.listener

○ d. services.ora

Question 42

Which of the following is true for MTS? [Choose the two best answers]

- ❑ a. MTS can increase performance significantly.
- ❑ b. MTS is required for connection pooling.
- ❑ c. MTS can support connection pooling and multiplexing simultaneously to increase the number of connections.
- ❑ d. MTS uses shared server and dispatcher processes to reduce the overhead of multiple connections.
- ❑ e. MTS is required when using ANO.

Question 43

The **CMAN_RULE** parameter SVR represents _____?

- ○ a. Destination server
- ○ b. Source sever
- ○ c. SID
- ○ d. Action

Question 44

When only one region is configured for ONAMES, how is replication between names servers accomplished?

- ○ a. All the names servers will replicate between each other.
- ○ b. No replication is necessary.
- ○ c. The root names server will handle replication between all the servers.
- ○ d. All the names servers will replicate among all the regions.

Question 45

Which of the following is used to interface with Intelligent Agent?

○ a. Net8 Assistant

○ b. Enterprise Manager

○ c. Performance Pack

○ d. Advanced Networking Option

Question 46

Which of the following commands is not a valid listener control utility command?

○ a. **lsnrctl stop**

○ b. **lsnrctl start**

○ c. **lsnrctl status**

○ d. **lsnrctl display**

○ e. **lsnrctl services**

Question 47

Which of the following is not a CMAN_profile parameter?

○ a. **LOG_LEVEL**

○ b. **PROTOCOL**

○ c. **AUTHENTICATION_LEVEL**

○ d. **SHOW_TNS_INFO**

○ e. **MAXIMUM_CONNECT_DATA**

Question 48

Which of the following commands will increase the number of dispatchers configured for MTS from 6 to 12?

○ a. **alter database set mts_dispatchers = '(PROTOCOL=TCP)(DISPATCHERS=12)'**

○ b. **alter system set mts_dispatchers = '(PROTOCOL=TCP)(DISPATCHERS=12)'**

○ c. **alter system set dispatchers = 12;**

○ d. **alter system set mts_disptachers = '((PROTOCOL=TCP)(DISPATCHERS=12)"**

○ e. **alter system set mts_dispatchers = '12,tcp'**

Question 49

Which algorithm is used for cryptographic checksumming?

○ a. RC4_40

○ b. RC4_128

○ c. DES40

○ d. MD5

○ e. ANO

Question 50

What is required in order to configure multiple listeners using TCP?

○ a. Separate hostname and port for each

○ b. Separate listener name and port for each

○ c. Separate listener.ora file and port for each

○ d. Separate TNS_ADMIN parameter for each

Question 51

The cmctl utility is used to control what background processes? [Choose the two best answers]

❑ a. listener

❑ b. dispatchers

❑ c. CMGW

❑ d. CMLSNR

❑ e. CMADM

Question 52

In order to set tracing on the client, which parameter must be configured?

○ a. **TRACE_DIRECTORY_CLIENT**

○ b. **TRACE_FILE_CLIENT**

○ c. **LOG_LEVEL_CLIENT**

○ d. **TRACE_LEVEL_CLIENT**

Question 53

When troubleshooting a problem, which of the following files can be configured to obtain additional trace information?

○ a. sqlnet.ora

○ b. listener.ora

○ c. cman.ora

○ d. names.ora

○ e. All of the above

Question 54

What is the function performed by Oracle Trace Assistant?

- ○ a. Create trace file on the client.
- ○ b. Create trace file on the server.
- ○ c. Format trace files.
- ○ d. Provide performance statistics for the dispatcher processes.

Question 55

Which of the following views provide tuning information for MTS?

- ○ a. v$mts
- ○ b. v$queue
- ○ c. v$session
- ○ d. v$mts_queue

Question 56

How can you configure logging and tracing for the client using Net8?

- ○ a. Highlight the Service Names icon and select General from the pull-down menu.
- ○ b. Highlight the Profile icon and select General Parameters from the pull-down menu.
- ○ c. Highlight the Profile icon and select General from the pull-down menu.
- ○ d. Select Test Network Connectivity from the Tools item.

Question 57

Which of the following Oracle products provides additional security? [Choose the two best answers]

❑ a. CMAN

❑ b. RMAN

❑ c. ONAMES

❑ d. ANO

❑ e. Net8 Assistant

Question 58

What tool is provided for Net8 file configuration?

○ a. CMAN

○ b. Trace Assistant

○ c. ANO

○ d. Net8 Assistant

Question 59

Which of the following settings will turn on multiplexing for incoming connections only?

○ a. Both

○ b. 0

○ c. 1

○ d. 2

○ e. In

Question 60

The default sqlnet.expire_time is _____?

○ a. 5 ticks

○ b. 1 tick

○ c. None

○ d. 10 seconds

○ e. 1 minute

Question 61

The key of data encryption is specified in which parameter?

○ a. **SQLNET.CRYPTO_SEED**

○ b. **SQLNET.CRYPTO_KEY**

○ c. **NAMES.CRYPTO_SEED**

○ d. **NAMES.CRYPTO_KEY**

○ e. **SQLNET.CRYPTO_CHECKSUM_KEY**

Question 62

If you want to configure logging and tracing for the listener process, where would you set the parameters?

○ a. sqlnet.ora

○ b. tnsnames.ora

○ c. listener.ora

○ d. init.ora

○ e. names.ora

Answer Key

1. c	17. d, e	33. c	49. d
2. a	18. e	34. b, e	50. b
3. b	19. c	35. d	51. c, e
4. d	20. d	36. b	52. d
5. c	21. c	37. c	53. e
6. d	22. b	38. b	54. c
7. b	23. b	39. a	55. a
8. a	24. c	40. c	56. c
9. d	25. a, b, c	41. b	57. a, d
10. a	26. b	42. b, d	58. d
11. b	27. b	43. c	59. e
12. a	28. d	44. a	60. c
13. c	29. c	45. b	61. a
14. c	30. d	46. d	62. c
15. a	31. e	47. b	
16. e	32. e	48. b	

Here are the answers to the questions presented in the sample test (Chapter 12).

Question 1

The correct answer is c. The **PRESPAWN_MAX** parameter is configured in the listener.ora file. It determines the maximum number of prespawned dedicated server processes that can be created. This is also the maximum number that the listener will maintain. When a connection request comes in, the listener can redirect the request to a prespawned dedicated process instead of having to spawn a process at that time.

Question 2

The correct answer is a. Net8 is used to establish connections between the client application and the Oracle database. The connection mechanism is transparent to the client regardless of the operating systems used at the client and server level. ANO is used for security. CMAN is used for cross-protocol connections and security. TCP is a network protocol, and svrmgrl is the server manager utility that is used with the database (not for network administration).

Question 3

The correct answer is b. The default port number of 1521 is required when you configure host naming.

Question 4

The correct answer is d. The NN (network naming) layer is part of the TNS protocol stack layer. If you were unable to answer this question correctly, you should review the various layers of the protocol stack and what each one does. (See Chapter 3 to review the basic Net8 architecture.) The other listed layers in this answer are NI for network interface, NA for network authentication, and NR for network routing. TCP is a network protocol.

Question 5

The correct answer is c. ONAMES stands for Oracle Names, a method to centralize the administration and configuration of service names. TNSNAMES is used for local naming and requires a tnsnames.ora file on each client. Host naming uses the default settings. Connection pooling has nothing to do with centralized configuration of service names.

Question 6

The correct answer is d. The **MTS_DISPATCHERS** parameter in the init.ora file is used to configure connection pooling. Except for the MTS_POOL parameter (which is not a valid parameter), the other listed parameters are used to configure MTS, but not connection pooling.

Question 7

The correct answer is b. The namesctl utility is used for Oracle Names. The command to start client-side cache is namesctl start_client_cache. The cmctl utility is used for CMAN. The lsnrctl utiity is used for the listener process. The svrmgrl utility is used for the database.

Question 8

The correct answer is a. The **SOURCE_ROUTE** parameter is configured in the tnsnames.ora file to force connection requests to attempt to use CMAN for connections. You should review each of the files in the appendices and be familiar with what each includes.

Question 9

The correct answer is d. The Support level produces the most detailed trace information for troubleshooting. Because the default is for tracing to be set to Off, you can obviously eliminate this as your answer, because no trace information is generated with the trace level of Off. The User and Admin levels provide information, but it's not as detailed as the Support setting. The trace level of 16 may be familiar to experienced users and will produce a very detailed report. However, for the purposes of this exam, you should answer that the Support setting is used to obtain detailed information.

Question 10

The correct answer is a. The CMAN product replaces the Oracle7 MultiProtocol Interchange (MPI) product. It is used for supporting clients with one network protocol with servers that use a different protocol. If you answered Two-Task, you have *character* and *network* protocols confused. Two-task will interpret one character set to another character set. You should have recognized that ONAMES and Intelligent Agent were obviously the wrong answers.

Question 11

The correct answer is b. Data encryption is used to encrypt data that is going through the network to provide data privacy. Data integrity deals with data that is modified. Authentication and authorization have to do with the user identification and object privileges.

Question 12

The correct answer is a. The Service Name Wizard is called by Net8 to configure service names. Do not confuse it with the Names Wizard which is used to configure ONAMES. ANO (Advanced Networking Option) is used for enhanced network security.

Question 13

The correct answer is c. DES is supported for 40- and 56-bit encryption. RC4 is supported for 40-, 56-, and 128-bit encryption.

Question 14

The correct answer is c. When you have finished configuring your parameters using Net8, you need to save your configuration. The Save Network Configuration is called from the File menu, and you should save your configuration before exiting. When you are presented with this type of question, the best thing to do is try to visualize what you are doing at each step and see if there is anything else that could be done before you exit. That will be your last step.

Question 15

The correct answer is a. The client/server configuration is an example of a two-tier architecture (client as one tier and server as the other tier). When using an n-tier architecture, you place the application on an application server or middle tier. Three-tier is a variation of n-tier.

Question 16

The correct answer is e. All of the listed parameters will enable connection pooling.

Question 17

The correct answers are d and e. When the connection request is picked up by the listener, it will either redirect the connection request to an existing process or spawn a new process for the connection. These are the only options for the listener to service the connection request. The only other action the listener can take is to refuse the connection request.

Question 18

The correct answer is e. Logging cannot be turned off on the client or for Oracle names. It can be turned off for the listener process by explicitly including the **LOGGING_LISTENER** parameter (set to Off) in the listener.ora file.

Question 19

The correct answer is c. The **REORDER_NS** command will issue a ping against each names server and order the connections from the fastest response to the slowest response.

Question 20

The correct answer is d. Oracle recommends installing CMAN on the middle tier. While this middle tier could also be the Oracle Names server, this is not the best answer because it assumes the use of ONAMES with CMAN.

Question 21

The correct answer is c. The services command provides information on the number of connections established and refused. The status command provides information on the uptime and services. No command provides information on all the listener processes for multiple listener configurations. The other two answers are obviously wrong.

Question 22

The correct answer is b. The **NAMES.DIRECTORY_PATH** parameter in the sqlnet.ora file should be set to ONAMES. This is the parameter that determines which method or methods should be used to resolve connection strings for connection requests. The tnsnames.ora, **SOURCE_ROUTE** is used for CMAN. The other listed parameters do not exist.

Question 23

The correct answer is b. The Two-Task Common layer provides character conversions. A previous question (Question 10) concerning network protocol conversion also listed two-task as a possible answer. If you were unsure of whether two-task common or CMAN was correct for the previous answer, this question could assist you. CMAN is not one of the possibilities here. The OCI and OPI and TNS are layers of the protocol stack. If you need to refresh your memory on the protocol stack layers, review Chapter 3. You should memorize the various layers and what each layer does. Even experienced Oracle database administrators rarely know all the layers and their uses; however, for this test you do need to know them.

Question 24

The correct answer is c. SecurID is an example of a token card. It has nothing to do with any algorithm for data encryption or with cryptographic checksumming. A biometric device would be something like a fingerprint scanner. A digital certificate is used for security using an authentication server. SecurID uses a card combined with a PIN for access (just as you use a bankcard and PIN for access to your bank account from an automated teller).

Question 25

The correct answers are a, b, and c. Intelligent Agent creates snmp_ro.ora, snmp_rw.ora, and services.ora files when it is first started. This type of question can be the most difficult because of the similarity of the answers. You need to look closely at the answers. You can eliminate names.ora because it has to do with Oracle names and not security. The rest depends on you remembering that it is snmp and not smnp.

Question 26

The correct answer is b. Each dispatcher will have a response queue in the SGA. Answer d is easy to eliminate: only one pmon process is required for your database. Because there are six dispatchers does not mean that you will need to configure six shared servers. (There is no direct correlation between dispatchers and shared servers.) Only one request queue configured in the SGA is used by all dispatchers and shared servers.

Question 27

The correct answer is b. A "tick" is equivalent to a ten-second interval, and the **TICK** parameter is used to configure connection pooling.

Question 28

The correct answer is d. The init.ora **MTS_DISPATCHER** parameter is used to configure multiplexing (**MUX**). Remember that multiplexing and connection pooling cannot be used together, but both require an MTS configuration.

Question 29

The correct answer is c. The default location is **ORACLE_HOME\net80\admin**. It will help if you can remember that, on a Unix server, your directory for Net8 is network, and net80 for NT. The default for Unix is **ORACLE_HOME/network/admin**.

Question 30

The correct answer is d. **TTL** stands for *time to live*, which is the parameter setting that determines how long connection address information should be maintained before it is refreshed. All of the other parameters listed are for the init.ora file on the server and are not used for Oracle Names.

Question 31

The correct answer is e. The number of sessions must be greater than the number of connections in order to allow connections to be shared. Therefore, the formula is sessions minus connections equals the number of waiting sessions that can be supported.

Question 32

The correct answer is e. The **LOCAL_LISTENER** parameter is used to configure MTS. The configuration for MTS is made in the init.ora file. If you had difficulty with this question, review the parameters for MTS in Chapter 7.

Question 33

The correct answer is c. The combination of Required and rejected will always result in a failed connection when you are configuring encryption modes with

ANO. If you had trouble with this question, review the combinations of modes in Chapter 11.

Question 34

The correct answers are b and e. The connect descriptor is composed of the SERVICE_NAME and CONNECT_DATA. While the HOST, PORT, and ADDRESS_LIST are part of the connect descriptor, the most complete answer is SERVICE_NAME and CONNECT_DATA.

Question 35

The correct answer is d. When you load a tnsnames.ora file into the regional database, the last step is to click on the Execute button. When it finishes executing the load, the work is saved and there is no need to use the Save Network Configuration option on the File menu toolbar. Review the Net8 Assistant screenshots to get a feel for using Net8. Even better, if you have access to Net8 Assistant, practice configuring Net8 using it.

Question 36

The correct answer is b. Oracle recommends setting the **LOCAL_LISTENER** parameter to your SID. While the **MTS_LISTENER_ADDRESS** can be used, it is there for backward compatibility with Oracle 7 and is not a correct answer for this exam. The other answers are not actual parameters for MTS.

Question 37

The correct answer is c. Both the CMAN server and the destination server addresses should be included in the tnsnames.ora file. For an example, refer to Chapter 8.

Question 38

The correct answer is b. A regional database is created as the repository for names server information.

Question 39

The correct answer is a. When local naming is used, a tnsnames.ora file must be configured on each client. This is a disadvantage, because any configuration changes must be made for all the client workstations. If you have 100 clients all using local naming and you decide to add a new database, all the clients need a change to their tnsnames.ora file in order to access that new database. While the sqlnet.ora file is configurable for local naming, it is only mandatory if the defaults are not used. Note the word *must* in the answers. The final two answers are not true: any port number can be used and multiple listeners are supported.

Question 40

The correct answer is c. Service names are configured using the Service Name icon. To create a new service name, you then choose Create from the File menu on the toolbar. If you missed this question, review the screen prints for Net8 Assistant.

Question 41

The correct answer is b. The snmp_ro.ora file includes a reference to the snmp_rw.ora file using the **IFILE** parameter. Note that this question can help you answer Question 25. The snmp.contact.listener and snmp.index_listener are parameters in the snmp_rw.ora file. The services.ora is the third file used by Intelligent Agent. See Chapter 9 to review the contents of these files.

Question 42

The correct answers are b and d. The MTS configuration is not a method to increase performance, but instead aims at supporting large numbers of users by configuring shared server and dispatcher processes that are shared by multiple connections. MTS can support an even larger number of users when configured with connection pooling. Connection pooling and connection concentration cannot be used simultaneously, even though both require MTS. The ANO does not require MTS.

Question 43

The correct answer is c. SVR is the SID. The destination is designated by the DST and the source by SRC. Action is abbreviated ACT and can be configured for ACC (accept) or REJ (reject).

Question 44

The correct answer is a. All the names servers within a region replicate to each other. The root region will replicate all that region's changes to other root regions.

Question 45

The correct answer is b. Enterprise Manager works with Intelligent Agent for job and event scheduling, reporting, and so on. The Performance Pack is a separate product for performance tuning. Net8 Assistant is used for configuration of the network files. The Advanced Networking option is a separate product and is used for added network security.

Question 46

The correct answer is d. Notice that this question is worded in the negative. The only command listed that is *not* a valid listener control utility command is **lsnrctl display**. The command to display information is **lsnrctl show**.

Question 47

The correct answer is b. All of the listed parameters can be configured in the CMAN_PROFILE with the exception of the **PROTCOL** parameter. If you had problems with this question, review the example of the cman.ora file in the Appendix E.

Question 48

The correct answer is b. The command to increase the number of dispatchers is the *alter system set mts_dispatchers = '(PROTOCOL=TCP)(DISPATCHERS=12)'*. By the number of examples using the **ALTER SYSTEM** command, you can eliminate the first answer. Because there can be dispatchers with multiple protocols, that eliminates the second answer because no protocol is specified. Answer D is eliminated because only TCP is used in the protocol specification, and not TCP/IP. Answer E is simply incorrect.

Question 49

The correct answer is d. This is another situation for which you need to memorize information but could rely on previous questions. Question 13 lists various encryption algorithms. This is asking for the cryptographic checksum algorithm. By referencing Question 13, you can eliminate the first three answers. Because ANO is not an algorithm, that leaves d as the only possible answer.

Question 50

The correct answer is b. When configuring multiple listeners, each must have its own name and port assignment. Each listener is controlled separately using its listener name. No two virtual devices should be using the same port. The purpose of configuring multiple listeners is to have multiple listener processes on one host. This eliminates answer a. While you can configure multiple listeners with separate files using the **TNS_ADMIN** parameter to point to the listener.ora file when performing lsnrctl commands, this is not required. Review the listener.ora file in Appendix A.

Question 51

The correct answers are c and e. The background processes for CMAN are controlled using the cmctl utility. The two background processes are CMGW and CMADM.

Question 52

The correct answer is d. To enable tracing on the client, you must set the **TRACE_LEVEL_CLIENT** to User, Admin or Support. The default setting is Off. The **TRACE_DIRECTORY_CLIENT** and **TRACE_FILE_CLIENT** are used to indicate where the trace file is to be written and the file name. Because the file name and directory will default if not set, they are not required parameters for enabling tracing. The **CLIENT_TRACE_LEVEL** is incorrect. Remember that the word *client* is at the end of the parameter and that the purpose of the parameter is at the beginning. This is also true for **LOG_DIRECTORY_CLIENT** and **LOG_FILE_CLIENT**, as well as the corresponding server parameters.

Question 53

The correct answer is e. All of the files listed have configuration parameters that can be used to obtain tracing information. If you missed this question, review Chapter 10.

Question 54

The correct answer is c. Oracle Trace Assistant is used to format trace files into readable text files. Trace Assistant does not create trace files and does not provide performance statistics on dispatcher processes. It does include performance statistics relevant to the network.

Question 55

The correct answer is a. V$MTS provides information relevant to tuning the MTS option. V$QUEUE contains information on message queues, and the V$SESSION contains information on all the database sessions (both dedicated and MTS connections). The V$MTS_QUEUE does not exist.

Question 56

The correct answer is c. In order to configure logging and tracing with Net8, you need to highlight the Profile icon and then choose the General option from a pull-down menu. Review the screen prints in Chapter 10.

Question 57

The correct answers are a and d. CMAN provides connection rules, and ANO provides things such as data encryption, cryptographic checksumming, and support for authentication services. ONAMES is used for central configuration of service names. RMAN is not a part of Net8; it is Recovery Manager provided with Oracle8. Finally, Net8 Assistant does help to configure security parameters; however, it does not in itself provide any additional security.

Question 58

The correct answer is d. Don't let the easy questions confuse you. Some of the questions simply will be very obvious. In this case, it is obvious that the answer is Net8 Assistant. You have various screenshots that show you what Net8 Assistant looks like, and this book has covered the various files that it will create and the parameters that are configured using Net8 Assistant.

Question 59

The correct answer is e. The IN value configures multiplexing for incoming connections. Both and 1 will turn it on for incoming and outgoing connections. Multiplexing is turned off by 0, and 2 is not a valid value.

Question 60

The correct answer is c. The default value for sqlnet.expire_time is none, which means that the default is not to have any expire time for connections.

Question 61

The correct answer is a. The data encryption key parameter is **SQLNET. CRYPTO_SEED**. The other parameters listed are incorrect.

Question 62

The correct answer is c. To configure logging and tracing for the listener process, you need to set the relevant logging and tracing parameters in the listener.ora file. If you had problems with this question, review listener.ora files in Appendix A and Chapter 10.

Appendix A
The listener.ora File

The listener.ora file is the configuration file for the listener process. The following is an example of the listener.ora file for multiple listeners (listener and listener1).

```
LISTENER= (ADDRESS=
               (PROTOCOL=TCP)
               (HOST=srv1)
               (PORT=1521))
STARTUP_WAIT_TIME_LISTENER= 0
CONNECT_TIMEOUT_LISTENER= 60
SID_LIST_LISTENER=(SID_LIST=
                    (SID_DESC=
                        (GLOBAL_DBNAME = PROD1.WORLD)
                        (SID_NAME=PROD1)
                        (ORACLE_HOME=/sqlhome/Prod/8.0.5)
                    )
                    (SID_DESC=
                        (GLOBAL_DBNAME = HR123.WORLD)
                        (SID_NAME=HR123)
                        (ORACLE_HOME=/sqlhome/Prod/8.0.5)
                    )
                )

TRACE_LEVEL_LISTENER=off
TRACE_DIRECTORY_LISTENER=/sqlhome/Prod/8.0.5/network/trace
TRACE_FILE_LISTENER=lsnrtrace.trc
LOG_DIRECTORY_LISTENER=/sqlhome/Prod/8.0.5/network/log
LOG_FILE_LISTENER=listener.log
```

```
LISTENER1= (ADDRESS=
            (PROTOCOL=TCP)
            (HOST=10.11.1.21)
            (PORT=1526))
STARTUP_WAIT_TIME_LISTENER1= 0
CONNECT_TIMEOUT_LISTENER1= 60
SID_LIST_LISTENER1=(SID_LIST=
                    (SID_DESC=
                            (GLOBAL_DBNAME = PROD1.WORLD)
                            (SID_NAME=PROD1)
                            (ORACLE_HOME=/sqlhome/Prod/8.0.5)
                            (PRESPAWN_MAX = 20)
                            (PRESPAWN_LIST =
                                (PRESPAWN_DESC =
                                        (PROTOCOL = TCP)
                                        (POOL_SIZE = 5)
                                        (TIMEOUT = 2)
                                )
                            )
                    )
                )

TRACE_LEVEL_LISTENER1= USER
TRACE_DIRECTORY_LISTENER1=/sqlhome/Prod/8.0.5/network/trace
TRACE_FILE_LISTENER1=listener1.trc
LOG_DIRECTORY_LISTENER1=/sqlhome/Prod/8.0.5/network/log
LOG_FILE_LISTENER1=LISTENER1.log
PASSWORDS_LISTENER1 = (password,oracle)
USE_PLUG_AND_PLAY = off
```

Appendix B
The tnsnames.ora File

The tnsnames.ora file is the configuration file for the listener process. The following is an example of the tnsnames.ora file for a Windows95 workstation.

```
# C:\ORAWIN95\NET80\ADMIN\TNSNAMES.ORA Configuration
# File:C:\orawin95\net80\admin\tnsnames.ora
# Generated by Oracle Net8 Assistant

CMEXAMPLE.WORLD =
  (DESCRIPTION =
    (ADDRESS_LIST =
      (ADDRESS = (PROTOCOL = TCP)(HOST = CM_SERVER)(PORT = 1610))
      (ADDRESS = (PROTOCOL = TCP)(HOST = LSNR_SERVER)(PORT = 1521))
    )
    (CONNECT_DATA =
      (SID = ORCL)
    )
    (SOURCE_ROUTE = YES)
  )

TCPEXAMPLE.WORLD =
  (DESCRIPTION =
    (ADDRESS = (PROTOCOL = TCP)(HOST = Production1)(PORT = 1521))
    (CONNECT_DATA =
      (SID = ORCL)
    )
  )

NMPEXAMPLE.WORLD =
  (DESCRIPTION =
    (ADDRESS = (PROTOCOL = NMP)(Server = FinanceServer1)
      (Pipe = ORAPIPE))
```

```
    (CONNECT_DATA =
      (SID = ORCL)
    )
  )

EXTPROC_CONNECTION_DATA.WORLD =
  (DESCRIPTION =
    (ADDRESS = (PROTOCOL = IPC)(Key = EXTPROC0))
    (CONNECT_DATA =
      (SID = extproc)
    )
  )

BEQ-LOCAL.WORLD =
  (DESCRIPTION =
    (ADDRESS = (PROTOCOL = BEQ)(PROGRAM = oracle80)(ARGV0 =
      oracle80ORCL)(ARGS = '(DESCRIPTION=(LOCAL=YES)
      (ADDRESS=(PROTOCOL=BEQ)))'))
    (CONNECT_DATA =
      (SID = ORCL)
    )
  )

SPXEXAMPLE.WORLD =
  (DESCRIPTION =
    (ADDRESS = (PROTOCOL = SPX)(Service = Server_lsnr))
    (CONNECT_DATA =
      (SID = ORCL)
    )
  )

TCP-LOOPBACK.WORLD =
  (DESCRIPTION =
    (ADDRESS = (PROTOCOL = TCP)(HOST = 127.0.0.1)(PORT = 1521))
    (CONNECT_DATA =
      (SID = ORCL)
    )
  )
PROD1.WORLD =
  (DESCRIPTION =
    (ADDRESS_LIST =
        (ADDRESS = (PROTOCOL = TCP)(HOST = srv1)(PORT = 1521))
        (ADDRESS = (PROTOCOL = TCP)(HOST = 10.11.1.21)(PORT = 1526))
      )
    (CONNECT_DATA =
      (SID = PROD1)
    )
  )
```

Appendix C
The sqlnet.ora File

The sqlnet.ora file is a configuration file used on both the client and server. The following is an example of a sqlnet.ora file for the client.

```
# \ORANT\NET80\ADMIN\sqlnet.ora Configuration

LOG_DIRECTORY_CLIENT = C:\orant\net80\log
LOG_FILE_CLIENT = sqlnet.log
TRACE_LEVEL_CLIENT = ADMIN
TRACE_DIRECTORY_CLIENT = C:\orant\net80\trace
TRACE_FILE_CLIENT = sqlnet.trc
SQLNET.ENCRYPTION_CLIENT = requested
NAMES.DIRECTORY_PATH= (TNSNAMES, ONAMES, HOSTNAME)
SQLNET.CRYPTO_CHECKSUM_CLIENT = required
SQLNET.CRYPTO_CHECKSUM_TYPES_CLINET = required
SQLNET.CRYPTO_SEED = ouerowuroj
SQLNET.ENCRYPTION_TYPES_CLIENT = required
```

Appendix D
The names.ora File

The names.ora file is the configuration file for the Oracle Names Server. The following is an example of the names.ora file.

```
# File:/sqlhome/oracle/8.0.5/network/admin/names.ora
NAMES.SERVER_NAME = NS1.WORLD

NAMES.ADDRESSES =
  (ADDRESS = (PROTOCOL = TCP)(HOST = svr3)(PORT = 1575))
NAMES.ADMIN_REGION =
  (REGION =
        (NAME = LOCAL_REGION.WORLD)
        (TYPE = ROSDB)
        (USERID = names)
        (PASSWORD = password)
        (DESCRIPTION =
                (ADDRESS = (PROTOCOL = TCP)(HOST = svr1)(PORT = 1599))
                (CONNECT_DATA = (SID = orcldb))
        )
        (DOCNAME = sbox)
        (REFRESH = 200)
        (RETRY = 2)
        (EXPIRE = 25000)
  )
NAMES.AUTO_REFRESH_EXPIRE = 25000
NAMES.AUTO_REFRESH_RETRY = 2
NAMES.CACHE_CHECKPOINT_FILE = cacheckp.ckp
NAMES.CACHE_CHECKPOINT_INTERVAL = 6000
NAMES.CONFIG_CHECKPOINT_FILE = configckp.ckp
NAMES.DEFAULT_FORWARDERS =
```

```
        (FORWARDER_LIST =
            (FORWARDER = (NAME = mainsvr.world)
                (ADDRESS = (PROTOCOL = TCP)(HOST = mainsvr1)
                    (PORT = 1588) )
    )
        )
NAMES.DEFAULT_FORWARDERS_ONLY = TRUE
NAMES.DOMAIN_HINTS =
        (HINT_DESC =
            (HINT_LIST =
                (HINT = (NAME = mainsvr.world)
                (ADDRESS = PROTOCOL = TCP)(HOST = mainsvr1)
                    (PORT = 1588) )
            )
            )
NAMES.FORWARDING_AVAILABLE = TRUE
NAMES.FORWARDING_DESIRED = TRUE
NAMES.MAX_REFORWARDS = 2
NAMES.LOG_DIRECTORY = /sqlhome/oracle/8.0.5/network/names
NAMES.LOG_FILE = names.log
NAMES.LOG_STATS_INTERVAL = 4800
NAMES.LOG_UNIQUE = FALSE
NAMES.RESET_STATS_INTERVAL = 4800
NAMES.MAX_OPEN_CONNECTIONS = 20
NAMES.MESSAGE_POOL_START_SIZE = 20
NAMES.TRACE_LEVEL = ADMIN
```

Appendix E
The cman.ora File

The cman.ora file is the configuration file for Connection Manager. The following is an example of the cman.ora file with multiple CMAN addresses and rules.

```
CMAN =
        (ADDRESS_LIST =
            (ADDRESS =
                    (PROTOCOL = TCP)
                    (HOST = appsvr1)
                    (PORT = 1610)
            )
            (ADDRESS =
                    (PROTOCOL = TCP)
                    (HOST = appsvr2)
                    (PORT = 1602)
            )
            (ADDRESS =
                    (PROTOCOL = SPX)
                    (SERVICE = CMAN)
            )
        )
CMAN_RULES =
        (RULES_LIST =
            (RULE =
                (SRC = hrwk1)
                (DST = server2)
                (SRV = prod2)
                (ACT = REJ)
            )
```

```
                (RULE =
                    (SRC = finwk2)
                    (DST = server1)
                    (SRV = prod1)
                    (ACT = ACC)
                )
                (RULE =
                    (SRC = server2)
                    (DST = 10.x.x.x)
                    (SRV = prod1)
                    (ACT = REJ)
                )
            )
CMAN_PROFILE =
            (PARAMETER_LIST =
                (MAXIMUM_RELAYS = 206)
                (LOG_LEVEL = 1)
                (TRACING = YES)
                (RELAY_STATISTICS = YES)
                (SHOW_TNS_INFO = YES)
                (USE_ASYNCH_CALL = YES)
                (AUTHENTICATION_LEVEL = 0)
                (MAXIMUM_CONNECT_DATA = 2048)
                (ANSWER_TIMEOUT = 10)
            )
```

Glossary

Advanced Networking Option (ANO)—An Oracle product that provides additional security through data encryption, cryptographic checksumming, and support for authentication services.

authentication—The process of verifying that the identities of the clients, hosts, and devices are correctly known as a prerequisite for allowing access to the database or system.

authentication services—This is the security method of checking the identities of users by configuration of a server that maintains information to identify the client.

authorization—The permissions given to a user to access or modify database objects. Oracle uses roles, profiles, and grants to establish access permissions.

bequeathed process—The process that is created to handle a connect request that is passed by a listener. A bequeathed process may also be created without using the listener for a connection request; such as a request which is made by a client that is signed directly onto the Oracle database server at the operating system level.

cache replication—The process of sending information to the local cache on another node.

catsnmp.sql—The script provided by Oracle to create the snmpagent role used by Intelligent Agent.

centralized naming—This method, used by Oracle Names, provides one central place where address information is configured and maintained. Client applications are pointed here to resolve service names.

client-side cache—This is the process of maintaining address information in the client workstation cache for a specified period of time. By using the client-side cache with Oracle Names, it is not necessary to go to the Oracle Names server to resolve every connection string.

CMADM—The connection manager administration background process that is responsible for handling administrative issues for CMAN.

cman.ora—The configuration parameter file used for Connection Manager.

cman_profile—The section of the cman.ora file that specifies the parameters relating to the behavior of CMAN, such as logging and tracing.

cman_rules—A section in the cman.ora file that allows security rules to be defined for accepting and rejecting connection requests based on the source, destination, and SID.

CMCTL (Connection Manager Control Utility)—The connection manager utility provides a command-line method for controlling the connection manager processes.

CMGW—The connection manager gateway background process that acts as the hub for CMAN requests.

communications daemon—The process configured on a node to provide an interface between Intelligent Agent and Oracle Enterprise Manager.

connection concentration—A feature supported by CMAN to handle multiple connection requests to a single server. This feature can be configured only for databases using the Multithreaded Server option (MTS).

Connection Manager—Oracle Software for multiprotocol support, security rules, and connection concentration.

connection pooling—The process that is configured with MTS databases to allow dispatchers to support additional connections. When a connection is idle, it may be temporarily disconnected so that another waiting process may use the connection.

cryptographic checksumming—A method provided by ANO of attaching a value to a data packet to ensure data integrity during transmission.

data encryption—A method provided by ANO for scrambling data during transmission in order to ensure data privacy.

data integrity—The security risk that data will be modified or interrupted during transmission over the network.

data privacy—The security risk that data will be viewed by nonauthorized users during transmission over the network.

dispatchers—The processes configured with the MTS option to receive incoming SQL commands and transmit them to the database. The dispatchers return the data from the Oracle database to the client application. Dispatchers handle multiple connections at one time.

Gateways—An Oracle product that provides an interface with non-Oracle databases.

hostname—The name of the server. The hostname is translated into an IP address.

host naming—The method of resolving connection requests using default values and the TCP protocol. This method is easy to configure, but it has many limitations.

Intelligent Agent—A smart process running on a server that performs a variety of tasks and monitoring actions.

listener—The process on a server that resolves incoming connection requests for one or more databases using one or more protocols.

listener.log—The file that contains information on errors and service activity for the listener process.

listener.ora—The configuration parameter file for the listener process.

local naming—The name-resolution method that relies on a tnsnames.ora file on each workstation to resolve the service name (connection string) into a connect descriptor (address information).

logging—A feature used to place errors, service activity, and statistical information into a file.

lsnrctl—The listener control utility is the command-line interface for starting, stopping, and viewing information on the listener process.

multiprotocol—The use of more than one network protocol. When more than one protocol is used, CMAN performs the translation between the protocols.

multiplex—The process of sharing connections that is supported by connection concentration and CMAN.

multithreaded server (MTS)— In Oracle, the process that allows multiplexing of database connections. Dispatcher and shared server processes are configured to support multiple connections.

n-tier architecture—The architecture that uses multiple levels. More specifically, a middle tier or application server that is used between the client workstation and the Oracle database server.

names.log—The file that contains information on the activities of the Oracle Names server.

names.ora—The configuration file for the Oracle Names server.

namesctl—The utility used to control the Oracle Names server background processes.

Net8 Assistant—The Oracle software that provides a GUI method to configure Net8.

Oracle Call Interface (OCI)—The layer of the network protocol stack that is between the application and two-task common layers on the client side.

Oracle Enterprise Manager (OEMGR)—The Oracle product that works with Intelligent Agent for job and event scheduling, report generation, and so on.

Oracle Program Interface (OPI)—The layer of the network protocol stack that is between the server and two-task common layers on the server side.

Oracle Protocol Adapter (OPA)—The layer of the network protocol stack that is situated between the network protocol and TNS.

Oracle Names—A centralized naming service used to resolve service names into connect descriptors. Oracle Names provides a method to centralize the configuration and administration of service names.

Oracle Service Name Wizard—The Oracle GUI tool, called from Net8 Assistant, to configure service names.

prespawned dedicated server processes—The dedicated listener processes that are created when the listener is started. The listener can redirect requests to these processes instead of creating a new dedicated process to handle the request.

profiles—The properties associated with a client or server. In Net8, the sqlnet.ora file is configured with parameters that determine behaviors such as logging and tracing. These are configured using the Profile icon in Net8 Assistant.

queuesize—The maximum number of connections that can be handled by the listener process at any one time.

regional database—The repository of information for an Oracle Names server.

request queue—The SGA area in which the dispatchers place SQL commands. The shared server processes pick up the requests from the request queue.

response queue—The SGA area for a specific dispatcher in which the shared servers place the results of a SQL command for pickup by that dispatcher.

reload—This command performs a shutdown of all listener processes except the listener addresses and rereads the listener.ora parameter file.

repository—The database where information is placed for use by Intelligent Agent.

root region—The top of the hierarchy, this is the region responsible for sharing Oracle names information with other regions.

Security server—A server that is configured as a centralized point for maintenance and configuration of users and the privileges assigned to them.

service name—A name for a connect descriptor that is easy to use and remember. The service name is used by the client application as the connect string.

services.ora—The configuration parameter file for Intelligent Agent that contains information on the services discovered by Intelligent Agent.

shared servers—The processes configured for MTS that handle requests from the request queue and return the results to the calling dispatcher's response queue.

snmp_ro.ora—The main configuration parameter file created by Intelligent Agent.

snmp_rw.ora—The secondary configuration parameter file created by Intelligent Agent.

sqlnet.log—The file in which information on errors and actions taken by Net8 for resolution of connection requests is placed.

sqlnet.ora—The configuration parameter file used to modify the behavior of Net8 (for example, to start tracing a connection at a specified level).

tnsnames.ora—A file that is used to resolve service names when the local naming method is used.

tracing—A facility that writes information about an operation to a file. This file can then be used to resolve connection problems encountered with Net8.

Transparent Network Substrate (TNS)—A layer of the protocol stack that works with any standard network transport protocol to provide Oracle connectivity.

trcasst—The command used for Oracle Trace Assistant to format trace files into text files that are more readable.

two-task common—The layer of the protocol stack that is responsible for resolution of differences in character sets and data types between the client workstation and Oracle database server.

two-tier architecture—Also known as the client/server architecture, this is a client workstation connecting directly to an Oracle database server.

Index

Bold page numbers indicate sample exam questions.